Stark
&Raving
Zen

Kristy Sweetland

Stark Raving Zen

A Memoir of Coming Alive

Kristy Sweetland

Cauda Pavonis / New Mexico

Published by Cauda Pavonis Publishing
Santa Fe, New Mexico
Copyright © 2020 Cauda Pavonis Publishing

The stories in this book reflect the author's recollection of events.
Some names, locations and identifying characteristics have been
changed to protect the privacy of those depicted. Dialogue has been
re-created from memory. Where actual names have been used, it is with
permission.
To request permission to use all or parts of the book, please contact:
coaching@kristysweetland.com

ISBN:978-0-9826769-5-0
Library of Congress Control Number:2019920734

Printed and bound in the United States of America

Illustrations: Nana Nishigaki
Cover Design and Logo: Nana Nishigaki
Author Photograph: Aaron Tompkins

Names:	Sweetland, Kristy, author.	Nishigaki, Nana, 1978- illustrator.
Title:	Stark raving zen : a memoir of coming alive / Kristy Sweetland ; illustrations: Nana Nishigaki.
Description:	Santa Fe, New Mexico : Cauda Pavonis, [2020]
Identifiers:	ISBN: 978-0-9826769-5-0 (paperback)	978-0-9826769-6-7 (ebook)	LCCN: 2019920734
Subjects	LCSH: Sweetland, Kristy.	Spiritual biography–United States.	Self-actualization (Psychology)–Personal narratives.	Self-realization–Personal narratives.	Private revelations.	Visions--Personal narratives.	Psychic trauma–Personal narratives.	Psychic ability–Personal narratives.	Neurasthenia–Personal narratives.	Mental fatigue–Personal narratives.	Adult children of dysfunctional families–Biography.	Travel–Psychological aspects.	Spiritual life.	Well-being.
Classification:	LCC: BF637.S4 S94 2020	DDC: 158.1–dc23

Dedication

Dedicated to my beloved Arya,

who absolutely provided me

safe passage between worlds.

My Bodhisattva,

I will love you

for eternity.

Introduction

In 2009, at the age of thirty-nine, I experienced a spiritual awakening so intense it blew wide my sensory channels, resulting in a psychic opening so volcanic it nearly destroyed me. This temporary insanity opened a portal into an ethereal dimension so beautiful and horrifying, I had no choice but to become a new person—my authentic self—to survive it.

I had a history of trauma, abuse, workaholism, anxiety, emotional avoidance, chronic repression—and ultimately suffered a severe professional burnout, which is what released that glorious wrecking ball. I was suddenly and terrifyingly free, not able to remain in my current field of veterinary medicine, which was the only life I had known. My entire identity was instantaneously wiped clean; I was a blank slate.

It was then that I decided to take a drive across the country, and midway I found myself unraveling so explosively, there was no halting the process.

Though I had been intuitive and oddly wired from the start, suddenly I was seeing spirits, having conversations with them, channeling universal messages, and hanging out with archangels and historical characters who'd been dead for two hundred years. I came face to face with mythological creatures and became one with nature. I traveled to heaven where I heard the voice of the cosmos, and to hell where I was terrorized by demons and darkness. My senses became so acute I could hear like an animal, unable to block out conversations between strangers fifty yards away. I had to face every single one of my fears…and learn to stop fighting or risk total annihilation.

I had to undertake my own Hero's Journey to reclaim my life, and I nearly died in the process. And though you will find that this book has been organized in accordance with Joseph Campbell's understanding of the Hero's Journey, it was the author Sharon Blackie who, after this book was finished, helped me realize that *Stark Raving Zen* is truly the Heroine's Journey, a feminine version of transformation that includes fire and fury, creation, enchantment, intuition, and mythology.

I was living in Minnesota at the time of my eruption, but this fantastic voyage through my own spirit and psyche took place in New Mexico, over a ten-day-solo car ride (with my dog Arya, who I believe literally saved my life).

The details of my story are wilder and more volatile than any fiction I could ever imagine. I survived, though it took two years to fully recover, and many more to continue assimilating what had happened to me through those mystifying ten days. A few years later, I received a master's degree in transpersonal psychology, which helped put back together the many truths of my once broken existence.

It took ten years to become healed enough to write this story, which began long before that fateful New Mexico date with destiny. It was an impossibly difficult endeavor, to immerse myself in the memories of my divine insanity: some excruciatingly painful, though thankfully preserved in journal notes and a blog I published at the time, *Stark Raving Zen*. But it never felt like the story belonged to me. It belongs to all of us, all who have or will navigate their own traumas, and commit to turning the soil in order to cultivate enchantment and indescribable beauty out of darkness and pain.

Some names and minor details have been changed to protect the innocent, including myself.

This is my story, my personal heroine's journey. This is how I came alive.

Part One

THE ORDINARY WORLD

"Don't ask what the world needs. Ask what makes you come alive, and go do it. Because what the world needs, is people who have come alive."

~ Howard Thurman

CHAPTER ONE

I crawled like a sloth into my bed. The full moon shone through my open window, its gauzy curtains gently wafting in the warm, midnight breeze. My senses filled with the briny ocean air of the New Hampshire Atlantic coast, an easy stroll away. I was thirty years old and felt much bigger than the evidence of my life. But if my place in the world had any real significance, I didn't see it. And why did I feel as though some enormous, formless thing was stalking me?

"What is it? What?" I mumbled to the frustrating emptiness, my fists clenched, trying to force it to speak. I threw the covers off, sick with the discontent of my morbidly stagnant existence. I sat up in bed, hugged my knees and compelled the gears in my brain to keep grinding. I pleaded with something inside of me: "Wake up!" I ordered. "Please. Do something. Lead me somewhere. I can't stand this." Relinquishing all responsibility to some invisible something—if I could only open to whatever answers might be waiting for me—I sent the invitation and remained in a perpetual state of waiting, primed for a response. I fantasized its arrival as a grand envelope waxed shut with the official seal of Purpose and Meaning (sound the horns!). I lay down, pulled the blankets up to my chin, and began to fade, allowing my mind to rest. So tired, I finally drifted and accidentally stopped forcing.

In the disembodied space somewhere between awake and asleep, something happened. Something touched me. And then something else touched me. Brittle hands, cold, hard, dry, like branches on a dead tree scratched at my skin, grasped feebly at me. Three skeletal hands pulled at me—one on my left arm and two on my right—wrapping bony fingers around my wrists, imploring me to follow. The energy was childlike, innocent.

I made my answer very clear.

"Don't touch me!" I yelled, horrified by the physical intrusion. I was wide awake now, sitting bolt upright, rubbing my arms where the hands had been, reclaiming my personal space. I recovered, embarrassed by my own histrionics. "Damn," I mumbled. I wrapped my trembling arms around myself, felt my heart drumming in my chest—I was suddenly freezing cold. I had asked for a response, an intervention for my life's frozen state—was that it? Whatever it was, I couldn't answer. A door had opened at my request and I slammed it closed. My body went limp with defeat. I somehow willed myself to go back to sleep.

When the sun rose, I woke with a grief hangover that enveloped me in depression. I wanted to be delivered from this life of terminal dullness. Something had been there for me last night, something with which I had a long-standing appointment, something just beyond my sight and my reach, something I had asked for, begged for even. But I didn't understand it, had no will to accept it, not enough courage. Those cold, scratchy hands...I was too afraid. "Give me time," I whispered into the morning sun peeking through my sheers. I hid my face in my hands. "I'm sorry if I scared you. Just give me some time. Whoever you are...please don't leave me." I felt the gentle retreat of whatever it was that had touched me last night. It was willing to give me whatever I needed.

CHAPTER TWO

Though I had never before experienced their touch, I was no stranger to spirits. My grandmother was an odd German medicine woman who stayed with my family six months a year on the golden plains of eastern Colorado, creating herbal tonics and poultices to treat our every ailment. Throughout my childhood she was there, a tiny hunchbacked thing, with long silver hair restrained in a braided bun at the nape of her neck. She wrapped her whole head in a nylon "kerchief" as she called it, tied and knotted beneath her chin. She had no use for beauty: she preferred to shuffle around in ratty slippers and housedresses with giant cardigans purchased at Goodwill. With only a few teeth left and refusing dentures, she looked like something straight out of Hansel and Gretel. But her smile was adorable, her eyes sparkled, and everyone commented that my Gramma was just about the cutest thing they'd ever seen. She had been married to my grandfather, whom I had never met, as he died before

I entered this world. My mother's father had been a troubled poet who gardened for the few coins he'd ever earn. Pursued relentlessly by his own dark demons, he was a monster of a man and despised by his own family, legitimately earning their hatred through a lifetime of sadistic abuse.

I knew very little about that though, because all the knowledge of my mother's lineage was locked up tight, a vault of protective secrets, gleaned only through rumor and whispers. This was my mother's strategy for keeping us safe. Questions weren't allowed. My mother's entire history seemed to be a psychological thriller with an R rating; no detail seemed to be suitable for children. Nothing was spoken. A tenacious detective searching for clues, I sleuthed fragments of stories, all of them gruesome, trying to piece them together into something that made some kind of sense. I catalogued them in my memory—they were not for public consumption. Most of the story scraps came from my grandmother, stolen from her by the forbidden questions I incessantly asked. Her treasonous revelations caused my mother to hiss at her when she thought nobody was listening. Once I heard her threaten Gramma that if she continued to talk about the past, she couldn't stay with us. I couldn't hear my grandmother's response, but it carried the tone of pleading; she did that a lot. This need for secrets was maddeningly confusing and only made my commitment to excavate that much stronger. I was a focused kid, and my curiosity was like the deranged monster in a horror flick—it just couldn't be killed. I wanted those stories. I needed them to feel like an entire person.

As it was, I had to be content with a few threadbare memories, none of which would ever be verified. I couldn't run anything by my mother for clarification or validation, knowing the hell Gramma would catch if I did. I couldn't risk her being sent back to South Dakota, the birthplace of my parents, where she normally spent the remainder of the year living with my aunt's family on their glorious farm in Aberdeen. I needed her here with me.

What I recall hearing several times was that she had met her husband, my grandfather, when he raped her in a train station. To make matters even more appalling, it was a gang rape. I didn't know much as an eight-year-old, but I was keenly aware that this sounded violent enough to keep it locked up tight in the family memories vault, not to be shared with another living soul. I was ashamed of this truth. It felt like a punch to the heart every time a friend would share their own origin story. "My grandparents met in World War II. She was a nurse, he a soldier. She saved his life," the little girl would say, pride leaking out through her words. Or, "My grandparents met marching for civil rights! They fell in love at first sight." "Just swell," I'd respond, doing my best to change the subject, hoping to God nobody would ask about my own grandparents.

Which they inevitably did. To which I once responded, "In a grocery store." Yes, I panicked. My diversionary tactics had failed, and I was now full blast in the headlights of their invasive curiosity, which reduced me to a bold-faced liar. "They bumped into each other as they were feeling around the produce section." I got no high fives for that one, but at least my shameful secret was safe. Boring is better than horrifying.

I received scraps of stories equally horrible—that my grandfather sexually abused his daughters, brutally abused his children physically, psychologically, and emotionally. He tortured all of them. I received no real details. My curiosity was my way of arming myself against that which stalked my family's history. I wanted to know how, why, when, and where. I wanted to know why Gramma couldn't protect her own children. But the reality was that I rarely received even a full sentence, just maddening hints stolen from broken facial expressions. The information I received was like the skeleton of a redacted newspaper. I could read a few headlines, but the stories were cut out by the family utility knife, for my protection of course. Little did they know, though, that keeping my own matriarchal history from me, an insatiably inquisitive child, was eroding the ballast of my psyche. Where some people felt the anchoring of a documented family history, I felt nothing but shame.

Gramma was a leaky faucet though, and the drips kept dropping. I was told my grandfather had dabbled with demon worship and then became so frightened by his own magic that he stopped. One night during a satanic ceremony, he telekinetically moved a lamp, and then as sort of a "Good Job! Bravo!" Satan himself made a personal appearance, slowly clip-clopping around the candlelit room on cloven hooves. Gramma crouched in the corner between the bed and the wall, praying to God, speaking in Pentecostal tongues, which she did regularly. Turns out my grandfather couldn't stand straight in the presence of Lucifer; he crumpled to the carpet, a babbling, bawling lunatic. Gramma, however, was on God's varsity team; her life was one long prayerful devotion. She prayed Satan away—he blipped out like an extinguished candle—then stood up, straightened her skirt, and went about her business. But my grandfather? The experience broke him. After that, he flip-flopped into a fear-based Holy Roller fundamentalist, but was no less brutal. He changed uniforms—he hid behind God but the evil remained.

My grandmother shared that she was regularly and savagely beaten, sometimes to unconsciousness. She would tell me these things in a sweet story-telling atmosphere, with cookies and cocoa and a smile on her face, which freakishly normalized these tales of brutality. Sometimes he would go on a drinking bender and disappear for a while. It happened after Gramma gave birth to a baby, when she was so sick with pneumonia, she couldn't produce milk. Grandfather told her he was leaving to get the doctor, but he never came home. There was no way to feed any of the children, no way to contact anybody, no way to escape during the extreme South Dakota winter, no way to keep the shack they lived in warm. By the time my grandfather came home, she was nearly dead. And he arrived to find her rocking the lifeless newborn in her arms, after she found him stone cold in his crib. She held him tight, refusing to release the tiny corpse. The good news is that the other kids somehow survived.

I didn't know how to navigate Gramma's expression upon delivery of this story. Was I supposed to smile along with her? I couldn't do that. Was I supposed to cry? I couldn't do that either, or the stories would stop. Were they even true? I had no way of knowing that. How could such cruelty exist in the world? In my own family? But still I listened, loving her more with each physical or emotional strike recounted, learning to hear her with a generous heart.

And her fourteen children…she loved talking about them. She spoke of the dead as if they were still alive. She lost the one son soon after he was born. She also lost two sons to murder and one to suicide.

I tried to ask my mother about this. How must this have affected her? The one who committed suicide was one of her favorite siblings. But all she ever said about him was, "He was sensitive. He couldn't find a way to heal from the injuries our father inflicted upon him."

"What kind of injuries?" I'd quietly ask, hoping to catch her off guard, searching for anything that could provide a clue to all these dark mysteries. But then she'd snap into a place of lucidity and shoo me and my ghoulish inquiries away, leaving me hungry and frustratingly unsated. The unknowing felt terribly unsafe.

Gramma shared with me on numerous occasions that she'd often wondered if her baby had truly died of pneumonia, or if he'd been smothered to death by one of her older sons who was just a toddler at the time. The baby wouldn't stop crying, and this particular toddler had a strong penchant for jealousy. She seemed to hold no grudge, mostly blaming herself for falling unconscious due to her own pneumonia, but her eyes filled with tears. Upon hearing this story, I tried to lighten things up, placing my hand softly on Gramma's knee. I leaned in, and tried to convince her that the baby likely did die of pneumonia—a thought that sat a fraction nicer in my stomach. But she held onto her pediatric murder suspicion like a dog with a bone. Who was I to argue? I was ten years old. I allowed her the alleged murder and kept listening, absorbing the horrors like a sponge.

Two of her living children were diagnosed with schizophrenia, and they all suffered from chronic depression. Many of them were genius-level brilliant, including the one she suspected of putting a pillow over the face of the crying baby.

My aunt, a diagnosed schizophrenic, spent most of her adult life in a psychological facility. I was never allowed to meet her, and as far as I know, my mother never spoke to her as an adult. I got the impression that she loved her but dealt with her like she dealt with everything else associated with the family, with dissociation and repression. She put her sister in a box labeled "don't open" and left it covered in dust on a shelf so high it couldn't be reached, and that was that.

I was fascinated by my aunt. I would stare at the old black and white photographs and wonder when exactly it was that her mind splintered. She was so beautiful, tall and thin with the perfectly sculpted hair of the 1950s, sporting pencil skirts and horn-rimmed glasses. I'd stare at her elegance and watch the progression from joy-filled, puckish, free spirit to all but dead inside, vacuously expressionless. Mother explained her away as she did her dear dead brother: "She was sensitive. She couldn't find a way to heal from the injuries our father inflicted upon her." My mother found a way to survive for a while, but she never found a way to heal.

It was Gramma who first told me that my grandfather's mother was Cherokee American Indian from northern Georgia, but back then the family wouldn't admit it because it was too dangerous to be identified as such. They were better off hiding behind their European roots and denying their indigenous blood. I was startled by the cowardly nature of this. And as much as I loved my Gramma, I sensed something in her delivery that made me feel like there was some dirty little secret I could never wash off my skin. If they were ashamed of themselves, they would be ashamed of me too. What must that have done to my grandfather, I wondered, being shorn of your heritage through cowardice and shame? How must this have contributed to his monstrous mental state? I never asked these questions out loud. I just lost myself in the anthropo-logical and psychological curiosities, making my own sense of things by assigning this secret as the cause of his brokenness. Once, I gathered up the courage to ask my sane aunt, the one who lived on the farm in Aberdeen, why it was that some of my uncles looked indigenous. Her response was, "Native American? No! That's just the swarthy look of the Welsh, dear." I looked up swarthy in the dictionary. I found some Welsh people in my Encyclopedia set. And then I silently shook my head and called bullshit. There was no penetrating this fortress.

I never talked about my fierce desire to know more about my possible native blood. I couldn't. I had to stay loyal to my Gramma, who would get in serious trouble if I ever started a sentence with, "Gramma told me..." But she was German. She didn't have to contend with the complexities of a secret Cherokee bloodline. Gramma did whisper when she told me about it and stressed the word Indian a little too strongly. It felt off. Or maybe I was too sensitive, just my insecure imagination. All I know is that I felt a bit like a piece of fruit gone bad—sweet smelling, but bite too deep and you were sure to find me rotten on the inside. Because if it was nothing to be ashamed of, why wouldn't we all just talk about it?

My gregarious Irish father, however, was more accepting in his inappropriate sort of way. Once he joked with me that in my mother's lineage there was "an Indian in the wood pile." I had no idea what that even meant, but he told me to keep it to myself. He'd wink at me, deflecting my attempts to gain further clarity. It's possible he just didn't know any more than I did. But in the summertime when the Colorado sun tinted my skin a dark mahogany, he'd scoop me up, kiss me on the cheek, and call me his little Indian, loud and proud. I never knew if he was actually referring to my unsubstantiated drop of Cherokee blood, or if he was just being his slightly racist, lovingly inappropriate self, but I liked to tell myself it was the former. I felt like a queen when my father said "Indian," not a cobweb-covered secret.

CHAPTER THREE

Demons and spirits followed Gramma—the presence of which a few of us witnessed as kids. I was the youngest of five, but it was a trait I would grow to share. One of my sisters wondered if this made her "evil," but to me, they never felt like they were Gramma's. It felt more likely that she was continually cleaning up my grandfather's mess, decades after his death. Gramma thought nothing of hauntings. I asked her once, "Do you believe in ghosts, Gramma?" She curled her nose, confused by the question. Of course she did. For some reason that comforted me. I also liked to think that some of the forces swirling around her were just our protective ancestors keeping an eye on us.

Some of them, though—yes, they were shady. I'm not sure why it was that I loved to be scared out of my mind, but one of my favorite childhood stories was when my older sister decided to have a sleepover in our grandmother's attached apartment. In the middle of the night a horned creature showed up, pacing the floor. Both my sister and Gramma experienced it, clutching each other as Gramma shielded my sister's eyes. My sister never saw the beast—Gramma protected her—but she saw its shadow on the moon-cast wall, wearing horns like a bull though the thing stood upright on two legs. They waited out its presence, but not quietly. My sister was a screamer. She woke the whole house while my grandmother spoke in strange tongues, trying to cast it out before it could do too much mischief. Maybe it was Satan again, I don't know. My sister was too traumatized to speak of it, which really frustrated me. I wanted to know everything— how it felt, how it smelled, how it behaved. Did it say anything? Again, no answers. Terror tends to render a person mute. I hated that. I was so eager to investigate this supernatural intrusion, oddly fixated on it. Knowledge was power, and in my household the reluctance to speak made me feel vulnerable to the unseen forces that seemed to prowl the shadows of my mother's line.

Perhaps I knew that one day the Unseen would suddenly become the Seen, and I'd have to cling to the edge of sanity while I watched my own mind's desperate attempt to make sense of an entirely new spirit-filled reality. Maybe on a deep, subterranean level I knew that I had to mine my elders for every bit of understanding I could, because decades from then I had a date with destiny poised to shatter everything I thought I knew about the world. It's possible I knew that someday this would mean life or death for me.

But until then, Gramma instructed us to chant, "I need thee, I need thee" whenever the demons would arrive. I asked who "thee" was—who do I need? And she informed me that I needed God, a constant presence in her life. When

I was truly in deep need, I thought the words "I need thee" sounded unclear and a little ambiguous. Even as a young girl, when the demons reared their heads, I felt more confident yelling "Be here NOW God, please!" It was important to be polite but direct.

My Gramma deeply formed my spiritual identity and my supernatural foundation. From the beginning, my relationship with Jesus was nothing short of rapturous. I seriously loved that guy. I prayed every night into the darkness and would often feel so much pure love in return that I would start weeping into my pillow, ecstatic tears flowing as I professed my devotion to this handsome man with a beard. I also considered Archangel Michael to be a very good friend of mine and a constant protective companion. I could see him in my mind's eye and was aggravated every time I saw an artistic rendition of him as some mealy blond cherub with soft white skin and a flaming sword. He was dark when I saw him. A certified smoldering badass with black hair and brown skin. I could feel him walking behind me, always there with me. I loved him deeply and suspect that's why I never feared the demons.

What was equally rapturous was my relationship to Mother Nature. I could talk to her, hear her, and find her miraculous beauty and spirit in everything—a hand-woven blanket, a favorite stick I had as a friend, a mud puddle filled with unidentified larval insects that I wanted so badly to get to know; if I could only speak their language! I was born an extension of the wild and always felt more at ease with the animal kingdom than with humanity. I felt that being human made me superior to nothing, that everything on this planet was a possible friend, and certainly my equal.

As a tiny nature-loving, praying girl with tanned skin, freckled nose and long chestnut braids, my tendency to hang out with Archangels definitely came from the influence of Gramma. It certainly wasn't my nuclear family, who as a group never displayed any more than a tepid relationship with Spirit. We read a verse from the Bible every Christmas Eve before unwrapping our presents, and we said a kind of run-on version of a Catholic before-dinner prayer, which went something like, "*BlessUsOhLorFoTheeThyGifs...*" completed in a few seconds. We were hungry. And that was the extent of the Sweetland family's spirituality, at least spoken out loud.

I learned more about the Divine from my grandmother than I did from the Catholic Church, which is what I was baptized into thanks to my father's Irish heritage. My church upbringing was great for theory. I memorized the heck out of a bunch of prayers, A+ grade there, but I never felt like I connected to the concept of God through Catholicism. I loved the ritual, the fanfare, the regal ceremony of it all. But I remember being told that Buddhists were evil, and that gays would go straight to hell along with people who had committed suicide. My brother was gay and my uncle had committed suicide, and I knew both to be incredibly sweet guys who would never harm a soul. Both had suffered enough without having a house of God pile on the hatred. Outside of church I asked a lot of questions about Buddhists, and I heard a lot of answers about being peace loving, respecting nature, practicing loving-kindness. My inquisitive mind just couldn't make the numbers add up. I needed to be reminded again and again why these people were going to hell. My connection to the church started to unravel.

I still went diligently to service every Sunday until I was

about sixteen years old, mostly because a boy I liked went. He was my neighbor, and I would peek through the curtains to see when he'd burst through his front door and trudge on down the sidewalk, off by himself again to attend Sunday service, hands stuffed deep into the pockets of his sweatshirt hoodie, smelling like stale cigarettes thanks to a chain-smoking parent, something we had in common. As soon as I'd spot him, I'd run out my door, coincidentally leaving at the exact same time he did. "We couldn't time this if we planned it!" we'd say to each other, shaking our heads, and I'd sit close by him, never right next to him, bashfully admiring him from the safe separation of a pew or two, savoring his ashtray scent as if it were a bouquet of roses. But we ended up moving across the state, and after that I fell away from the church. Catholicism by itself just wasn't as compelling as my beloved favorite boy.

I made a conscious decision to fully separate from Catholicism at the age of nineteen after I watched my mother die. I thought it would be a good punishment for God, who had clearly taken her from me in the most horrendous way possible. My grandmother had died a year earlier, an arcadian exit at my aunt's farmhouse in South Dakota, going to sleep at night and never waking up. Of course the angels would arrange such an exit for her; she'd never removed the Team Jesus letter from her varsity jacket. My mother's death was not peaceful at all, and after the trauma, with a heart thoroughly crushed, I staggered away from the priests and the incense and the lightheadedness from the incessant standing, sitting, and kneeling.

With both my mother and Gramma gone, I had no further access to the truth of my lineage. I had no relationship with anyone else in my mother's family, and if I had they wouldn't have shared a thing. The answers I had sought among all the whispers and the secrets and the half-truths had gone to the grave. My father had fallen deeply into alcoholism years before, but was even worse after my mother's death. Her loss also proved to be too large of an obstacle for my siblings and me to navigate gracefully. Like so many mothers, she was the glue. We all drifted into our own separate lives, and our father isolated himself to an unreachable degree. By the age of twenty, I was on my own. Thank God for good friends who taught me how to balance a checkbook and that sheets actually needed changing every now and then. I watched them. I watched their mothers and learned what I could. My memories became my only parental companions, and I searched them for whatever useful lessons I could find.

CHAPTER FOUR

*I*n the early years of my childhood, we lived a chaotic life. My mom and dad seemed to despise each other, and there was a constant energy of seething discontent in our household. My parents had come together so many years before, drawn by a force of nature that felt like survival for both. They clung together with an early love so fierce that my dad braved the disapproval of his entire family, who were scandalized by my mother's Protestant upbringing. She converted to Catholicism, and they married. But it all collapsed into ruin when their family inheritances caught up with them—mental illness for one and alcoholism for the other. My father was comfortable doling out abuse; my mother was comfortable receiving it.

My mom cried more than she smiled, and my dad was destructive toward everyone and everything, chain-smoking Pall Malls and drinking Coors beer on a near-constant basis. My dad's addiction to alcohol caused a lot of job losses and many moves. By the time I was eighteen, my family had lived in four different towns with eight changes of address. I learned to make friends easily, but I constantly felt out of control. I battled anorexia in high school and developed obsessive compulsive disorder (OCD) at an early age. Cleaning was my thing, constant cleaning. And drinking was my thing. My senior year I was 5'5" tall and weighed in at 100 pounds. I wouldn't eat all weekend so I could afford the booze calories.

I used to love to stare at my own skeleton in the mirror, digging my rapidly disappearing form. I loved to view my razor-sharp pelvic bones, outlining my iliac crest with my fingertip. My clavicles and ribs were favorites too. I was able to insert my hand underneath my ribcage and grab onto that bony case that protected my heart and lungs. I loved the feeling of hunger; it made me feel in control and alive. But after a while the hunger just went away. My body stopped expecting to be fed.

During the week, I ate nothing but one small bag of Cool Ranch Doritos and one Diet Pepsi a day. My mom and dad would cry and plead for me to eat. Wow, the high of that control. They weren't fighting anymore; instead, they were aligned with a single goal—get their daughter to eat.

I remember a time as a small child when I was once again witnessing my parents verbally destroying each other, their biting expressions of hatred just too much for me to bear. In a fit of desperation, I threw my empty plastic cup across the room. Sitting at the kitchen table eating my lunch on the front lines of the battle, it involuntarily flew from my hands in frantic rebellion. I said nothing, terrified by my own action. They froze and looked at the cup rolling across the tile, then at me, then at each other. They began a horrible attempt to act their way out of the war, their faces twisted into forced smiles—like a fifty-ton truck attempting a U-turn at seventy miles per hour—awkwardly patting each other on the back to show me they were on the same side, cooing at me that this is just how mommy and daddy talk sometimes. The pain in their eyes was intolerable. I knew their reconciliation was a ruse, but they didn't fight again for at least that day.

But anorexia was way more powerful than chucked tippy cups.

I starved myself from ages sixteen to nineteen, until my mom died...and then the need to punish my parents for their weaknesses fell away and my cruelty to my own body lost its charge. I stopped binge-drinking alcohol as well. That too lost its charm, although on the rare occasion when I did drink, I drank too much. I still loved the high of an occasional escape; anything to bypass the reality of my loneliness and loss.

As a young woman suddenly alone, I patched the hole in my heart with work. Veterinary medicine quickly became a surrogate for my lost family. I got an Associate's degree and became a licensed veterinary technician. It was mostly left-brain work: looking through microscopes, conducting blood tests, taking and developing x-rays. It appeased my constant desire for structure and control, and I adopted my workmates as my new family. I loved it at first. It didn't take me too long to numb a bit to the pain of the animals. Even the most severe cruelty cases stopped crippling me as much as they had been, and that felt like a victory. I was involved in their recovery and care. I was really good at what I did, and that made it all worthwhile.

Through my twenties I appeared to keep it together. I had learned to stuff all my emotions into one tightly wound explosive device, and I kept it controlled and dormant for a full decade. The chronic repression—my mother had taught me well—caused a death of sorts, and my twenties were spent in a zombified state of callous disregard, completely detached from my spirit. Even so, I knew that I would need for there to be more to my life one day. So despite the fact that I was working nine to five in a Minneapolis general practice and nights at a veterinary urban emergency hospital, I went back to the University of Minnesota to complete a bachelor's degree in psychology.

My penchant for order, organization, and structure made me an excellent manager of all things. By the time I was twenty-seven years old, I had moved into administrative roles in veterinary medicine. I became even more analytical as I lost my physical connection to the animals and replaced it with office work. I became robotic, totally disconnected from feeling. I watched myself start to unravel, like a slow-motion movie reel, and felt helpless to stop it. I found some solace in shopping, a new addiction that seemed to keep me alive. Buying things tricked me into feeling something like a heartbeat.

At the same time, I became highly nonsocial, severely introverted, and completely lost contact with my best friends and family. I had been in a long-term relationship with a much older wealthy man who would not accept the outward expression of any emotion other than sweetness and joy. I was feeling none of that, so I worked hard to pretend to be something I wasn't, when all I truly had inside was heartbreak. I learned to fill the void by filling the shopping bags. I had so much credit card debt it caused a chronic dread; the accruing interest felt like a predator constantly stalking me.

The shopping was a crudely placed bandage, just barely

stopping the hemorrhage. I felt nothing for myself, but at times the pain I felt for others was crippling. I had long ago suppressed my own pain; instead I concentrated on the lives of others so I wouldn't have to process my own personal traumas. Sometimes I'd obsess over a person's obvious tragedy, other times I'd feel for a person just standing in line at the grocery store. I would get pulled into their painful smile or a stranger's moment of displayed vulnerability and make up stories, projections, about their struggles and attempts to hold their life together, their heart hanging by a thread. Or was it my heart hanging by the thread...?

I had this tendency as a child too. I didn't know what to do with all that pain and neither did my parents, so they decided the best thing to do was to just protect me from whatever they could. There were certain subjects of conversation not permitted in our household due to their debilitating effects on me. The Holocaust, for one. Animal cruelty. Or nuclear war—I was inexplicably obsessed with it. On a few occasions I remember accidentally watching things that sent me into hysteria. My poor parents had no idea what to do with this sobbing rag doll of a thing who couldn't stop feeling for that little gazelle who was killed by the lion on *Wild Kingdom.* Or the ending of the 1977 version of *Last of the Mohicans.* Or a news story about a geriatric homeless woman with a rotten head of iceberg lettuce she'd found in the trash, her dinner for later. She looked too much like Gramma. That wrecked me. "There's no nutrients in iceberg lettuce!" I pointed and yelled at the screen, parroting what I'd been told, expecting my mother to fix this tragic mess of an old woman's life.

When these episodes hit, I would be wracked with such uncontrollable sobbing that my siblings would clear the room, their discomfort palpable, and my parents would look at each other with a sort of desperation like, What the hell? How do we stop this? They had no idea. At one point my mother became so desperate over my hyperventilation that while my father rocked me in his arms, she actually raided the Christmas closet and shoved a premature stocking stuffer into my hands, a classic distraction move. They were tiny pastel-colored plastic barrettes with little animals on them. It worked. I learned that a shiny new thing took the pain away.

This lesson would prove to be a bitch to unlearn.

Part Two

THE CALL TO

"At any moment, you have a choice that either leads you closer to your spirit or further away from it."

~ *Thich Nhat Hanh*

What is the knocking at the door in the night?

It is somebody wants to do us harm.

No, no, it is the three strange angels.

Admit them, admit them.

~*D. H. Lawrence*

CHAPTER FIVE

The explosion of my psyche, as I knew it, was by any definition atomic. At the age of thirty-nine the amalgamation of a lifetime of confusion, emotional and psychic repression, and the early trauma of my mother's gruesome death shattered my world. The eruption was sudden but had been smoldering for decades. In fact, the fuse was lit while I was still in my crib.

At the age of about two years, I had my first conversation with the spirit world. My crib stood next to my parents' bed. Three feet away from my sleeping mother, the wooden spindles of my confinement separated us. I reached out silently into the dark, extending my small hand, telepathically imploring her to wake up. No luck. In the lonely darkness, I curled up and drifted off to sleep.

Deep in the night I woke up, blinking my eyes, staring at the ceiling, blanketed in blackness. My heart was racing. The nightmare was still fresh. Goofy, the Disney character, had been chasing me down an abandoned city street. I had the amiable Pluto galloping loyally by my side. I couldn't get away. Every time I dodged Goofy's terrifying grasp, he was right there again with those big floppy shoes and white gloved hands. I escaped to the waking world and tried to reorient myself.

The beating of my heart and the sounds of my own rapid breathing broke the silence. When I shifted, the vinyl covered crib mattress made too much noise, so I lay unmoving. In the stillness I heard something, a strange shuffling sound down the hall, outside the bedroom. My ears strained to identify what it was. I wanted to believe it was my older brother Scott, who was around six years old at the time. I was always comforted by his presence. A calming and loving brother, all sweetness and fearless adventure—it wasn't unusual for him to roam around the house at all hours, unable to sleep.

I called out to him with my mind, not expecting him to hear but too afraid to make a noise. The sounds were getting louder, closer, coming down the hall now. I heard a muffled conversation and a woman's voice say, "Be careful." The energy felt foreign. It wasn't Scott.

I froze, my heart pounded, my head craned to the left; I lay wide-eyed trying to visualize the door in the darkness. It was opened a crack. Go away. Please go away, I begged silently. The noise dissipated but the presence was still there. Time seemed to stop, and I waited for what felt like an eternity. Were they gone? And then I stopped breathing completely as I watched the silhouette of the door slowly swing open into the black room.

Three forms soundlessly entered. Still too afraid to move or cry, I stared at my parents, silently imploring them to wake up. Generally, my mother was extremely sensitive to the needs of her brood even in a deep sleep. Throughout our childhood all we normally had to do was step silently into her room at night, awakened by a stomachache, and before we could yelp a "Help me!" she'd be instantaneously wide awake, tending to our hurts. Tonight however, three strange people were ambling around the bedroom and neither she nor Dad sensed a thing.

They were talking now, the intruders, close enough for me to see that they were women. Voices low, they were speaking with no concern for my completely unaware parents. The women seemed to be in disagreement. I couldn't understand much. I shut my eyes tight and played dead, holding my breath and fearing they'd hear my beating heart.

When I opened my eyes, they were peering around my crib rails, one on my left side and two on my right, speaking to each other in harsh whispers. They had odd attire on their heads. Hats? Large black somethings, and black dresses. I was certain they were witches.

"This one." The oldest one peered down at me with a scowl on her face. Rigid and unforgiving looking, she scared me the most.

"Yes!" The youngest one had a playful energy. She nudged her sister. "Look at her!" She cooed down into my crib, stroking my cheek. She grabbed the rails of my confinement, bouncing up and down on her toes and making no attempt to contain her excitement. She was beautiful. Pure love was in her eyes and her touch was warm, not like I'd expect a witch to feel. I remained silent. I couldn't have made a noise then even if I had wanted to.

The third sister looked into my eyes and said, "It's an honor." Tuning out the other two, she seemed to be in a world of her own. I felt reverence from her, awe and gratitude. She wouldn't touch me. Her demeanor was respectful but distant; she treated me like royalty.

"I'm not sure," said the scowling sister.

"You're not sure she's our girl?" the pretty one said.

"No. I'm sure she's our girl. I'm just not sure she'll do it." She shrugged, only minimally interested. A calming energy replaced my anxiety. They had been assigned to watch over me. Two of them were clearly taking their assignment seriously. The third was conflicted.

The reverent sister silenced the other two with an elegant wave of her hand. "She'll do it. No question." And then she leaned into my crib, her face inches from mine, and stared into my eyes for what seemed an eternity. When she spoke, I understood every word. "Listen. We're going to leave you alone now. Someday we're going to be together again; a long time from now. You remember us, okay? You remember this."

They all stared at me. By now I was standing up, grasping the crib rail, no longer afraid. The pretty sister stroked my cheek again. "She's just a baby," she said, softly kissing my forehead, then holding my face with both hands to soak me up. The other two gently pulled her away and all three filed out of the room. I stood at the crib rail with my tiny hand extended out toward the open door. I felt so lonely at their departure. I didn't utter a sound to my parents. I didn't try to wake them.

I wouldn't blame you for not believing me, but nearly fifty years later, I still remember every detail, though I'm aware it seems impossible. Of course, I have no further memories from this age and despite decades passing, the details never dim, not even a little. A memory from my crib, stamped upon my brain, and it would take nearly a half century before I would arrive at any solid understanding of who those women were.

Confounding and utterly enchanting, their visitation planted a seed within me. It was a reminder of the secrets found in the blackness of the night; mysterious things never meant to be remembered had I not been ordered to do so. Inside of me that seed grew. There was more to this world than we might allow ourselves to experience; disruptions in the glassy stillness of everyday consciousness happened all the time. The spirits of that experience were guardians who would stay with me, bearing silent witness to my life with an alcoholic father and a chronically depressed mother. Through the years of teenage anorexia, escapism with alcohol, and a sense of constant loneliness (though I was surrounded by many who loved me), the three spirit women would be there. They knew me. They reminded me of my worth, my preciousness, my gifts... the royalty of the human spirit. They were near me, constantly guiding me to the shores of safety with flames illuminated by my own inner light, always reminding me that I had a purpose, even if I didn't yet know what that purpose was.

CHAPTER SIX

*F*ast forward seventeen years from that spirit encounter. I was a teenager, beginning my college sophomore year. After a persistent cough lasting no longer than an average flu, my mom was diagnosed with stage-four adenocarcinoma of the lungs. She had gone to the family practitioner thinking she'd pick up some cough syrup, and the x-rays instead revealed her rapidly impending mortality. It was considered incurable, but they agreed to chemotherapy on the off chance a miracle would occur. They said if we were asking for the truth, she'd likely be dead within six months.

At the time, I worked at a B. Dalton Bookseller happily stocking shelves, working a register and hoarding in the back room more books to buy than my minimum wage would ever pay for. I received the call informing me of my mother's imminent demise as I was preparing to go in and work the night shift. My father's voice kept running through my mind, snippets of a nightmarish conversation. "The most aggressive form of cancer…Successful treatment is unlikely…Kristy, she probably has a short time left."

Still frozen in shock I went to work, only to thaw out midway through my first hour. The thought of my mother dying was more than I could bear, and I began sobbing among the books, upsetting the shoppers and getting the paperbacks soggy. My manager took me aside, my face smeared black with mascara, to ask me what was going on. She promptly sent me home when she realized my issue had clearly surpassed her knowledgeable grasp of the self-help section.

My mother was sweet and kind, intelligent and artistic. Allegra Lenore Goheen, she was named after laughing Allegra, Longfellow's daughter in the poem "The Children's Hour."

How did Gramma know her laugh would be her trademark, explosive and infectious, like raucous water sprites playing just a little too loud? Or did the spirit of Longfellow's Allegra take root in her the moment she was named? Either way, her laugh caused a noisy unladylike ruckus that I often tried to temper. Myself a dignified quiet child, her unbridled joy embarrassed me.

But she had a darker side too, a constant shadowy presence. Her middle name was Lenore, and though it wasn't the origin of her name, she embodied the energy of Edgar Allan Poe's "The Raven," which felt even more apt. No one could emulate the darkness of Poe like my mother.

Poetic and creative, my mother demanded of us tolerance and love of all beings. She was a gifted painter, oil her medium, and spent her time in front of her easel, quietly singing to herself with the voice of an angel while she created her personal masterpieces. Bringing her vibrant and whimsical landscapes to life was what anchored her to this planet. As much as she loved her children, it was her art that kept her heart beating.

How could I possibly live without her?

She tried hard. Her open mind was always searching for the next best possible but simple solution to her chronic depression: the only inheritance from parents who raised her in devastating poverty and staggering abuse. As she grew up, most people were brutal to her for being so poor. When she told me that, I wanted to go back in time and cause great suffering to all who had disrespected her. It sickened me that she grew up with cruelty on all sides of her, in and outside her home, never a respite, a constant onslaught.

My mother was a giant to me, nearly six feet tall with size ten feet. My father was only five feet seven, which caused her to hunch over a bit trying to mask her great height. I tried to walk with a straight spine around her, to encourage her to carry herself with pride. She wasn't willowy. Large-boned and often fifty pounds overweight, she marveled at her petite daughters. I was the tallest of her three girls at 5'5", all of us small-boned, small feet, thin. She called us fairies and delighted in her love for all of her children. Our mother was beautiful, with raven black glossy hair and dark mysterious eyes, though she seemed to want to hide her beauty from the world. Maybe it was safer that way, buried underneath rags for clothing and a hunched posture. Maybe she inherited that from Gramma too. But depression was her constant companion, unspoken grief and tragedy her signature. She tried so hard to duck, hide, and run from it, constantly evading, never having the courage to stop and face it, to have a conversation with it. Because if she went back to the origin of it, if she unlocked that door and entered it, I believe she thought she'd end up like her brother or sister—dead by her own hand or insane.

One time she became certain the solution to her depression was hug therapy and insisted that everyone in the household engage in a two-minute hug once a day. This came with a lot of teenage eye rolls, but we accommodated the request, and I secretly liked it. She then began extolling the miraculous virtues of creative visualization and started to meditate daily. It was right before she was diagnosed with cancer that she finally sought a psychologist's care and was told she had clinical depression. So began her inaugural journey of selective serotonin reuptake inhibitors. She felt confident and optimistic for about one week—and then the coughing began.

Since she considered herself a visualization pro, I was convinced she could think her way out of this cancer mess. With my paltry paycheck I bought my mother a copy of Bernie Siegel's *Love, Medicine and Miracles* and was certain she would beat the army of cancer advancing across her organs if only she could think it so. But like Patton's soldiers, the cancer advanced, putting up its flag of victory when each organ fell. Her lungs were gone. Her liver. Then the lining of her stomach. The chemotherapy did nothing but eat a hole in her chest where the implanted port-a-catheter failed. It did a nice job of eradicating her hair too.

Six months after her diagnosis, we went as a family to the oncologist to check the progress of her chemotherapy. He threw the CT scans on the viewer to show us the battle was officially lost. Her lungs were solid with tumor. They glowed white on the screen, an otherworldly abomination. At first sight I thought somebody had done us the favor of coloring in the lungs with a luminescent marker, you know, to show us where they were. But no, that silver glow was the vast metropolis of cells refusing to die, multiplying like the walking dead, deformed and hungry, demanding more and more of her as sustenance for their needs, consuming her very life. Didn't they realize that if they destroyed all of her, there'd be nothing left for them, that they'd die too? But cancer never thinks in those terms. It just keeps marching and expanding and battling and multiplying.

Time froze as I stared at the pathology replacing my mother's lungs. I could hear somebody talking, but I couldn't process the words. They sounded garbled and distorted. Bile rose up my esophagus and I felt my neck muscles tighten like a hand grabbing me around my throat. Reality check.

The chemo and radiation therapy would stop. No use wasting good chemicals on the imminently dead. The oncologist, sick of losing the battle to cigarettes, turned to my father—the only smoker in the household—and quietly hissed, "How does it feel to know you killed your wife?" Our mouths dropped open in a collective gasp of disbelief. His job done, he said a final goodbye to my mother. He patted her on the shoulder and unceremoniously stalked out of the exam room, leaving us to simmer in the stew of the poisonous reality of second-hand cigarette smoke. Nobody had pointed to the cigarettes previously, but we were all thinking it. The terrible and awesome doctor shined an overt spotlight on the elephant in the room to a family that had perfected the art of secrets and repression.

God! Finally somebody told the truth.

Friends and family members had been speculating, "Gee, do you think the cancer was genetic? Was it caused by the fact that she was chronically overweight? Maybe it was that she was an oil painter, constantly inhaling turpentine fumes and such?" To which I would silently scoff, "OR maybe it was because for the past thirty years she's inhaled the equivalent of a pack of cigarettes a day, along with the rest of us."

Honestly, even as a teenager, I knew it was likely more complicated than that. I'm sure it was some combination of all of the above, but the man in the white coat assigned my dad the full weight of the blame, and even if it was something that none of us dared utter out loud, we'd all been thinking it. Our mother was dying from the most aggressive form of lung cancer in existence, a royal and devastating gladiator of destruction, and she had never smoked a cigarette in her life. Dad smoked a monstrous amount every day. The action of being called out by an oncologist with an ax to grind, in front of his entire family, essentially killed our father that day too.

CHAPTER SEVEN

Within a short span of that fateful exam, my mother died in the presence of my oldest sister and me, leaving this world screaming and choking on her own blood. The cancer had destroyed so much of her liver that disseminated intravascular coagulopathy, the inability for blood to clot, was the final result. My ultimate moment with my mother was like some scene cut from a Stephen King horror flick, too gruesome for cinema. As my mother's crimson blood repainted the white sterility of the hospital floor; every red blood cell jumped from the sinking ship, pouring from her ears, her eyes, her nose. I drowned out the sound of her screams and the sight of her exsanguination by clinging to the wall, clamping my eyes shut and repeating a mantra over and over: "There is no God, there is no God, there is no God." Traumatized beyond comprehension, wild with grief, these words were all that made sense to me in the face of something so utterly hideous and heartbreaking. If there was a God, how could He/She/It possibly be overseeing this? And what in the hell was Archangel Michael doing while my mother was enduring this horror?

My eldest sister Tracy clung to my mother's hand, escorting her out of this world, refusing to look away, her guardian angel. Covered in our mother's blood she cooed to her, "Let go, let go, let go, we'll be okay, let go," while the hospital staff hysterically ran around bumping into each other, their white nursing shoes squeaking and slipping on my mother's blood covering the floor, throwing her this way and that, seemingly getting their punches in before the reaper won the battle, as if they ever had a chance against this.

If I had been a bit standoffish in the recent past, a bit noncommittal, in that moment I officially broke off my love affair with Jesus, furious that pain like this existed in the world, furious that this out-of-body experience was me witnessing my own mother's horrible death. She had been saying to me over and over, "I'm peaceful with my death. I have totally accepted my death." And yet the moment death came for her, she was anything but peaceful. I was furious at her too. I was furious at the entire universe.

I took a long hiatus from my spirit then. I closed off completely. I shut down, went numb, and dissociated from feeling. My father drifted away into unreachable nothingness, ravaged by his own guilt and alcoholism, having treated my mother with disdain and barely concealed hatred for most of their life together. In the days before my mother died, she told me that the way Dad had cared for her through the last six months made up for all the years of abuse. He absolutely doted on her.

I couldn't forgive him so easily.

If my father's cigarettes had killed her body, his constant cutting insults had done away with what had remained of her psyche long before. I never believed his crocodile tears of mourning; I saw no reason to. I just couldn't, though I tried.

Shortly after my mother died, I was desperate for connection, any connection, and I tried to reach my father on the telephone. Again, no answer. After too many unsuccessful attempts I drove ninety minutes to his dreary garden-level apartment to make sure he was okay. I found his car in the driveway, a brand-new blood red Ford Mustang purchased with the insurance money from my mother's death, and saw him sitting at his kitchen table through the plate glass window out front. It felt good to see him, even if he had ignored my phone calls. I ran inside the unsecure apartment complex to knock on his door.

Nothing, no response. I knocked again. No answer. What the hell, Dad, I thought, knowing he was inside, sitting four feet from the door. So, I went outside again, to peek through his plate glass living room window. His back was turned to me. He was moving, so I knew he was alive. I knocked on it. Again no response. Didn't even turn to see who it might be. I went back to the door, now furious and confused. I knocked again and again, now yelling, "Dad! It's me! It's Kristy!"

He never opened the door. I gave up, retreated to my car, leaned my head against the steering wheel, and wept. The sense of abandonment felt like a hand around my heart crushing my life force, looking me straight in the eye while I struggled to breathe, all the while sneering, "You. Don't. Matter. You never mattered."

And I still couldn't shake this stupid feeling that my mother had left me intentionally, that she died to get away from him.

My siblings and I separated too. The rapid progression of our mother's death was too painful a reminder; we couldn't dissociate so easily in each other's presence. We couldn't forget that we had lost everything when we looked into each other's eyes.

CHAPTER EIGHT

I entered a state of perpetual drift.

Because I became so distant from my own spirit, trying desperately to numb out, my inner world tried to take over, and my dreams took on a new life. When I fell asleep, I felt spoken to. I felt a universal connection in my dreams: a loving, protective force, caring for me.

In the daytime hours I buried myself in my work, and at night I curled up in the fetal position; I had no energy to grimace my way through pretended good times with friends, though I did force myself to do a little of that.

Mostly what I wanted to do was be with my mother through her extensive collection of books, feeling held by her through the words of her favorite authors: Daphne Du Maurier, Edgar Allan Poe, Mary Stewart, F. Scott Fitzgerald...They brought back memories of her peacefully reading, which felt a lot better than the visions of her tear-stained puffy face or the trauma of watching her bleed to death through her screams.

But when I slept, I dreamed, and the dreams started to transform me.

At the age of twenty-one I had a dream experience that brought me a little bit back to life. Like the Three Sisters, the dream entered my bones, acting as permanent guidance, an antidote to the numbness.

At first it seemed like a typical anxiety dream, something I frequently had. I was running away from someone dangerous—a dark silhouette of a person who was close behind me. It was dawn, which I found interesting—not the common anxiety-ridden, pitch-black backdrop. I got to my car and began fumbling for my keys to unlock the door. He was getting closer. I kept fumbling. Terror rising. I could hear his breathing. Hysteria mounting…then everything froze. Everything but me. Time stopped. I could reach out and touch my statue-like pursuer. But he couldn't touch me. I looked around, puzzled.

A voice said, in a rather bored tone, like a behind-camera movie director speaking through a megaphone. "It's your dream. Just open the door. You don't need *keys* in dreams." The voice seemed impatient, a little exasperated, as if this was our fiftieth take and he could no longer bear it. He wanted so desperately for me to get this, to believe in my own power.

I listened to him. I tried the door. It was open.

And then everything started up again, time whirled and the madman was still coming. Reaching for the door, I opened it and jumped in, securing it shut behind me. But here I was, fumbling with the keys again! Couldn't get them in the ignition! The door was opening! I dropped the keys! He was reaching in. I….

Everything froze again.

Oh God. I braced myself, preparing for the director's voice. "It's *YOUR* dream. Just drive the car," the voice boomed.

I shut the door, pushing my attacker outside. I said out loud to myself, "It's my dream. You can't touch me. You can't hurt me." Without keys, I started the car by willing it so, and peacefully drove up and over a big hill to an immense rainbow over the horizon.

"There's no going back. You've arrived," the voice, finally satisfied, assured me. And somehow, I knew exactly what he meant. I had to choose a life that meant something. I had to become complete. I had to get to know myself and accept all parts of what I found there. No secrets. I had to own my life, my gifts, my perceived brokenness. I felt flickers of hope after this experience, but I had absolutely no idea how to do what I was being implored to do. This male voice inside the dream felt like a guardian of sorts. I did feel less abandoned after meeting him, less alone. A tiny flicker of light had illuminated inside of me.

After that, with the guidance of my dream director (always the same voice), I acquired the ability to control my actions in my dreams. If I needed to fly, I'd fly. If I wanted to morph through a brick wall, I'd do it. If I wanted to hover invisibly to get a better look at something, I'd float. "It's my dream" would forever remain with me as my cue to take any action I wanted or needed in a lucid dream state. I was learning to create a whole new universe inside of me.

Around this time, I also experienced three precognitive dreams, each one of them about a phone conversation predicting an actual identical phone call that I awoke to. In the first dream, my sister called to tell me she was in the hospital in premature labor. I awoke from this dream to the sound of my phone ringing. It was my sister calling to tell me she was in the hospital in premature labor. In the second dream my father surprised me by calling to tell me he had gotten a new job, so he'd be moving closer to me. I woke up to a phone call from my father, telling me exactly that. And in the third dream, I received a long-distance call from one of my best friends. She was calling to tell me she was pregnant with her second child. In the dream she passed the phone to her husband who gave me the information. Again, I woke up from that dream to a ringing phone, and to this very friend who said, "Hold on, George wants to tell you something." Her husband then told me Shari was pregnant with their second child.

This path of precognitive breadcrumbs led me to a state of wonder. I knew how special these experiences were. Without shocking me too badly or scaring me senseless, they were just enough to keep me fascinated by their intuitive mystery.

Yet they were also incredible enough to override my left brain's tendency to tell me I was making it all up, or imagining things, or fabricating it all somehow, or the favorite of analysis: it was just coincidence. The brain can't easily discredit a pattern of concrete information being dreamed five minutes before an actual phone call comes through.

I was learning. I was growing. And most of all, I wasn't alone.

CHAPTER NINE

I'd spent my life ignoring or consciously hiding my spooky side, which had entered my life when the three ghostly women slipped into my parents' room during my toddlerhood. At the same time, that experience surpassed everything else in terms of how I viewed myself, my inner identity. But I had feared rejection, had thoughts of craziness, that I was just being self-aggrandizing…. Sometimes I even feared that others would accuse me of making it all up, as if their thinking it would make it true. It was easier to say nothing.

I did tell one, maybe two very close friends, and preceded my sharing with, "Okay, it's possible I'm crazy, but…." This approach somehow painted my revelation with a self-deprecating humility I thought I could live with. If I kept it safe, protected, it couldn't be taken away by disbelief or denial or rejection. But it was like trying to contain Niagara Falls in a fishbowl. My intuition didn't just fade away. It continued to build, becoming stronger and more volatile through denial.

My dream director—for lack of a better term, the voice in my dreams—became my parent then, my teacher. Every night was a life lesson, a blueprint for direction. The strong male voice became common to nearly every dream. Like sitting through university lectures, I learned the contents of my own soul by way of this voice. Cutting through the pain and the loss and the dysfunction, it seemed to be a voice of higher reason.

I never gave the voice a name. I never attempted to understand it. And I never spoke of it. Whether or not the voice was some aspect of me, or something external to me, I didn't much care. I only knew it was supporting me, keeping me alive. But always in the back of my mind was the face of my aunt, embattled by schizophrenia. Though no details were ever shared about her circumstances, I knew enough to keep quiet. The word institutionalized packed a powerful punch. Was she just like me? I knew my mother's family had suffered unthinkable traumas delivered by a demonic father. I experienced nothing with my own father that compared to their hell, though my experiences were bad enough. But despite their horrors, had they been born with simple peculiarities, like I seemed to have? Maybe the severities of their traumas turned these peculiarities against them. I know my beautiful aunt's voices told her to do horrible things to herself.

The voice in my dreams never spoke of destruction or harm. I knew I wasn't crazy. I knew that conversing with voices—the Three Women and the deep male voice, considering them my teachers—could be perceived as crazy. But I knew I wasn't. I also knew that the average crazy person didn't believe they were crazy. So, to prove my sanity, I kept mostly quiet. I did so for decades; I'd been groomed to harbor secrets. And besides, I reasoned with myself, they were just dreams.

CHAPTER TEN

My deeply guarded spiritual identity notwithstanding, I remained in a life that wasn't working for me. By now I was in my late twenties, working in veterinary medicine at a referral hospital on the affluent seacoast of New Hampshire. It was stressful and fairly cutthroat. I had the constant impression that any one of my coworkers would have gladly thrown me under the bus for kicks. And I was no better. I became competitive and ego-crazy, vying for the bosses' approval like a street orphan desperate for coins. I made no real friends in New Hampshire; all my relationships there went no further than skin deep. It's no wonder why. The two romantic relationships I had endured thus far in my adult life had been sheer madness. For the past seven years my fiancé, Theo, and I had struggled to make our loveless relationship work. He was ultra-controlling. I was completely detached. I slipped further and further into depression, living in empty isolation, rarely in contact with my siblings or my dearest lifelong friends.

It was when I turned thirty that I vowed to reconnect to something, anything, to make me feel alive again. I joined a spiritual mail-order book club and became enamored with quietly thumbing through their monthly catalogue. No longer lost in the numbness of my twenties, I was starting to stir, feeling the nudge to find meaning. I knew there was something I was supposed to be doing that went beyond my unfulfilling career in veterinary medicine—which had become more about navigating the mine fields of human coworker drama than actually caring for the animals. The intuitive experiences of my life, which seemed to be fueled by my love of nature, were the only things keeping me ticking at this point. I was feeling the pressure to make meaning of my life. Though I had somehow managed to be born without the desire to have kids—I never paid attention to my biological clock—I always had the sense that I was meant to birth something into this world. The dawn of a new decade often has the potential to set off internal alarms. But kids? I knew I would never embark on that journey.

The truth is, I think I was born devoid of that "must procreate" instinct because there was something else in my grand plan, something I had chosen to bring to life before I entered this incarnation. The Three Sisters and my relationship with the spirit realm only served to further that sense. But what was it? It wasn't clear. Here I was, thirty years old. I had an empty relationship, no real direction, nothing to be truly proud of, totally unplugged emotionally. If I died tomorrow, I thought, I'd be disappointed in this failed life, with nothing to show for it. And I was terrified of death after watching my mother die. I was absolutely blind with fear at the mere thought of my mortality.

I had to find my way back to my whole self, as the man in my dreams had instructed. I realized then that I wasn't afraid of dying. I was afraid of not living, remaining in this treading-water, zombified state of absolute nothingness, wandering the void.

I started voraciously reading spiritual books, anything I could get my hands on. I began to search for everything that made me feel alive. One line here, one concept there, a paragraph that made me weep for no clear reason. There wasn't a book I chose that didn't somehow offer me at least one valuable clue.

I found a book on Zen Buddhism and was introduced to the concept of the Four Noble Truths, roughly translated to:

1. *Life is suffering.*

2. *There is a cause to that suffering,*
   which is seeking control and being
   excessively attached to silly things.

3. *There is an end to that suffering, and it's*
   about detaching from illusion and silly things
   like material goods and rampant judgment.

4. *The path of Buddhism leads*
   to the end of suffering.

Mind sufficiently blown. Could it really be that easy? Nothing had ever made so much sense.

As a spiritually numb, heartbroken, anxiety-ridden control freak, I diverted my full focus to Buddhism and bought every Zen book I could find, because it felt like a direct path out of the abyss. I read each one two or three times, barely understanding them but simultaneously witnessing what I considered impossible—my constant state of fear was loosening its grip.

All hail Buddha. Siddhartha's concepts were stitching back together my unraveled heart.

CHAPTER ELEVEN

With just the slightest change in spiritual chemistry, I became a little stronger. My anxiety no longer completely shut me down and my inner world, my spirit world, ignited. My strong desire to *plug in* to life awakened within me a new dimension of intuition. A little terrifying, beautiful, and breathtaking all at once, that intuition first appeared in the same manner as everything fantastic that had happened in my life, in a dream.

I woke to darkness. Wait. Was I dreaming? I couldn't tell. Where was I? I appeared to be in my New Hampshire bedroom exactly as it was in reality, and yet it felt completely unfamiliar. I was alone. I stood up and felt my way around the bedroom in pitch darkness. It was darker than it should be. Where was the moon through the skylight? I heard a buzzing, and I kept pacing and pacing—back and forth—breathing deeper, hoping my anxiety would dissipate. I closed my eyes to calm myself. It wasn't working. My fear grew heavier, my insides filled with static electricity, and the buzzing screamed louder with the conversation of spirits. "Breathe…just breathe, Kristy." I tried to equalize. I couldn't. I felt stretched and pulled apart by the vibration.

I leaned my hands against a heavy dresser to steady myself and looked in the mirror. I could barely see the reflective outline of my body in the dark. I said out loud, "What do you want? What is it that you want?" There was silence but for that awful buzzing like the cicada symphony that had permeated the scorching Colorado midday sun of my childhood. I kept staring and looked closer. My reflection began to change. It was getting wider, morphing grotesquely, my features swollen and distorted. And then it quickly returned to normal. But now I was no longer looking at the mirror.

I reeled backward and stared into the face of a tiny second version of me.

There was no angst in her. No discomfort. She crouched in front of me, perched upon the dresser top, and looked directly into my eyes.

"You asked me what I want. I want to be free," she said. "That's what I want."

She leaped off the dresser, madly hopping around the room. She leaped with ecstatic joy all over the bed, the chairs, the armoire…laughing hysterically, a tiny imp's laugh. Full of spirit, never having known sadness or frustration or doubt, she was a feral thing, wild, untouched by pain or trauma. She glowed silver blue in the moonlight that poured once more through the skylight. She shrieked with exuberance and unsuppressed mania. I stood there horrified while she danced and jumped all around me, and I felt my soul excised from my physical form.

I screamed. "NO, you can't!"

She stopped and crouched again in front of me. She said, "Yes I can. I just did." and continued to dance, leap, laugh, and glow with the power of her freedom.

I chased her. I tried to catch her. In the darkness I cracked my shin on the corner of the footboard of the bed rail and fell to the floor. I had never felt such fear! It was like witnessing my own beating heart being ripped out of my chest. "You have to get back inside of me!" I screamed, clutching at my painful shin. I grabbed at her. She was too fast, too nimble, too small. I kept trying. I was sobbing now, crying so hard I couldn't see. I was a heavy soulless beast; my insides torn out. I finally caught her, hugging her to me tightly, awkwardly attempting to stuff her back in, but I couldn't. She squirmed, "No, silly!" she said, slightly offended and a little embarrassed for me. She freed herself from my needy grasp once again.

She was the perfect manifestation of love. I cannot describe how she made me feel. It was like trying to catch a real live version of myself as a tiny child, not confined by the safe boundaries of memory or fable. I felt nothing but terror at our separation. I couldn't remain upright any longer. I collapsed, sobbing as she danced and sang and laughed hysterically at her freedom, barely noticing me.

She paused at my histrionics. "Why would you want to contain me?" she asked sweetly, only mildly curious, trying to be kind.

Hiding my head in my hands, feeling ugly and grotesque, still crouched like Gollum, I lifted my face and said, "Please come back. I can't keep you safe when you're out like this. I just can't keep you safe unless you're within me. Please, please just come back to me." I hung my head, too weak to speak, humiliated by what I felt in the face of this little being's fierceness and courage. Could she truly be me? Where did she get her strength? My consciousness followed her around the room like an eager puppy, leaving me a repulsive empty vessel.

And then it was still. No more buzzing. Just silence. I felt tiny hands softly clasping mine. She gently cupped my chin and slowly pulled my head up. I was staring her in the face again; her tiny black eyes glowed and sparkled, dancing in the moonlight. There was no memory of fear or loss within them. Could she possibly be me?

She stood only as tall as I was crouched, and she paused there, lovingly holding my hands. "I don't want to be safe. I want to be free. I want us to be free. I will never leave you. But I don't want to be safe, Kristy. I don't want to be caged." She hugged me and we became one again, my spirit delivering her own blueprint for survival, and then reuniting with me in good faith. She knew I had heard her. She trusted that I would stay true to her.

And then it was over. I woke up.

Sunlight spilled through the curtains, diluting the darkness, and my face was streaked with fresh tears. Confused and terrified, I threw my covers off, swung my legs around and rested my feet on the plush carpet. My hand flew up and instinctively covered my mouth as I tried not to scream. I had an enormous bruise on my shin where I had collided with the corner of the bed rail in my…dream? I was awake now, I knew that. I also knew that where I had just been was no dream. I wasn't fully back in our world yet, and I knew that as well. I was sort of half out and half in, between this plane and hers, straddling two realities. Where had I been? I awoke with new eyes. The darks were blacker and the lights were brighter, the colors more vibrant. I was sick with confusion.

I got out of bed and walked around the house, shin throbbing, feeling like an open portal to anything and everything. With effort I closed that portal and forced myself to go to work.

Overnight, my life had changed.

Part Three

THE REFUSAL OF THE CALL

Leave the situation or accept it. All else is madness.

~ Eckhart Tolle

CHAPTER TWELVE

The blossoming of my own spirit was keeping me warm while what was left of my relationship with my fiancé struggled for life with a weak and thready heartbeat. We had been engaged for several years, though never actually planned a wedding. I was twenty-three when we started dating and had recently lost my mother. He was a man, not a boy, who actually had his shit together.

On our second date he flew me from Minneapolis to San Francisco for dinner at Stars. We spent the night at a magnificent and exclusive private resort on the Pacific Coast. The next day, he whisked me back home. My life became a series of "I-can't-believe-this-is-happening" moments. Moving from a life of lack to one of abundance blinded me, so much so that I didn't catch the warning signs, present from day one. Things moved fast, and within a few short weeks I had moved out of my tiny one-bedroom basement apartment and into his 5,000- square-foot house in an affluent Minneapolis suburb.

We were horribly mismatched during a time in my life where every day of my young existence felt like trying to survive with a mortal wound: dragging my body along, attempting to hide the wide swath of my blood trail, hoping it wasn't too great an inconvenience for those around me. It felt doomed from the beginning, but for the sake of survival, I wanted it to work. I played along. I was mostly dead inside, so how could I even know what I wanted?

Fast forward eight years and, suddenly, I cared. At thirty years old, I could not play my way through this dysfunctional charade any longer. I was in the process of waking up, and it made me sick to live a lie. Frustration, confusion, fear... it was all starting to thaw after years of icy numbness. Like frozen, blue fingers recovering from frostbite, the pain was unbearable.

But I was starting to understand my value. By making the choice to resurrect my own lost soul, even if I had no idea where it would lead me. Things were changing. I felt worthy. My senses were beginning to sharpen. As my awareness strengthened so did my strangeness. I began to feel the frequent sensation of an unseen presence close by, which made my hair stand on end and gave me goose bumps so exaggerated they stung. At the same time, my scalp would tingle and burn with the sensation that my skull was growing faster than my skin could accommodate, like my whole head was about to split down the center at the part of my hair.

I often felt like something was watching me, like I was never alone. I hated to wash my face at night because I feared as soon as I leaned back up over the sink and opened my eyes there'd be a visible form behind me, reflected in the mirror. I doubted my heart could take that. I was getting used to their presence, but I still had rigid boundaries. For example, I had recently determined that touching me wasn't allowed.

I was trying to process all the changes that were happening; I was clearly in some kind of a psychic growth spurt. I began to leave my body, to astral travel, something similar to the lucid dreaming I had become comfortable with, but also very different. It felt more real, less abstract. I knew nothing about this and seemed to have no control over it; and at first, like everything else, I was afraid of it.

When I first experienced this wondrous new ability, I was taking a nap on a blustery, New Hampshire spring Saturday. Theo was traveling on business, which he did frequently. As was common, I had the house to myself. It was one of those rare days where I felt totally content, happy in my own skin, grateful to be alone. It was raining outside, grey and gloomy with a heavy fog shrouding the pine forest around me. I felt nothing but light. I had my independence all weekend, answering to nobody. All I wanted to do in this moment was take a heavenly nap calmed by the sound of torrential rain. I padded lightly around the house closing all the windows so I wouldn't awake to a flood.

I had just read an article about a great relaxation method that entailed lying down and letting each body part sink into the bed, feeling oneself get incredibly heavy, visualizing one's skeleton forming a deep impression in the mattress. From my feet on up to my head I concentrated on the relaxing heaviness…calves, knees, pelvis, hands, arms, torso, shoulders, neck…I let them all sink into my mattress like a delightfully numb dead thing without a care in the world. This was awesome. The plan was, once my body felt like a heavy lump, I was supposed to spring back and release my concentration, feeling light and free. I was all the way up to my head when the deafening buzzing began.

I wasn't happy about this uninvited intrusion, and suddenly felt paralyzed as the jarringly discordant sound of cicadas took over, blocking out any ability to think or process what was happening. I started rising, leaving my physical body, which remained there in its peaceful heavy deadness. Like a dog on a slippery marble floor, I desperately tried to dig my nails in, to stay grounded, connected to myself, but it wasn't working. I was completely out of my body, looking down at my own form lying there on the bed, seemingly asleep, drifting two feet above my physical being. The panic I felt didn't match the Buddha smile on my resting face, and the incongruence of that sickened me.

I screamed.

I shrieked like a wailing banshee, trying to wake myself up so I could stop this separation. I felt the embalming of my soul, sucked out of me by some invisible instrument. I continued to scream and desperately reached for my body, but I was rising and getting further and further out of range. Now ten feet above myself, there was no use in resistance. I couldn't reverse this. Whatever was happening, I surrendered to it. I remembered the tiny version of myself imploring me not to fear it and gave in. "I just want to be free." I remembered her words, closed my eyes, and released my need for control.

I flew. Shooting around the house at the speed of light, covering every room of the large colonial in what seemed like under a second. I relaxed. This was getting fun. Why was I always so afraid? How could I have resisted this? I watched my dogs sleeping next to me, two elegant sighthounds, my cherished Borzoi and Saluki, but they gave no indication they sensed me. I stopped and hovered above their slumbering forms, calling out to them. Nothing but snores.

I went whirring around the house again, testing my wings. It was just like what had happened in my dreams, but this was so clearly not a dream. I observed my cat, Matisse, stopping to hover over him as his tiny grey form, curled in a soft circle, napped among the pillows on the elegantly overstuffed living room couch. One of his eyes snapped open. He could see me! It startled me, which was clearly nothing compared to the effect I had on him. All puffed up, but too afraid to move, head low and ears pinned back, he growled, staring right at me while issuing a puritanical hissing of "Off with you, demon!" I felt bad. He wasn't having nearly as much fun with this as I was. So as not to bother him, I decided to leave the house for a quick spin around the neighborhood. As I accelerated, Matisse leaped off the couch and chased me across the room, unable to decline an exhilarating pursuit of his phantom mama.

By phasing through the wall—something I had done a million times in my dreams (had that been practice for me?)—I was now outside, hovering over my beautiful battle-grey house with black shutters, speeding around the block in a fraction of a second. I watched a woman walk her German Shepherd in the rain, glanced in the neighbors' window and saw them in conversation, peered into a squirrel's nest at the top of a balsam fir tree—it was all riveting. But taking a floating stroll around the neighborhood wasn't enough. I devoured this newfound freedom and had an insatiable desire for more.

I shot straight up, like a rocket from Cape Canaveral, and watched as my house got smaller and smaller until it was reduced to the size of a Monopoly playing piece. I saw the New Hampshire beach stretching wide before me, the Atlantic Ocean roiling in the spring storm. A humpback whale breached twenty miles out, exuberant and graceful, the breaking waves massaging her silver skin. I reached my hand in the direction of the whale, now just a speck on the water; I felt so connected to her and hoped she could feel my love.

As my trajectory continued, I saw the outline of the United States, of North America, and continued to fly higher, unfazed by the thinning atmosphere. I watched the earth slowly spin from the deep comfort of cosmic blackness, and still I wasn't ready to go home. I stopped and found myself floating.

I rested there, feeling like I was back inside my mother's womb. I could sense my body regenerating and healing from the enormous pressures that gravity puts on a body, a soul. For what felt like an eternity I drifted, free from any stress or strain, pain or anxiety, with nothing to fear or be hurt by. For the first time in my life I felt at home.

I never wanted to leave. Pulling myself away from my cosmic drifting felt like leaving the arms of my beloved mother. I had the sense she was there, too, fully healed and radiant, a flickering star but immortal in her beauty, no scars inflicted by the traumas of her human life, her embattled lineage. I didn't want to leave, but I knew it was time because I felt a strange sensation in my solar plexus, as if somebody down below were pulling me back by an invisible cord. I left the deep cosmos and reentered the earth's atmosphere, finding my house safely held by the surrounding fir, cedar, and pine-forested neighborhood. I phased back in through a wall, no need for doors.

"This is so strange, believe me, I know," I said to my cat who was once again stalking me, horrified by my transformation.

I hovered over him as he stared at me wide-eyed, until it all became too much for him. He hissed, swatted at the air, and tried to run away, scrambling on the granite surface of the kitchen counter, losing his balance and falling directly into a large plant underneath, breaking off a significant branch. "Dang it, Toosey," I said to Matisse as I hovered over the plant, assuming I was unable to touch the branch with my unearthly form, sad that it had to withstand an injury like that. "I'll put you in water when I can," I lovingly assured the stem and left the kitchen.

Taking one more spin around the house, I returned to my bedroom. I wondered if I could manipulate things physically and decided to conduct an experiment, attempting to shut the bedroom door. I was able to! After the incredulity of this entire situation, for some reason that really thrilled me.

The sound of the closing door woke the dogs, but they still gave no indication they could see me. They watched the door, disoriented with sleep, but ignored my invisible specter. I hovered over my sleeping body, wondering how I'd get back in. Did I just kind of drift down on top of myself or what? I noticed that my body had turned to lie on its right side since falling asleep, so my back was to the alarm clock. Before I attempted my redock into the mother ship, I glanced at the clock. 2:43 pm. I lowered down, effortlessly merging with my body, and instantly woke up, all parts of me reunited.

I lay there blinking myself awake, unmoving, a quiet "holy shiiiit" forming on my lips, unable to suppress a smile. I noticed the door to my bedroom was shut. "I really did close it!" I said out loud. Seva, my Saluki dog, was lying next to me on the bed, staring at me nonchalantly. Still thoroughly fascinated I said to her, "I'm going to turn around now, and if the clock says 2:43, I'm gonna lose it."

My mouth dropped open. The clock read 2:43. I sat there wide-eyed, gaping at it, unable to make any sense of this incomprehensible out-of-body field trip. I jumped out of bed and opened the door. There was one more thing to check.

I made my way down the dark staircase. It was still storming outside, with rain battering the windows. Matisse was scrambling around, hissing, still all puffed up. I tried to lighten his mood, murmuring, "It's all fine, Baby, it's all fine," letting him know I was no longer a specter. "I'm back, sweetheart." He stared at me, unsure. I turned to walk down the hall on the way to the kitchen and paused before I entered the room. I took a deep breath and walked through the doorway.

The large broken branch, forlornly on its own, lay next to the plant. Potting soil was scattered across the room, with little kitty footprints clearly visible. I started to shake, the reality of this sinking in, and bent down to pick up the branch, putting it in a vase of water to root. A strange combination of laughing and crying erupted out of me and with it a sense of pure joy, uncontaminated by doubt or disbelief.

Mind. Officially. Blown.

There are some experiences so reality bending that, try as it might, the analytical brain can't elbow its way into the story to explain it away as something we ate, something we made up, or something we misunderstood. I wasn't thinking about this experience in the context of "God," physics, neurophysiology, psychology, or anything else. My only thought was that I had absolutely no understanding of what this was or what could possibly be causing it, and that realization felt like magic. Normally insatiably curious, I found this mystery so unique that I didn't much care about the answer—the question itself was glorious. Where had I gone? And how? I entered the unknown, the unexplainable, and I came back, as far as I knew, completely intact. I had cruised some realm of the inner cosmos and found nothing to be afraid of.

Deep down, I sensed that all of this was somehow connected to my deeply intuitive identity, the one I had kept hidden for so long. It would no longer be contained. It wanted to be free, not relegated to the cellar of my psyche. And this, the human spirit as a living, breathing entity, was what intuition truly looked like. I trusted that someday it would make sense to me. For now, it didn't need to.

CHAPTER THIRTEEN

My astral traveling happened more and more frequently, and though I'd love to say it was all cosmic bliss, it occasionally spiraled into some dark places, including sharing the tragic experiences of perfect strangers.

It had been a normal Friday at work, nothing to report, an uneventful but hectic day at the New Hampshire veterinary hospital. Feeling exhausted, I made no plans that night beyond returning home to Theo and an early appointment with sleep. I curled up in bed, trying to decipher my latest book on Zen Buddhism, but after just a few pages I found I couldn't keep my eyes open. I gave up, turned the light off, and zonked out in a couple of seconds.

I dreamed I was in South Boston. In the dream I was walking, fully aware that a group of three teenagers was following me. It was dark—the middle of the night. I was walking on a long, straight path, with brick walls on either side of it. There was no escape but to sprint forward, and I was not particularly optimistic I could outrun them. I tried to talk myself out of the fear that they were predators. Perhaps they were just back there walking…but the hair standing on the back of my neck told a different story. I wondered if perhaps they were the kind of men who got off on walking silently behind a woman, just to cause her terror. I hoped this was the case. Maybe my fear was all they were looking for. Turns out they were looking for more.

"At least they're not going to rape me," I thought, as I lay on cold, filthy tile in the slow black tide of my bleeding wounds. Where was I? A locker room? A bathroom? It was daylight now and the sunlight forced its rays through grimy windows. They were stabbing me, again and again. I curled up into a fetal position, so they kicked me. I tried to stay focused on the pooling blood, which had a rainbow sheen and created something kind of beautiful before me. I heard wild screams coming from my larynx, but they didn't seem like my own. They kicked me where they had stabbed me. And then they stabbed me some more, five times in total, across my lower back and butt, as I had curled up to protect my vital organs. Their violent act felt initiatory, as if they were trying to prove something. They either knew how to avoid my death, or they were just exceptionally bad at killing a person. Whatever their motive, at least they left me with that—my life.

By now I was taking it stoically, pure logic guiding my experience. *Don't fight back. You have a better chance of surviving that way,* I advised myself. It was easy for me. After the initial shock of the assault I seemed to be simply observing my own attack, free of any emotion but empathy. I felt intense love for myself, having to endure such a trauma. I kept whispering, over and over, "I love you, I love you, I love you," trying to calm the screaming voice I was somehow connected to.

I have always had the ability to evaluate my dreams while they were occurring, like watching a movie with the director giving running commentary throughout. But I wondered how it was that in this dream I could feel so sticky with viscous blood. I mean, this was all just a dream, wasn't it? I felt the searing heat of the stab wounds and thought to myself, *I'll never again wonder what getting stabbed feels like.* Searching for a silver lining in this horror, this pathetic observation was the best I could do. I felt the pain. I felt the blood, the coldness of the ceramic tile below me, the shoes kicking my spine. I felt them rifle through my pockets looking for something to steal beyond my blood and dignity. But I felt no emotion—no fear, no anger—just the physical manifestation of this assault—I was completely sheltered from the psychological horrors of it. I was like a ghost, a drifting witness to human trauma with no attachment to the pain.

And then I woke up, back in my bedroom. It was an early weekend morning.

I lay there blinking, breathing heavily, struggling to reorient myself to the so-called real world. My senses remained on high alert as I sat up and shook my head to shake off what I had just experienced. I felt around my lower back. No stab wounds. I looked under the covers. No sea of hot, sticky blood. I lay back down and stared at the ceiling. "Well, *that* sucked." I said out loud, trying to stay light. "What the hell was that all about?" My heart was pounding out of my chest. By this time in my life I was at least used to the unexplained.

I got out of bed and followed the scent of freshly brewed coffee, still disoriented and shaky. "Dammit" I said, as I navigated the staircase, carefully feeling my feet connect with the thick white carpet. With each step I dug my toes in, trying to stop the current, to come back to Earth.

The *Boston Globe* was on the kitchen counter. I poured my coffee and leaned against the cabinet to peruse the front page. And then I dropped my freshly filled coffee cup to the unforgiving hardwood floor.

What I had dreamed last night was a headline on the front page of the Globe. Every detail there: South Boston, stabbed five times in the lower back and buttocks, three young attackers, robbery the perceived motive. I devoured the words before me, my mind scrambling to understand it. The victim was in critical care, and like the attackers also a young male. Theo came sauntering in with the sound of the dropped cup. "What the hell?" he pointed to the enormous coffee mess.

"He'll be okay!" I assured him. I shook the paper in my hands, pointing to the article about the young man whose stabbing I had endured with him. "He'll have a lot of pain to recover from, he'll be there awhile, but he'll be discharged. He'll be okay. There'll be psychological work, a lot of that to undergo, but the kid is going to be fine." I don't know if I really knew that, or just hoped it.

Theo looked at me as though I'd completely lost my marbles. He slowly shook his head, refilled his coffee and made his way back to his reading chair in the living room. I proceeded to clean up my spill, sopping up the coffee flood in a daze without explaining anything more. There was no point. I thought nobody was capable of understanding this. Even I was incapable of understanding. I was in this baffling state alone, my solid version of reality slowly unraveling, my brain being pushed to navigate this metaphysical obstacle course.

I was alone, but for the mysterious young man about whom

I have wondered since sharing that experience with him. The overwhelming sense of love I felt for myself during the dream was transferred to him upon reading the article. I felt like I knew him, like we were connected. And I somehow hoped that while he was enduring what he was enduring, he felt that love pouring out of me, witnessing his horrors, sharing his physical pain if not psychological, trying to soothe him, just a boy. I hoped he heard the mantra, "I love you, I love you, I love you," and that somehow helped him heal.

As was my pattern, I wanted it to mean something.

I was an empath, I knew that. Feeling experiences for other people was a trait I seemed to have been born with. I just never knew it could be experienced to such a degree. Now that my eyes were fully opened, and I was willing to explore this new world inside of me, I was discovering so much. Love and wonder and gratitude were easing out my previous foundation built of hopelessness, fear, and sadness.

I was becoming psychically agile, stronger. I couldn't know that all of this was practice. I couldn't know that in ten years, at the age of thirty-nine, I'd be connecting these teachings, each experience a thread in an elaborate universal tapestry, weaving an impenetrable protection that would literally keep me alive from terrors, real dangers I couldn't possibly comprehend.

CHAPTER FOURTEEN

*I*t was a few weeks before my thirty-first birthday when I dreamed of a man. We were naked, floating in the cosmos. It was dark, but also illuminated by stars flickering like candles above and below. I was straddling him, and we were making love, my tanned and toned long summer legs wrapped around his muscled back. Arching my spine, he was kissing my neck, my tousled hair trailing down my back. He was beautiful and powerful, with a shaved head, and he delivered a sense of wild ecstasy I had never experienced before. He was the full embodiment of the divine masculine, and drove me mad with desire.

"This is love?" I contemplated in shocked wonder, feeling the full force of it. "Because if this is what love feels like, I have clearly never felt it."

I woke up, lying next to a man I knew could never understand my spirit. It was over. After the usual heartbreak surrounding the dissolution of an eight-year relationship, I handed over the diamond platinum ring and we went our separate ways.

I declared to the Buddha that I would gladly spend the rest of my days single if it meant not having to compromise another day of my life living with a man who wasn't capable of truly knowing me. And within six months my cosmic dream man walked into my workplace for a job interview. Shaved head, 6'2", a muscled Adonis, impossible to miss. The women I worked with gestured behind his back. "Hire him!" they mouthed, with wild eyes and goofy smiles, silently nodding. He was a wonder to behold, a god in the presence of mortal men.

I didn't hire him, because I was out of my mind with desire the moment I saw him, and I felt that clouded my ability to judge his eligibility. There must be a sexual harassment lawsuit in there somewhere, but I hired a sweet and highly capable woman instead—who only lasted a few months and then decided she was moving to Arizona. Tentatively flipping through my filing cabinet, I found the man's resume. I called him. He was still interested.

There was no halting the irrepressible force that brought us together. Within a few months of stoically working together and trying to maintain professionalism, we said, "Definitely not stopping this," and gave ourselves to the waves washing over us, allowing the tide to carry us out to sea, right off the cover of a corny romance novel. He was also navigating a fractured engagement, way too similar to mine, but there was no denying this thing. The mad love we felt was nothing short of karmic.

Waking tangled up next to Aaron, legs and arms a jumbled mass, involuntary smiles across our faces, the unstoppable reflex of joy, desire never waning, was an introduction to the full capacity of my own heart. I explored his body with a hunger I'd never come close to experiencing before. I was insatiable. He was perfect, beautiful, powerful and sexy, hand delivered by the Buddha only after I'd made the universal declaration that I was good on my own. I realized that I had never been in love before, though I'd been engaged twice (my first when I was way too young, to a train wreck of a man addicted to every drug imaginable), as had he. *Third time's a charm* for us turned out to be less cliché and more of a portent. His was the kind of stunning beauty that turned heads wherever he went. He was smart and funny and compassionate and kind. He loved animals as much as I did.

I couldn't *believe* he was mine. Until I said, "Never again," I thought I was destined for felons and control freaks.

We never even had a real date. We moved in together as soon as we made the decision to jump into each other's arms, and within two years we were married.

There were no hidden skeletons. It never went south. Don't get me wrong; it wasn't always easy (it never is). We started our relationship a few months before the planes wreaked their havoc on September 11. Having experienced that horror from too close in New Hampshire, I resumed the confusion of my psychic evolution, which felt like psychological unraveling as I struggled to meet my true destiny.

CHAPTER FIFTEEN

For three consecutive nights after the New York Trade Center collapsed to the ground of its beloved city, I dreamed I would go back to the same empty room in a still-standing twin tower. It was just me and the expansive, sparkling view of New York City at night, sitting at a lone desk in the middle of one giant empty floor. It was dead quiet. I could hear myself breathing, my own heart beating. Then "ding!" and an elevator door would open allowing a wave of thousands of people to come flooding into the room to surround my desk. I had a little pad of paper and a pencil. I was sweating profusely. They all ran at me, shouting things: "Tell him I never meant to snap at him that morning!" "Tell her that I love her more than anything and will never leave her." "Tell him that his plane ticket is in my filing cabinet at home and that he can't be afraid to fly after this! Okay? You tell him!" And there I was, hearing thousands of requests all at once, furiously trying to scribble all these notes for all of the living loved ones and then losing the words to the buzz of the swarm, the sound of spirits, the deafening drone of a million cicadas. I couldn't do it. Surrendering my pencil, I'd give up, declare defeat, and wake up to a pillow soaked with tears and nothing helpful to hang on to. The spirits of these murdered people carried no anger, no misunderstanding, no confusion…they asked for only one thing and that was to relay a one-sentence message to their beloved. The energy of these tragic strangers flooded me, and I was left with a broken heart and crushing frustration. I had no idea what to do with this.

"You're wasting your time!" I yelled to whatever something might be listening. "I don't know what I'm doing. I'm sorry. I don't understand."

Aaron and I moved to Minneapolis around this time, because after the tragedy all I wanted to do was be closer to family. My sister and father lived in Minnesota, and Minneapolis felt safe and familiar. Aaron was eager and ready for a change, having never lived anywhere but Boston. The novelty of the move energized us. Though everything was going all right, the old feelings of emptiness inside of me were rekindling; the frustrating feelings of not connecting with something I was supposed to be doing were becoming stronger.

And although I had no idea what any of it meant—and certainly not all of it was pleasant—after experiencing some of the unexplainable things that had happened to me over the past few years, another banal day at the office became nearly unbearable. The spirits made everyday living seem incurably boring.

In Minneapolis I took a job with a toxicology center, a corporate poison control center for veterinary and human medicine. Within a few years I was supervising the veterinary division. Aaron was getting tired of my "what is the meaning of my life" laments because they weren't going anywhere. I was talking in circles, never actually straying from my deeply worn rut. He was as frustrated as I was at my own inability to tap into the path of my life purpose and never really understood the search for it in the first place. To him, this concept of purpose felt like an abstract excuse for not digging into the life I had right in front of me, but purpose stalked me like a jaguar, and I couldn't ignore it even if I tried. And I knew it had nothing to do with what I was currently doing in my career. I hated my job. I hated it so much I could barely get up in the morning, and I could only do that with the help of a handful of prescription pills. By this time, I was seeing a psychologist for severe depression and a psychiatrist for my OCD, which had worsened due to stress. They'd see me every week, ask how the drugs were doing, and then pat me on the back, shove me out the door, and say "Go get 'em Tiger!" It was a nightmare. Not one of my therapists ever asked me if my life was working for me the way it was. Not one suggested a career change. Because I looked good, wore expensive clothes (that I couldn't afford), and was somewhat professionally functional, there was clearly nothing to see here…move along. Of course, I never shared with any of them my tendency for peculiar experiences. Those belonged to me and no one else.

I was driving home from a therapy session one evening, contemplating my earlier workday. In my corporate job, it was EPA reporting time which meant my days were spent in tedium, reviewing hundreds of cases—most of which involved accidental chemical exposures having happened to people and every species of animal. Like most other days, I had lost my temper with a coworker; likely some inane irritation had stoked my talent for sarcastically dismantling a person with surgical precision. And then I'd cool off and feel horribly guilty. Needless to say, I would rather not have revisited the fond memory of the few hours past and found myself instead wondering about my therapist's theme of the day—battling my inner demons. Should I be assertive, I wondered? Should I be passive? Is my assertiveness bordering on aggression? Am I passionate? Or just plain obnoxious? Who the hell am I, really? I was a jumbled collection of fractured pieces not forming a coherent whole. And why was it that in corporate America I was constantly rewarded for being mean? I was treated like absolute royalty. Make way for Queen Bitch in the Prada boots with four-inch heels.

These thoughts then led to the obvious progression of my next wandering thought, which was, "If I had to pick an animal that was stuck inside of me, what animal would represent me most accurately?" It took less than an eighth of a second for the answer to pop.

A claustrophobic porcupine on methamphetamines.

I laughed out loud and victoriously smacked the steering wheel, loving the visual!

A perfect analogy! I pictured the fractious animal's gritted teeth, her determination to challenge the confines of her very limited space. Tiny paws pushing, pushing inside my ribcage, spines bristling, likely the cause of my chronic heartburn. Having discovered my inner porcupine, I was suddenly struck with regret.

"Why a porcupine?" I lamented, barreling down the Minneapolis highway ten miles over the speed limit. Why not a hummingbird, flitting here and there, delicate yet full of action, never disturbing her surroundings. Graceful. Magical.

Capable. A hummingbird hurts no one's feelings. A hummingbird gets stuff done!

A porcupine?

Why not a mink? Luxurious and dignified, never losing her cool unless cornered. The Grace Kelly of woodland creatures. A mink would be soft and warm inside my rib cage. She'd never cause me heartburn.

Nope. I was a hopped-up prickly porcupine.

And therein lay my turmoil. I was constantly wishing I was what I am not.

To quell the inner porcupine and to fill the empty chasm, I continued to shop—not exactly what my therapist had in mind. The Mall of America—a mall so large it has its own police force and zip code—was located right next door to my office tower. As I battled the soul-killing frustration of this work, convinced it was destroying me, it was nothing a trip to Nordstrom for an expensive pair of shoes couldn't remedy—nothing except for my husband's rage every time I came home with another shopping bag. Bloomingdale's, Macy's, it didn't matter; they calmed me and enraged him.

Then there was the dread of tomorrow, which brought another workday. The new shoes would pump me up until 10:00 am or so, when I'd drop like a stone and start looking forward to the next purchase.

"Do you *combine?*" My cute pharmacist coworker said in her thick Minnesota accent. She twirled around in her chair, curled her hair with her finger, and snapped her gum with an impish grin on her face.

"Do I what?" I had no idea what she was talking about.

She leaned forward. "Do you combine?" She pressed. "Do you put all your purchases in your smallest shopping bag, so your husband thinks you had a minor night at the mall?" A few women around her, eavesdropping on our conversation, nodded their heads in agreement, eagerly awaiting my answer.

Jesus, this was apparently an epidemic.

CHAPTER SIXTEEN

The years progressed, and I was traveling a lot for my job. My periods of absence, the shopping, my chronic unhappiness, the high stress...all of these things were eroding my marriage. Painfully distant, Aaron would go to one level of the house, I'd stick to another, and we barely said two words to each other. The cosmic sex stopped. The involuntary smiles stopped too.

And the longings continued. I was afraid to leave my job because I made what I considered to be a lot of money, at least too much to comfortably walk away from. Of course, I spent more than I earned to manage my stress, which caused more stress only alleviated by more shopping, and on and on the vicious and mindless cycle continued. This was not my purpose. I wanted to serve humanity; I just wasn't sure how or by what means. I wanted to make the world a better place, not spend my time choosing between the red shoes or the purple. Dammit, I wasn't this superficial. There was an entire world inside of me that I wasn't accessing.

So, in my desperate attempt to crawl out of the blackened abyss of my own depression, I decided to play around with the idea of expressing myself through writing, the one thing that consistently made me feel alive. I contemplated starting a blog. As I sat on the couch, I thought to myself, "What would my blog be called?" and instantaneously, a title came to me.

Stark Raving Zen.

I *loved* it.

The name ignited something inside of me. A knowing, an understanding. I was Stark Raving Zen! Two forces battled for control inside of me—one pleading for me to let go, simplify, detach from all the bullshit, find my peace, live my purpose—and the other resisting the unraveling, unhinging, and crazy terrified of the thought. Because how could I do any of that without making enormous and risky changes? I started to write. It was only supposed to energize me a little. But with just a few entries I became lost in a new passion. I was finally learning how it felt to express myself. For the first time in my life, I was telling the truth about my life, and I didn't care who judged me for it.

Part Four

MEETING THE MENTOR

"When you demand nothing of the world, nor of God, when you want nothing, seek nothing, expect nothing, then the supreme state will come to you uninvited and unexpected.

~ Sri Nisargadatta Maharaj

"People say that what we're all seeking is a meaning for life. I don't think that's what we're really seeking. I think that what we're seeking is an experience of being alive… so that we actually feel the rapture of being alive."

~ Joseph Campbell

CHAPTER SEVENTEEN

*P*rior to starting my blog, I kept the details of my inner life locked up like Fort Knox. But when I turned thirty-five, a glorious state of authenticity began to drift down upon me. Guided by the power of this new creative outlet, I began to loosen my grip just a bit and told two people about my inexplicable experiences—my husband and my sister Jill.

Jill was three years older and the closest to me in age. We had a personal history of retreating and advancing, retreating and advancing—deciding we'd be close and then pushing each other away when one of us expected too much—like two stone pillars severely lacking in the family intimacy department. But I loved her dearly. My ailing father, and Jill, and her brood of children, were the primary reasons why I moved back to Minneapolis after 9/11. I needed to feel like I had a family.

Telling Jill and Aaron a few of my stories was liberating for me, and so healing. I began tentatively, expecting to be shot down straight out of the gate with something like, "It was something you ate…just a coincidence…you likely imagined it…." But instead I found the opposite. They asked questions, they were hungry to hear more, they were beyond interested and utterly fascinated, trusting, and believing.

I told my sister over hot tea, late at night in a Japanese restaurant. We closed the place, finally having to be shooed out the door. Tucked in a small booth, Jill's eyes teared, partly because she felt sad that I endured these confusing and terrifying experiences alone, and partly because she was sick with envy.

My husband reacted exactly the same, locked in eye contact in front of a roaring fire in our warmly lit den, trying to assess my words as something he could believe or not. He chose belief, fully supporting my need to talk about it. Then he got a faraway look in his eyes, became quiet, and spoke of his desire for something equally fantastic to happen to him. The sharing of my stories rekindled our cosmic flame. Enchantment brings everything back to life.

It blew my mind that somebody would envy an experience of astral traveling to the body of someone getting stabbed. But I guess the human spirit craves the great mystery invoked in certain types of sanity-questioning experiences. The reality of wonder, getting a quick taste of the divine or perhaps even some super-cool law of physics that just hasn't been explained yet, can produce the most euphoric of highs. I had to admit that even at their most terrifying, these experiences left me wanting more and struggling with the density of normal existence. Heavy gravity left me flightless until the next mind bender came along.

Nothing felt random. It all felt purposeful. Something or

someone was leading me somewhere, providing an instruction manual. I felt enrolled in some kind of trippy metaphysical flight school, seemingly from the moment I was born. No hallucinogens required.

Call it my super-control-freak nature, but I never had any desire to take any kind of drug beyond the use of alcohol, which for me was bad enough. I also had the burden of watching all the catastrophic consequences of heavy drug use through my first fiancé's tragically disastrous life. Drugs repulsed me because I blamed them for systematically destroying people I loved, for causing me so much heartbreak and rage and confusion. So I'd never had any experience with a recreational drug outside of liquor; I'd never even smoked pot. But all the personal reasons aside, I think I knew from a young age that on some level my brain was wired differently and messing around with drugs would be a colossally bad idea for me.

Right at the moment, however, nothing much was happening on a metaphysical level. I just kept showing up to my job in corporate toxicology, with relentless stress and anxiety as the result. Already three-quarters burned out when I left New Hampshire, I was attempting to squeeze a few more drops out of a repressive career, in a field that was way more stressful than anything I had experienced before. Each day felt like one of those brutal scenes in a movie where the horse is running and running, and the person on the saddle just keeps whipping and whipping. There was only one possible ending for me, and that was total burnout.

By this time, my blood pressure was skyrocketing, and I was suffering from nearly constant migraines. I became volatile and so depressed I could barely leave my bed. I was still seeing a psychologist and a psychiatrist, because my OCD was now at a monstrous level. I'd spend hours cleaning the house and then cleaning it again, and then just a bit more, and then I'd start all over again. The skin started peeling off my fingers from all the cleaners, and I took pleasure in discretely chewing off the rough patches and jagged edges. Finally, I discovered rubber cleaning gloves, and at least was able to lesson the destruction of my poor hands.

After a few years in Minneapolis, my husband and I chose to move to a small town outside the Twin Cities Metro area to be closer to my ailing father, who was losing a valiant battle to cirrhosis of the liver and emphysema. My commute doubled, but I found greater peace in the quiet farming community with rolling hills and maple trees. My house became a peaceful haven—helpful, but not a complete remedy for the struggles I faced daily at work.

I walked my dog a lot. By this time I shared my life with a spunky American Staghound. There was a state recreational park just minutes from my home, and when the seasons allowed, I was always there on my days off. I had my favorite five-mile loop, and it became my morning ritual. The riparian forest was old and beautiful, with mainly deciduous hardwoods bordering the massive Minnesota River, and there never seemed to be anyone else there. It centered me, healed me, kept the thread by which I perpetually hung at least somewhat fortified.

It wasn't long before I discovered the forest to be completely enchanted, haunted, which brought me right back to the dimension of the fantastic that had been closed to me by the stress of my work. Strange and thrilling things started happening in those deep woods, and I was blessed to have my beloved dog with me as I walked my daily miles with nothing but birdsong and rustling leaves for sound.

I could feel myself waking up again.

CHAPTER EIGHTEEN

*L*ike anyone who spends a lot of time in the woods, I experienced magical things that happened within the purely mundane realm of nature, and I was grateful to witness them. Like the day I watched a garter snake having fifty wriggling babies right on the path in front of me, all squiggly, sprinting their way into their new life on planet Earth. Or the little red squirrel, speeding along his arboreal highway, who took a wrong step and fell right down out of the sky, onto the back of my giant dog. Stunned, and a hunter by nature, he was too surprised to move, his big eyes bugging out of his head, not looking at the thing on his back, but at me instead, as if to say through frozen, gritted teeth, "What. Is. It?!" The little squirrel froze too, clearly understanding he was riding a predator, then shook his head and scampered off Finlay's back, furiously chirping like an obscene rodent sailor, fluffing his fur and hightailing it back into the trees, never to be seen again. I laughed so hard I nearly cried at my dog's dramatic yet subdued reaction, and Finlay, buoyed by my excitement, gave a wide smile and hopped a little; he was always a good sport, always ready for the adventure of what came next.

Finlay was enormous. He stood as high as my ribcage and had more muscles than a steroid-addled weightlifter. I never had much concern alone in the woods. This dog was bred to hunt coyotes and wolves, and it wasn't a distant ancestral memory for him. He came out of the womb ready to rumble.

It was a mid-May morning in our cherished forest together when I started talking to my spirits again. I felt connected in here, free, my scientific professional brain relaxing its grip on my heart. Playing a childish game that even I considered silly, I asked whomever may have been listening (I had no solid sense of "God") to "Let me see something really special, something I've never seen in nature before, and I'll be extra grateful!" or something like that. Feeling wondrous and peaceful, I closed my eyes, allowing Finlay to guide me, not stressing about anything at all, no expectations, feeling the leaves crunch beneath my feet. And then my giant dog froze.

I opened my eyes. Finlay was staring about ten feet in front of us, directly into the forest. "What is it?" I asked him, fully aware that a dog like him, a sighthound, has 20/20 vision from a mile away, so it was very likely I wouldn't catch his train of vision. "What do you see, Fin?" I squinted into the distance, patting him gently on his powerful ribcage, feeling his heart pounding. He looked at me and took one step closer then looked again, harder, as if to say to me, "It's *RIGHT THERE!*" And then I saw it. Literally three feet in front of my face, a magnificent mink clinging to the side of a tree—two feet long, nose level with me, perfectly camouflaged, the color of tree bark.

I held my breath and backed up, not out of fear but respect. This was one of the most beautiful creatures I had ever seen. I would have walked right by her had Finlay not stopped me, if perhaps I hadn't asked the spirit realm to show her to us. I felt so honored, so blessed, my heart felt like it would explode with wonder. We all froze together, the mink's black diamond eyes sparkling, her perfect little round face completely still, the flash of tiny white fangs protruding.

Finlay wasn't wanting to chase her or even step any closer. He remained totally silent. The mink, a species that is generally ferocious when threatened, didn't utter a sound and made no attempt to move. I stood back, satisfied with my respectful four-foot viewpoint. The mink clung there, frozen, with eyes wide. She seemed more curious than terrified, although I'm sure she was both. The sun rays danced across her, running their fingers through her luxurious fur—her energy flowed in waves of radiance, and all of nature worshipped her utter perfection. I talked to her quietly, just a few words. Every time I said something, she cocked her little head at me. "You're beautiful." Head to the right. "I have never seen anyone more beautiful." Head to the left. "Thank you for allowing us to see you today." Head to the right.

I didn't want to, but out of courtesy to her I finally dragged myself out of her tractor beam. The last thing I wanted was to cause her stress. I bowed my head to her, hand to heart, excusing myself from her presence and wandered back through the woods in a euphoric state of complete awe at the beauty of nature. My mind was thoroughly blown from the coincidence—was it just coincidence?—of asking to see something unusual and having nature overdeliver to such an incredible degree in less than ten steps. The beauty of this coincidence was compounded by the memory of the visualization exercise I had done in my car weeks before, when I longed to be a mink or a hummingbird rather than a hopped-up porcupine on methamphetamines. Was this my inner mink? Was somebody trying to tell me something?

I went to work the next day, still high on life from this direct contact with nature, and I told my boss, a clinical toxicologist, what had happened. He replied, completely bypassing the fact that a mink is an extremely rare wildlife sighting, "I'm sure it just froze because it was afraid. Nothing unusual about that."

Wow. Way to completely diffuse the magic of the moment. He looked at me incredulously, like, "Why are you telling me this, you wacko?" I returned to my cubicle and with that, I was back in the sterile realm of toxicology.

But the woods kept delivering. The next time I hiked through, I stopped for a moment to let Finlay scratch his ear, which can take a while when you have stilts for legs and tiny feet angled like running blocks. While I paused there, enjoying the sun on my face, something enormous blew by my head. It was so loud, like someone standing right next to me swirling a rope with a heavy rock attached to it. I felt and heard the wind rush by my face and then a gentle brush on my cheek, but saw nothing! I gasped, putting my hand to my face.

Finlay had no reaction at all. He didn't see it or feel it, or if he did, he didn't respond in the slightest, which for a sighthound is a very unlikely scenario. It was terrifying. It was as if a large invisible raptor had just swooped by a half an inch from my head! I know peregrine falcons can dive at over 200 mph; would this be beyond the visual acuity of a human? Where did it go? We were in dense trees, not the diving backdrop of open air and skyscrapers, so what are the odds a falcon could swoop into the deep forest, missing all the trees, then swoop back up without a human or a dog detecting it? I'm generally so in awe of nature that I believed this could have been a natural, albeit fantastic, experience, but it confused me so much that it left me wondering if this thing could have been supernatural. Still astonished, I continued my walk with a deep sense of fear and confusion. I felt firmly rooted in reality yet at the same time I seriously wondered if I'd just narrowly escaped death. That invisible, giant raptor thing—whatever it was—nearly crashed into my skull! My stomach twisted. I had been through enough disorienting experiences by now to know that sometimes I teetered right on the line between two dimensions.

Still in that numinous space, I came around a corner and froze again, inhaling with another gasp. My heart could not catch a break but was once again whipped into a full gallop. Finlay remained unfazed. Fifty feet ahead of me, up in a giant maple tree so large it created a covered canopy over the trail, were twenty or thirty indigenous men of various ages—hanging out, sitting, standing on branches, crouching, some kicking their feet. They were laughing and yelling at each other, clearly having a peaceful good time in the tree. I couldn't understand their language. Dakota? Ojibwe? I could only take a romantic guess based on the region's history. They were so real, every bit as solid-looking as you or me. At first, I truly believed they were living people, here in flesh and blood. I wasn't worried. These guys seemed to be just taking a break, having fun, and were uninterested in me or my dog. At this point, my left brain was dragging behind, still trying to process the experience from a few steps before. I stood there looking up at them—not so much afraid as overwhelmed—when one of them looked down at me and casually said, "Hello," in English.

As soon as my ears registered the sound of his voice, all of the men vanished. Or perhaps they were just no longer visible to me, I don't know. Finlay never skipped a beat. If he had heard them or seen them, he just wasn't all that interested, preferring instead to sniff the forest floor. I stood there staring up at the tree, wondering just how much I could process at once, and if they were still there just beyond my vision. I remembered my oldest brother Jeffrey's theoretical explanation of my experiences with intangible things—spirits, ghosts…I didn't know what to call them—and it moored me in this moment of silence. He had studied astrophysics at Columbia University, and his brilliance provided an anchor for me. An atheist who did not believe in the concept of spirits, he once tried to explain to me a controversial scientific theory that certain people are somehow wired to be able to see across dimensions, gaining momentary glimpses into other worlds, only to readjust back to this dimension with painful confusion. My brother isn't emotionally demonstrative, so his attempt to cast light on a perplexing and chronic experience for me I found to be touching. He never said, a) you're flakey or b) you're insane—and I was so grateful that he allowed me my reality, and my experiences, even if he chose to discount what I was seeing and experiencing as a connection to the spirit world.

Since I was always apprehensive about external judgment, seeing people who were *there one minute and not there the next,* was an experience I generally kept to myself. That night I casually told my husband I thought I had seen something but passed it off as the workings of a stressed brain that had just been asked to process the unexplainably disturbing *whooshing* event.

Shortly thereafter, I experienced another visitation in these woods, and it managed to surpass the last. Walking along the path in the quiet of midday, I suddenly heard a horse running behind me, fast and out of control. I didn't have time to turn around. Finlay reared up, his hair standing on end, and tried to turn to face it. I felt the earth tremble beneath its pounding hooves right behind us, felt its furious breath on my neck, heard it scream. I literally dove out of the way and landed flat on my chest, knocking the wind out of me. The leash still connected me to Finlay who had retreated before me, crashing through the dry leaves, panting, terrified, only to turn around to...nothing.

No horse, no sound. Nothing but dead quiet.

This time I knew with certainty that Finlay had experienced everything I had, because his response was faster than mine. I sat there in the cool grass, trying to comprehend, my mouth opening and closing like a gasping fish. Finlay stood panting, eyes wide and completely confused, snapping his head right and left in a desperate attempt to locate the specter. We were both shaking. I sat there until my heart slowed and my breathing calmed.

I got up and stretched my legs. I felt Finlay all over to be sure he was okay. He was fine. He carefully tip-toed around the path, sniffed the grass, and seemed to be wondering if the mad beast would return. I said out loud, "A phantom horse. *Really?*!" The sound of my own voice calmed me down, but I was still shaking. Finlay refused to continue our walk. Like a hot-blooded racehorse, he was easily frazzled. I stood with him, gently smoothing the hair on his head and running his silky little ears through my fingers. I told him it was okay, and he looked right into my eyes in utter disbelief, as if to say, "Seriously? Is that thing coming back?"

He collected his wits after a few more minutes and shook himself, trying to remove any remnants of the baffling ghost-horse. He forced a couple of yawns, trying to reset his nervous system. We started walking again, slowly, and in just a few steps came upon a gravestone, right off the path. I had been by it a thousand times before but had never thought anything of it. This time, I stopped. I crouched down and brushed off the dirt. It looked ancient. I could barely read it, but it said something about a young woman who had died in her early twenties in around 1800, almost 200 years before.

My head became filled with blurry visions of this beautiful girl laughing, riding, smiling atop her horse, galloping across the prairie. The gravestone said her cause of death was unknown. "Maybe it had something to do with a horse?" I said to Finlay. My legs buckled and I sat there in awe at the memory of what we had just experienced. Finlay was calm, lying beside me, carefully grooming his paw.

They were starting again, fantastic anomalies were reaching out of some dream world and pulling themselves into my consciousness. I felt a peace wash over me, not a resistance. By now I was thirty-eight years old. Nearly a decade earlier in New Hampshire, I had told the dead thing that reached for me with cold, scratchy hands, that I wasn't ready. Or maybe, at that time, I was the cold scratchy dead thing…desperate to come alive.

I was ready now. My soul was alive. I felt it with all of my heart. "I'm not afraid," I said to the forest. "Do you hear me? I'm not afraid."

CHAPTER NINETEEN

As much as these phantasmal nature experiences enlivened me, I still hated my work so badly I could barely muster the physical and psychological effort required to get myself there. I was floundering, struggling, and totally disconnected from my veterinary career.

My bosses became less accommodating, and my inability to do my job became more evident. My blood pressure was raging out of control no matter what I was prescribed. I didn't know what to believe anymore. If I were to believe my CEO, I was a flawed individual, and as an employee, I certainly had become that. But throughout my career I had always been the perfect one, the overachiever, the one everyone could count on, the workaholic who answered emails at eleven at night or four in the morning. My "perfection" was the foundation of my entire identity, but now I had become so imperfect. I just couldn't bear the emergence of this flawed persona or witness my psychological downward spiral. My spirit was breaking entirely. I hated this person I had become, this person who couldn't keep up, who couldn't pretend her way through life any longer.

I began a regular habit of calling in sick, coming in late, leaving early. I told my superiors I was struggling and that there were certain duties I didn't feel I could handle right now. They didn't relieve me of those duties. Instead, they pushed me harder. Like most executives, they had no understanding of severe psychological burnout. They became more and more disillusioned with me. This machine, this previously perfect employee, was becoming such a disappointment. I'd been the Golden Child throughout my veterinary career; and now it was all unraveling.

I woke up one morning and shuffled my way to the kitchen as usual. I opened my cupboard and placed the usual containers of pills on my spotless countertop. Effexor, Wellbutrin, Lisinopril, hydrochlorothiazide…. This cocktail of antidepressants and antihypertensives would get me through the day. I put the pile of pills in the palm of my hand and stared at it. It suddenly felt so ridiculous to be living a life that required all this chemical assistance; a life that might so easily be redirected if I could just jump tracks and start over. "I can't stand it," I said to my husband who was leaning against the counter, drinking his coffee, watching me stare at the pharmaceutical silver bullets in my hand. "I think I'm going to die." Never a good crier, I felt a single methodical tear march stoically down my face.

I'd said these things countless times before, but today Aaron changed his script. Instead of giving me the usual pep talk, instead of giving me the support he thought I needed, he said something new.

Just one word.

"Quit."

"I can't quit." I snorted and quickly wiped away the one rogue tear. Is he serious? I thought to myself, squinting my eyes at him, searching for evidence either way.

"Quit," He said, "I'm serious. I can't take it anymore. I can't take watching you slowly die. You were burnt out eight years ago. Quit."

"But how will we manage? How will we survive?" Inside I was begging for him to continue with this permission, this radical decree; but my brain continued to replay its *does not financially compute* memo over and over inside my head.

And then with words that completely broke me free of the pattern I'd been languishing in for so long, and launched me into a powerful new odyssey of discovery, he said, "I don't know Kristy. But I don't care. I don't care if we lose everything. It's just *stuff*." He gestured wildly, encircling the exquisitely decorated house. "You've got to do something about this life, this work that you hate."

A glorious inferno ignited within me.

I drove straight to the office and tendered my resignation. My boss sputtered and stammered, completely flummoxed. He said he didn't accept it. Like a bad comedy sketch, I literally chased him around the office trying to get him to take the letter from my hand. There was no way I was changing my mind. Afterwards, he pulled several people into his office. "Did you know Kristy was leaving?" he drilled them. With shrugs, their answers were variations of "No, nope, no I didn't." And they were absolutely telling the truth, because even Kristy didn't know Kristy was leaving.

And with that, I pulled up anchor and set sail into my new

world. Had I known what I was willingly entering into, I would not have had the courage. I was heading straight into a spiritual, physical and psychological experience so intense that on a good day I would wonder if I had lost my mind, and on a bad day I would wonder if I'd survive. But on the worst days, I truly wondered if I was already dead, wandering the *bardo* lost and alone. I became immersed in a world I had previously only been allowed to glimpse, lest I lose my footing in this world and my sanity, and never be able to return.

I called on my Zen tools. Non-attachment: my identity is not my career. I won't disappear because I've quit the only life I have ever known. Mindfulness: stay in the moment, stay connected only to what is real in each present moment.

CHAPTER TWENTY

*I*n absolute silence the sun peeked through the pale yellow floral curtains of my bedroom, rubbed its eyes, and thought about rising. After spending a short stint in the professional purgatory of my two-week notice, I woke up to a strange mix of elation and terror when I realized I was officially unemployed. What the hell had I done? And then—why the hell hadn't I done this ten years ago?! Back and forth I swung between feelings of illumination and freedom followed by dread, loss, and panic.

My identity was my connection to veterinary medicine. Twenty years before, when I had lost my mother to cancer, lost my entire family it seemed, veterinary medicine became my new tribe. It cared for me, accepted me, took me in with all of its strange smells, fascinating questions, and intellectual challenges. Who was I if I was no longer connected to veterinary medicine? It felt so free, but it also felt like I was falling down a black hole into nothingness. I had no idea what I was going to do next.

The sun had barely risen, and my husband had left for work an hour ago. I lay there alone, wrapping myself in the soft dimness, trying to process the full scope of this newness. I felt a strange prickling sensation across my entire body, and the familiar buzzing of my early thirties began. I let go, feeling I had nothing to lose. The hands, the cold scratchy hands that once seemed so horrifying to me now felt completely different. They were warm and soft, delivering energy with comfort and love. I felt their message, "You are not alone." Three hands held me, one clasped around my left wrist, one around my right bicep, the third gently and reassuringly on my right shoulder. They didn't feel like banshees this time. They felt like soft angels imploring me to keep going. I wasn't afraid. I was ready for this.

"Where am I going?" I quietly asked in the darkness.

And I sensed their silent response, "Wherever you'd like to go."

Arya, my new puppy, snuggled up next to me, resting her silky chin on my neck. I felt a level of peace like I had never felt before. Finlay was stretched out at my feet. My entire body seemed to exhale, and I relished the early morning darkness with my two dogs sleeping next to me. I was suddenly free to be whatever or whomever I wanted. Maybe for the first time in my life I could actually be myself. But I didn't have to figure that out right now. For now, right here in this moment, I was a blank slate, and I had only puppy breath to contemplate.

CHAPTER TWENTY-ONE

Months before my departure from my job, I had fallen in love with a pup that had wiggled her tiny way into my heart through a simple photograph. I'd been in love with sighthounds for a couple of decades—they are my true spirit dogs. But the breed to which I feel the strongest ancient karmic connection is the Egyptian Greyhound, otherwise known as the Saluki. My precious Seva, my first Saluki, lived to be sixteen years old and had died a couple of years earlier. She struggled with the usual geriatric maladies, including arthritis and increasing dementia. We did everything we could to keep her comfortable but one day, as she lay on her bed next to me, I asked her to tell me when it was time for her to go. In a split second her whole body appeared to ignite in flame—not as a horrific image, but as an eternal spirit. As soon as I registered the shift, it was gone, and my precious Seva was back in her rickety physical form. I knew it meant that her answer was, "Anytime now. I want to go." I felt her dementia was a symptom of having two feet in this world and two feet in her next. I called a dear old friend, a veterinarian, to come to our house and help her pass on to her next life in the comfort of her own home. Finlay was a puppy then, around ten months old, and we had him temporarily in his kennel in the family room so we could focus on Seva at her time of parting. The moment Seva's spirit left her body, Finlay began barking and howling in his kennel, either desperate to say goodbye, or perhaps wishing her bon voyage.

Seva had felt like a guide for me, a wise Sherpa. I adopted her shortly after I'd lost my mother and it felt like it was me and her against the world. She was stubborn and callous and hated just about everyone on the planet except Aaron, who entered her world when she was ten years old, and me. We loved her more than anything, and I mourned her terribly. So much had happened in my life in those sixteen years she shared with me, including breaking up with my longtime fiancé and meeting the love of my life. When we moved from New Hampshire back to Minnesota, it seemed it was finally time for her to get off this earthly ride. For so many of her years, she had held me together.

So, when Delilah, the breeder from whom I'd adopted her, sent me an image of a day-old Saluki baby that looked exactly like Seva, I knew she had to join our family. It didn't take much to convince Aaron and before I knew it, I was flying to Los Angeles to personally escort our new baby home. When I arrived in LA, Delilah welcomed me into her home of Salukis, some of them distant relatives of my beloved Seva. Meeting my new puppy was love at first sight. I watched her for hours, becoming more and more smitten. Finally, the babies reached their daily energy expiration and collapsed for the evening, curled up around their mother's warmth. I collapsed too, my heart full, and went to sleep that night directly beneath a garden-level, open window that had no screen. I was too in love to be bothered by such a detail.

The next morning I woke up at the crack of dawn to catch my plane, had a quiet moment with my new puppy's mother, promising her that I'd care for her baby as if she were my own, promising her that she would never want for anything. She growled at me then, just in time for Delilah, more than a little eccentric, to come rushing into the room, asking, "What did you say to her?! Apologize at once!" And though I felt that I had said all the right things, the truth was I was taking a mother's baby, through no choice of her own. For that, I did deeply apologize, and I felt a little sick about it. The breeder scooped the pup up and placed her in a travel bag, shoved a tranquilizer in her mouth and rushed me out the door.

By the time we got to the airport I thought my puppy was dead. I had never seen an animal so young be so sedate, which was extremely disturbing, being that I worked in veterinary medicine. I called my best veterinary friend, and she told me to keep rubbing her to keep her stimulated. I was horrified. I boarded the plane and kept her on my chest, warm and safe, bouncing her and patting her ribcage. The flight attendants never suggested I place her under the seat for the four-hour journey, and near the end of our travel time, she perked up some. A little drunk, she tried to focus on my face, going a little cross-eyed then wall-eyed before she finally made eye contact. I named her Arya, after the Buddhist goddess, Arya Tara, who is described as a loving star by which to navigate.

From the moment she entered our lives she performed that role to a literal extent I never could have predicted. At the time, we were just delighted she was here with us. Finlay, the enormous warrior, treated her like fine china; he was so delicate and tolerant with her. She was a princess from a 1,000-year-old Egyptian lineage. She was magic. Pure joy.

CHAPTER TWENTY-TWO

So there I was—unemployed, on my first week untethered and drifting—sitting at the computer late in the evening while the office window next to me rattled and creaked. I paused and took a deep, relaxing breath, savoring the feeling of being warm and safe while the snow piled up outside. The Minnesota wind howled like a feral thing, in true January form. I was so content. The raging tempest drove me further inside myself, where life in this moment felt real and raw and uncensored.

I was surfing the internet, following up on a term a friend had recently used: Spiritualism. I wanted to learn more about it. I hadn't had much contact with anybody in the first days of my unemployment because I found myself frequently swatting away biting comments from misguided people. The conversations were getting familiar:

"So, what are you going to do now? What's your plan?" concerned ally would say.

"I really want to write, for now. Figure some things out," I'd reply.

"Write what?" (Abstract ideas were not going to cut it.)

"I'm not sure. For now, I'm writing a blog. Getting comfortable. You know, just figuring some things out."

"Well that's not going to buy groceries," they'd snort, peering into their crystal ball to view their version of my future, the one where I starve to death due to my own ridiculous folly. Sometimes I sensed they actually looked forward to this ending, as if the version where I pulled myself out of this broken life and found stability and happiness was way too disruptive of their worldview. People can't just start over, can they? How reckless. How irresponsible. How arrogant. Insane even.

I couldn't argue with them. Perhaps complete destruction was exactly what I was headed for. But at the moment, I couldn't think that far ahead.

I had found my way to an image on the internet that was making my hair stand on end. I froze, electrified, staring at it while the wind still howled outside. Three women in a black and white image from 1850. They had period hair styles with large elaborate buns. Every sense of my being knew these women. Their outlandish hairstyles were what my eighteen-month-old self had interpreted as hats. These were my women from the crib incident decades before. My mind locked onto that image. Without a doubt, I knew them.

Named the Fox Sisters, they played an important role in the creation of Spiritualism, the belief that spirits of the dead have the ability and desire to communicate with the living. The two youngest Fox sisters, Maggie and Kate, were notorious for allegedly communicating with the dead and became world-famous mediums. They claimed that certain "rappings" on walls and furniture were spirits revealing their presence to the living. Their oldest sister Leah managed their careers and for many years they had great success. In 1888, however, Maggie and Kate revealed that their rapping phenomenon was a hoax and demonstrated how they pulled it off. Later Maggie attempted to recant her confession, claiming to have been coerced into declaring her life a lie by those who considered the entire idea evil. But it was too late; they were exposed as frauds and publicly ruined. Within five years all three sisters were dead; they ended their days in abject poverty.

This blew me wide open.

Though the details were very different, this felt like my story. I never claimed to understand any of the things that I had experienced. I certainly didn't share them as fact or fiction. I never spoke of them at all. But the worldview which would be so quick to label me as crazy for having these experiences, which forced me to suppress this side of me entirely, didn't feel valid to me either. It felt too simplistic, like a lazy explanation. "You're insane" began to feel like a cheap response to anything outside societal agreement or scientific understanding. And I sensed that millions of others across time had experienced and were experiencing these same restrictions, fearing for their reputations (or their very lives) should they step out of the shadows and claim their full intuitive experience.

The Fox Sisters. They needed me to…what? Heal them in some way? Heal myself in some way? They were my women, the women who had connected me to my own secret supernatural world. They had peered over my crib and invaded my consciousness when I was just a baby. Here I was now, ready to claim my experience. No more secrets. No more fear or shame. The Salem witch trials had been over for three hundred years. Why were so many of us still retreating into the safety of conformity, and that dreaded word—normalcy? What was I afraid of, besides an inexplicable sense of complete and utter annihilation?

I decided in that moment that I needed a journey of discovery. I needed to go back to visit my puppy's breeder in California, but not to get another puppy. She was a highly intuitive psychotherapist who also happened to be an esteemed Tarot card reader. The Fox Sisters needed me to do something, and for now I determined that my first step was to take ownership of my own intuitive/empathic abilities. In so doing, I would write about it, freeing others to do the same. The Fox Sisters just needed me to *be myself,* and write about it, though as yet I had no solid understanding of who my authentic self was. I had been living (mostly) in an analytical world, on a foundation of logic from which I had learned to completely suppress and deny the truth of my whole self, my intuitive self.

I finally had a plan. I would leave in a week, drive to California, learn Tarot, be gone a month or so, and then drive home—a new woman with a shiny new life. Aaron was a little disillusioned with the thought of me being gone for a month, but he knew I was floundering and fully supported anything I felt I needed to do to find clarity. We agreed that I'd take Arya with me. She could see her mother again and she was too young, ten months at the time, to be left alone all day while Aaron was at work. The truth was, Aaron knew she would be a perfect road-trip partner. He didn't want me to be alone. Honestly, the thought of me and Arya on the open road delighted me. Our big adventure. I was so excited, feeling the heartbeat of purpose.

To my bold suggestion, the Saluki breeder gave a resounding yes. There were organizational things she needed help with, and I could do those things in exchange for room and board and my Tarot lessons. My family was horrified. My Ivy League brother Jeffery, sarcastic and mystified by what he deemed to be my increasing nonsense—and steered by his own succinct scientific opinion—snorted, "Los Angeles is the last place most people would choose for a spiritual quest." But I was certain this was my next step. Meanwhile, my siblings discussed in private whether or not it was time to seek professional intervention.

My sweet brother Scott snuffed that talk with his own observation about the writings in my blog, *Stark Raving Zen*. He said, "I don't know what's happening with Kristy, but I do know she's giving people hope, making them feel better about their own lives. Who am I to question that? Who am I to label that unwell?" The consensus was to let me be.

CHAPTER TWENTY-THREE

I chose to depart in five days, which gave me time to finalize some things and make the needed preparations. In our household I was the one who paid the bills, balanced our checkbook, and managed our finances. I was meticulously detailed and scheduled every payment over the next month, writing out checks with the proper dates and creating a calendar for Aaron. Each bill had a sticky note attached that notified him exactly when to mail it. I wrote lists for which plants to water when, what books I suggested Aaron read while I was gone (to explain what I was going through), how best to care for the cats and Finlay in my absence, and probably countless other inane management suggestions that he was so good about quietly ignoring. My OCD was alive and kicking and not quite collapsed yet; my detail-driven left brain was still dominantly running the show.

Curled up a few nights before my departure, my comforter pulled high up to my chin, I had the bed to myself while Aaron watched TV in the den. It was dark and quiet. I could hear the soft cadence of Finlay's breathing as my warrior angel lay protectively stretched out on the carpet beside my low platform bed. I slid my hand out from my warm cocoon and rested it on his ribcage. I felt his lungs expand and contract, and a feeling of gratitude came over me, gratitude for him, gratitude for love itself. I felt solid, like my presence on this planet just might have been more than chance. For the first time in my life, I felt that I was on the precipice of meaning. Not much was happening yet, but I had walked through a new doorway. I was okay with not knowing where it led.

The pattern of Finlay's breath comforted me, lulling me into a trance-like, theta-brainwave state: that lovely stepping-stone of consciousness just prior to sleep. In that gauzy between-world place of formlessness, I experienced something new. The same voice that had instructed me so many times in my dreams was suddenly clear as a bell, a man talking directly to my left, so distinct it was as if I had a microphone in my ear.

"Go find your spirit, Child." Calm and placid, like a deep-voiced Zen monk.

It shocked me wide awake. I sat bolt upright, sending Finlay onto his feet to wonder what the alarm was. And then a protective warmth spread throughout my entire body, a feeling of love like I had never experienced before. I was loved. I was love itself. I wasn't alone, had never been alone.

And I was officially, truly, hearing voices.

CHAPTER TWENTY-FOUR

I had a bachelor's degree in psychology at the time, which was just enough to offer me a little comfort when certain unexplainable phenomena occurred. Hearing voices, typically connected to schizophrenia, is one of those things that puts you on the fast track to the psych ward in the view of many traditional psychologists. But schizophrenics suffering auditory hallucinations often hear malevolent voices. "Command hallucinations" refer to voices that command a person to do something, generally harmful to themselves or others, and can be terrifying and confusing. In psychological pathology, the voices a person hears can be insulting, ridiculing, and brutally damaging. Hearing voices should not be confused with our inner dialogue. Everybody experiences inner dialogue; it tells us that our brains are functioning, that we're thinking. But some people hear distinct voices that are indistinguishable from that of a person actually speaking. And what is mind-blowingly fascinating about this, is that brain studies done on people who hear these voices reveal that when they are listening to them, the parts of the brain responsible for processing real speech are actively engaged, even though nobody else in the room is talking or hearing the voices.

It is also widely understood that a psychologically healthy portion of the population—depending on the research, anywhere from 8–16 percent—can also hear these invisible mysterious voices. Not considered pathological, the voices are generally helpful. They guide and gently inform with love and wisdom. People who can hear such voices, people like me, have often experienced trauma in their lifetime; according to traditional western psychology, the voices are thought to be the manifestation of chronically repressed emotion. But emotions don't have voices, so why does the language center of the brain fire up when they're being heard?

All I know is that when I experienced this moment of clairaudience it felt like one of the greatest gifts I have ever received, because there was nothing my brain could do to discount it. It was so real, so loud, so crisp, just like the experience of seeing people who aren't physically there. They don't flicker in and out like a puff of colorful steam—they are solid, like any other person you come in physical contact with. Hearing this voice in my ear felt like receiving an ancient skeleton key to one of the universal mysteries, only to open the box and find more mysteries. But the sense of overwhelming love that came with it was enough to empower me for all my days. I felt a truth; I knew I wasn't crazy.

Clairaudience gave me a sense of affirmation, of confidence. With all the financially risky decisions I had been making, with all the insights that came pouring through when I quit my job, there was always an inner dialogue that screamed something like, "What the hell are you doing?! Have you gone mad?!" But when the clairaudience happened, those voices grew still. It was as if the process of higher consciousness just wiped the slate completely clean, and I had to admit that something bigger was at play here.

My intuition was getting stronger, being refined.

So I decided to explore a little bit, to test my wingspan. I asked several friends if they'd mind doing an experiment with me. Would they give me an item belonging to someone in their life they had lost, and let me see if I could contact them through dream? Though several agreed to play, I chose only two. I wanted to keep this small and simple.

The experience was profoundly intimate, and I connected. I received clear messages through my dream state, highly detailed information that I was to specifically relay to both people, things my friends had never shared with me. Distinct visions, like snapshots in their histories, very specific fragments of their being—a love of sunflowers, a project one of them was working on before he died, a rare phobia of Ferris wheels, a betrayal...I went into the whole project flippant and curious. "This is what I got," I began, proceeding to relay everything I had been shown and told, not having any idea if any of it would be meaningful to either friend. I had nothing to lose. No pressure, these were friends of mine. Had I scored a zero out of hundred, they'd still love me.

But I quickly realized the gravity of what I had done when each woman collapsed, incredulous under the weight of what I had shared; the visions, the snapshots were profoundly meaningful to each of them. They cried, and one, an atheist, shared her sense that she was having what she referred to as a reverse crisis of faith, meaning suddenly her worldview had been so shaken she didn't know what to believe. I understood the heavy weight of this responsibility and felt foolish for having been so flippant about it.

I had never tried to harness this. I had never tried to control my intuition on demand. Having done so now, I was awed by it, and a little afraid—of what, I'm not sure. Had a deceased father really spoken to me? Or had I just telepathically mined his daughter's memory field? How did this work? How did I know this stuff?

The Fox Sisters were strong within me, and I started to feel the physical manifestations of spiritual energies. Whenever the Foxes were around, or any other spirits, I'd begin to violently shake with such force my jaws would tighten, my teeth would clench, and my muscles would spasm so forcefully my back felt like it would break. I felt an ice-cold sensation around my upper cervical vertebrae as if someone had opened the top of my neck and poured freezing cold water down my spine. Arya knew right when it was happening and she'd jog over to ground and comfort me, licking my face. She knew how to make the tremors stop. They were uncomfortable, but I accepted them as part of the growth process. It felt like learning to ride a bucking bronco. I only hoped that one day I'd be able to endure them more gracefully.

The next day I was leaving for California, on a freedom adventure. I felt so unhindered, excited, so thrilled to be alive.

That night before nodding off to sleep, the voice returned. Loud and strong, in my left ear. He said, "The man who taught you, the teacher in your dreams...go find him."

I replied, "Is he you?"

"Go find him," was his only reply.

Part Five

CROSSING THE THRESHOLD

"Who are you?" said the Caterpillar…

"I—I hardly know, Sir, just at present," Alice replied rather shyly,

"at least I know who I was when I got up this morning,

but I think I must have changed several times since then."

> *~ Lewis Carroll,*
> *Alice's Adventures in Wonderland*

CHAPTER TWENTY-FIVE

*M*y tiny emerald green station wagon was filled to the brim and parked in my driveway. I projected my giddy anticipation onto it, feeling its excitement, animating it to life with the promise of adventure. I had no idea how long I'd be gone, but my thought was a month or so. How long does it take to learn the art of Tarot? My plan was simple: clear my head, take one step, find a new path, begin again, start over.

Along with the usual supplies, I packed an entire crate full of books that I was eager to read when temporarily settled in California. I created the coziest, most comfortable little resting place in the back seat for Arya, my sweet companion. She, however, preferred to sit shotgun with me in the front seat, which I wouldn't allow. The potential deployment of the airbag was too dangerous. Disappointed, she settled into her backseat nest as I said goodbye to Aaron and Finlay, both concerned for my safety. Finlay was feeling left out, and Aaron was living in a constant state of conflict. "Let her go" and "keep her safe" were both fighting for dominance, but the truth was, it wasn't his choice, and he knew that. I had to go. I had to do this. He hugged me forever, kissed the top of my head, and told me a month was too long, to just get back home as soon as I felt I could. I promised I would.

Finlay wasn't so easily appeased. I kneeled face to face with him, and whispered in his silky ear, "I love you more than words can say, but you can't go on this particular adventure, Fin." He hated all vehicles, became horribly car sick with any drive longer than fifteen minutes, and couldn't be trusted around the California dogs. My friend made it clear—bring the Saluki, leave the Staghound—he wasn't welcome. My sweet warrior boy. I took one of his spare collars and attached it to my rearview mirror. Maybe he could somehow follow along through its connection. And besides, it made me feel safer seeing it there.

I waved to the males I was leaving behind as I backed out of the frozen driveway—just my girl Arya and me, on a journey to reconnect with my intuitive feminine self, leaving the structure and analysis and day-to-day order behind. For the first time I could remember, I felt totally and completely un-burdened. I could breathe. My senses were waking up and everything felt sharp and defined. I felt like I could fly. Tears came to my eyes. That girl I was, that woman I became, who had spent her life locked within the iron bars of restriction and repression, fear and hopelessness, had found a way to open a door. Who knows where it would lead, but as I stared out into this new, enormous world, filled with so much po-tential, I was being reborn. There was so much to be terrified of—where was I going, what was I doing, how I was going to support myself—but I couldn't focus on those things. I was numb to every sensation but the one within the realm of purpose. I'd spent a lifetime feeling unplugged, lost, dead. I had to find my connection, whatever that even meant. I had to find it if I was going to come alive, stay alive.

Driving away through the cloud-covered, lifeless tundra of southern Minnesota, I felt unstoppable. I suddenly had no ability to live anywhere but the here and now. And right now, for me, was what I had been fantasizing about for twenty years. I was doing what I wanted to do. How had that become such a radical concept in my life? It was exhilarating.

Arya was content to be close to me, nestled in her spongy bed and blankets in the backseat. Within ten miles she was snoring.

Listening to New Age music on my satellite radio while feeling the rhythmic cadence of tires on the seams of the open highway, my body fell into a bizarre state. I thought to myself, "Oh yes, this must be what relaxation feels like." But something else started happening. When I was in this relaxed state, I would feel an angry buzzing in my head and then a gentle pop, like a soap bubble softly bursting as it drifted. I would experience a brief dizzy spell, just a split second, and then, glorious then, a euphoric poring forth, a potent release of the most powerful sensation, just pure joy, happiness, love… but so intense it felt chemical, drug-like. The whole experience lasted only about three seconds. It was as if my brain experienced a tiny orgasm. Was this the pure sensation of brain chemistry finally finding the freedom to express itself? Was I finally experiencing something other than my addiction to stress? I didn't know and I didn't care. As strange as it was, I figured nothing that felt that good could possibly be harmful. I considered it a bonus and just kept driving.

CHAPTER TWENTY-SIX

*E*ight-to-ten hours later, I completed my first day on the road and arrived in Lincoln, Nebraska to stay overnight with some friends. Earlier that day I had stopped to visit my friend Michele in Iowa, and she had given me what she called a passage key, something to help me transition into this new life. I wore it around my neck and felt its love radiating. It was beautiful. Michele had been following my *Stark Raving Zen* blog—daily musings about the spirit world, my revelations about breaking free, the importance of non-conformism, and the dangers of consensus reality. She truly wanted to "get" all of this, but it was a lot to take in, and I could feel her concern. Sun poured through the lace curtains of her exquisitely decorated little farmhouse. I felt her gaze, a little too earnest, as though she were looking for direct evidence of insanity. She couldn't quite tell; nobody could. Even I felt that I was straddling the line, but when I saw the confusion of others, I could pull it all together and alleviate their concern with a show of the old Kristy, the *normal* Kristy. See? Totally sane. I had done it all my life. I was practiced.

Michele had an enormous Great Dane. He leaned against me trying to sit on a lap not anywhere near large enough to accommodate his two hundred pounds. Arya was completely uncomfortable with this giant, limiting her response to an occasional sideways glance. I think she was pretending he was an illusion, and I could almost hear her mantra, "You're not real. You're not real. You're not real…"

I stayed only a short while and was eager to get back on the road.

As she said goodbye, Michele said, "I worry about you, on this trip all by yourself. I want you to be very, very careful. Please tell me you will, Kristy."

I assured her I would absolutely be careful, but that I was untouchable. Woe be to those who would attempt to harm me. Archangel Michael was always within earshot. This I believed with certainty. I hadn't had much contact with the archangel in twenty years, but suddenly I felt him again.

I saw the look on Michele's face. Oops. I let the crazy slip through. I gave her a quick final hug and jumped in the car. I waved her concern away as if swatting a fly. "I'll be fine!"

CHAPTER TWENTY-SEVEN

*T*hat evening, sitting with Lisa and Harry in their brightly lit dining room in Lincoln, Nebraska, I gently played with the passage key Michele had gifted me. Lisa and Harry are mystics, so I felt like I could give them the full force of my spirit talk and they'd be perfectly comfortable. In fact, months earlier, Lisa had introduced me to a mythical creature called the *cadejo* from Central American and southern Mexican folklore. Half dog, half goat, they can save or destroy and will show up out of nowhere to do either.

I was so enamored of this mythology that Lisa made me a tiny tile with a leaping *cadejo*, carved in glass. It was a talisman for my journey. Holding it in my hand, I watched the light dance across its multi-colored surface and felt its pulse, protective and magical, smooth and cool, healing to the touch.

Harry and Lisa were so supportive and loving that it was hard not to feel buoyed by their energy, even after a long day of driving.

We cleared the table of what had not been devoured for dinner—imported olives, rare cheeses, artichokes, pepperoncini, an assortment of delicious spreads with tiny knives and homemade sourdough bread. I was so full of deliciousness I could hardly move. Harry moved my wine glass a few inches to the left and spread a map out to see where I'd be heading over the next couple of days. He pointed to a location on I–25, at the border of Colorado and New Mexico. His tone changed and took on a hint of warning.

"Be careful here. The pass at Trinidad. It's challenging. But once you cross that pass, you'll be free." He was referring to the steep grade. He kept pointing, tapping the location on the map, his reading glasses working their way down his nose.

Lisa protested. "It's fine. It's not that big of a deal. Why are you making such a big deal about that pass?" She shook her head at Harry as if he were the crazy one now, concerned he might be scaring me.

Harry pointed to the map then, saying "Trinidad," and it suddenly reminded me of a dream I'd had a month earlier in which Harry kept repeating something like, "Trinity, trinity" while I wandered through a post-apocalyptic, dystopian hellscape. At the time, I had no idea what the hell he meant. I had awakened from that terrifying dream feeling highly disturbed.

They continued their banter, but I had checked out, lost in the familiar buzzing in my head; yet it felt different this time, more intense. Since recalling that dream, it felt as if something was trying to butt into my consciousness, take over. I felt perfectly aware. I remained the person seeing through these eyes, but somebody else was trying to take the wheel. It felt like trying to suppress a massive yawn, frustrated but euphoric at the same time. I just couldn't stop it. And then a breakthrough voice, in my left ear again, "Trini..." but I was aware that this couldn't happen in front of Lisa and Harry—still having the "Don't scare her..." "I'm just saying..." argument in the background. I forcefully blocked out the psychic intruder, but not before I clearly heard the voice say something like "Trinidad," or was it "Trinity"...? I interrupted before the transmission was complete, but it carried the vibe of warning.

I spoke over Lisa and Harry. "That pass is going to be important for me," I said in a half daze. I held my passage key still hanging around my neck. "It's a passage for me." They stopped talking and waited for me to say something next. But the experience of wrestling the other consciousness out of my head was so depleting, I could barely string two words together. I folded up the map, somehow managed to thank my hosts for an amazing culinary feast, feigned a massive stretch and excused myself for the night.

Arya and I woke with the sun, had a wonderful breakfast with Lisa and Harry—homemade cinnamon rolls, and waffles sprinkled with tart cherries and dark chocolate chips, swimming in butter and drowning in Vermont maple syrup—and then packed up to leave. This time it was Harry who said, "Be careful. I've had some experiences...You just don't ever want to take these things lightly. This shamanic stuff is nothing to play around with." His tone was eerie and portentous, but I shook it off and tried to comfort him. I was totally okay, I assured him! I was on a departing train and the track was already laid. There was no choosing another direction. And shamanic? I didn't even know what that meant. I certainly wasn't labeling any of this outside of perhaps my description of *Stark Raving Zen*: finding inner peace through the portal of my outer chaos.

Like a bird following breadcrumbs, I was still living moment by moment, never questioning why it was that my brain had suddenly changed to enable me to do so. After a life directed by the constant warnings of "what if" and the siren calls of "if only," how was it that I was suddenly not afraid to do this wildly outlandish thing and all the while feel the unbreakable confidence of an archangel? I wasn't in a state to question the whys of the strange head sensations, the episodes of euphoria, the voices in my ear, and now the struggle to keep my mind mine. I just walked forward. I was an open portal, noticing every tiny detail, seeing waves of light with new eyes and hearing radio waves with new ears. I felt transmissions between the notes, encoded in a musical diorama as if there were a 3-D world just below the surface of every piece of music I listened to. I just accepted all of it because I believed that this is what being human was supposed to feel like. Not the crushed, condensed, ball of dark frustrating hopeless energy that my life had previously been. I refused to believe that this newness was pathological when the experience of the old was so depressing. Why would I want this to stop? Why would I want anyone to "help" me with this?

I was drinking all of it in with the fervor of a person having wandered the desert for nearly four decades and having finally found the oasis she always knew was there. For the first time on all levels I believed it was worth it to be here on this planet. How could I accept warnings in the face of this? I was worried about nothing. I felt impervious to my family's lineage of pain. I was free of the crippling fear and grief, the dark, grey depression and the relentless anxiety, the black hole I could never crawl out of. How could this freedom be insanity?

CHAPTER TWENTY-EIGHT

I stopped at a gas station to feed the belly of my little green station wagon. The credit card feature wasn't working on the gas pump, so I had to walk inside. A young woman behind the counter closed her calculus textbook. She was a sophomore in college, I heard her tell the person ahead of me in line. She was pretty, seemed polite and cheery, and wore her long blonde hair in a no-nonsense ponytail. As I made my way to the front of the line, I slid my card to her right at the moment I had one of those head pops of euphoric rush. "That'll be $34.50!" she chirped while writing something down to the left of the register. Basking in the glow of whatever curiosity was happening in my brain, I thought to myself, *Wow. Cheap gas.* It was more expensive in Minneapolis.

Without looking up at me she said, "Yes! Well, that's good to hear!"

The person behind me in line leaned forward and said, "*What's* good to hear, darlin'?"

The young woman looked confused. She pointed to me and smiled. "She said the gas was cheap, and I thought that's good, right?"

The woman behind me said, "She didn't *say* anything," and squinted her eyes with a slightly bemused are-you-a-little-soft-in-the-head look on her face.

And I, still bathing in a state of euphoria gushed, "But I thought it! She literally read my mind." I didn't think anything of the "Guard Your Crazy" rule at this point; usually I wouldn't consider revealing such a thought in a gas station in Nebraska. But by now the young college student was white as a ghost and looked like she was going to pass out. Tiny beads of sweat squeezed out of her forehead. She looked confused and a little sick from the whole exchange. I felt like I needed to protect her from the woman behind me, who was now sneering at me like, *Great. You're both fruitcakes.*

I said to the young woman behind the counter, "You're telepathic!" as I strolled out of there, marveling at the wonder of it. What a way to start day two of my magnificent adventure. As I buckled myself in and pulled out of the gas station, my phone vibrated, alerting me to a text. It was Shellie, my childhood best friend from Colorado, and my host for that night. "Be careful on the road! We're supposed to get a blizzard this evening."

Onward to my next destination: Limon, Colorado—my childhood home, a tiny town on the eastern plains. I hadn't returned since our moving van had pulled out of the long driveway twenty-five years earlier. On our way to northern Minnesota to start the next family chapter—dad had taken a new job—I remembered the vision of Shellie, my longtime best friend, peddling her bike behind us as fast as her little legs could spin, getting smaller and smaller in the rearview mirror. I was holding back tears while she furiously waved. It was still so fresh in my mind's eye. I remember buying myself a stuffed toy unicorn at the five and dime to keep me company on the long drive to our new home in Minnesota. I held onto him tight.

Colorado will forever be the place of sunny skies for me. Back then it was too early to understand the full effects an alcoholic father would eventually have on the family. That truth would bloom in Minnesota. That instability would eventually make me a pro at the moving thing. Though there was plenty going on under the surface, at the time I still believed my dad was a hero and our life was perfect.

But children have perceptive powers way beyond the confines of their conscious understanding, and I admit I felt confused at an early age. When I was around seven years old, I woke to shouting in the dead of night. Somebody was trying to break into the house! I sneaked down the dark hallway to peek down the stairs and saw my father battling to keep the front door shut, fighting that good fight in his boxer shorts. My father had always been a physically powerful man, once a semiprofessional baseball player and also a pugilist; I thought nobody stood a chance against him. But the unfathomable was happening as I watched the stranger on the other side of the door outpower my father. It was taking everything my father had to keep that man from entering our house, while he shouted to my mom, "Call the police!" He would then resume his battle, yelling at the man behind the door. I was terrified but could not look away. I stayed in the darkness, crouching behind a corner. At one point the man trying to get into the house slipped and his head hit the hardwood floor, right inside the door, but my dad slammed it anyway, crushing the guy's glasses. By then I was out of my mind, certain my dad was going to be killed by this man right in front of my eyes, but the glorious sound of the cavalry—sirens blaring and lights flashing—signaled that we were saved.

The policemen overpowered the guy, dragged him to his feet, handcuffed him, and secured him in the squad car. They then stayed to calm my father. "Jesus Christ!" my dad laughed with relief, trying to act cool with the cops—ever the man's man. "I heard a knock at the door, so I just cracked it to see what this guy wanted, he smelled like a distillery, and then all hell broke loose!" After labeling my father's decision a certified bonehead move—never answer a knock from a strange man in the middle of the night—they told him they were glad he was able to keep him out, made sure we were all okay, and left with that devil in their squad car. I hated the man for scaring me so badly, for threatening my family, for making my dad fight.

My father gathered all five of us children and made sure we were okay. My mother held me to stop me from shaking, and we finally went to bed knowing that our father was about as badass as they come. I was glowing, feeling that I had just received living proof that there was nothing from which my father couldn't protect us.

The next day the police called to give my dad the lowdown. This guy was totally inebriated and thought he lived there. He couldn't figure out who was in his house trying to keep him out. Dad sympathized with him. They threw him in what my father called "the drunk tank" for seventy-two hours and dad went to see him in jail.

What the…

I couldn't figure out why our father was being so damn forgiving to this man who nearly gave his youngest child a heart attack (I can't speak for the effects on the rest of the family). It felt like a betrayal. And then I felt it. Just a twinge on the inside. Dad relates to this guy. Dad drinks too much too.

And so began the metaphorical struggle, my father forever fighting his alcoholism like he did that poor adrenaline-fueled drunk at our door. The irony of that foreshadowing was heartbreaking. Dad could protect us from anything, except himself.

But now I was on my way back to Colorado. I had no idea what I would find there.

It's a long, tedious drive through Nebraska on Interstate 80. I set the cruise control and it seemed as if I never even turned the wheel for hours. I was feeling the bliss of the open road, checking the rearview mirror to see Arya all curled up in her backseat luxury accommodations. She had more blankets, pillows, and cushions than she could possibly use, but Salukis like their comfort level on the verge of ridiculousness. She slept there, pampered and loved, keeping me tethered to this world as everything inside of me fought to drift up and away like a helium balloon liberated from a toddler's sticky grasp.

I drove on with my meditative music and the trance-inducing cadence of four wheels on the seams of the highway. I felt a little sick passing the Nebraska cattle yards (for hundreds of miles). This wasn't the free range of the West, but small fenced areas with more cattle jammed into them than seemed even remotely humane. Cows walked around in mud and muck, but then I saw something that hit me like a line drive to the solar plexus. I pulled my car off to the side of the empty interstate and turned off the ignition.

I was a meat eater. And here I was, staring at two calves play-ing. Playing! In this hell hole of a mudlot that they just hap-pened to be born into, they were playing. They would chase each other and kick their feet in all directions and then chase some more, leaping, cavorting, having what would universally be recognized as a blast...and the only reason they were here was to be eaten. They were born into this literal shit hole to be killed and eaten, with nobody acknowledging they were living beings, babies, who *liked to play*. Nobody considered that they valued their lives, that maybe their mother valued their lives.

Always an animal lover, I was floored by the sudden incon-gruence. As a meat eater, I was contributing to this. How had I never seen it before?

My heart raced as I watched them continue their game, tripping in ankle-deep sludge, jumping back up, their entire existence played out in a fifty-by-fifty-foot square. Just babies. I was horrified. There was no more numbness to protect me. I had been asleep and now I was truly awake. I realized what a psychological rift this had subconsciously been causing in me. Throughout my entire life I'd struggled on and off to stop eating animal products but had never found the willpower to do so long term. But sitting here in my car on the side of the highway in Nebraska, watching these two babies feel joy, created in me an evolution that could not be suppressed this time. I finally got it.

As a little girl I collected stuffed animals. I had hundreds of them. When they started to overtake the house, my mother would secretly cull the herd, taking some to Goodwill, think-ing I wouldn't notice. I would. I screamed and wailed at their loss, horrified that these little beings could possibly be mishan-dled, thrown away, unloved. So I started putting "spells" on my stuffed animals. I would visualize a bubble around them and say an incantation, "May you always be safe, happy, and loved, no matter where you find yourself." Before I drove away, I put my spell on this cow herd. I visualized the babies in a sparkly pink bubble, extra fortified.

I saw our existence as being so interconnected—every species, every kingdom just one silken thread of a giant spider web. I didn't want horror in my system any longer. I wanted compassion instead.

I called my husband to tell him of my epiphany. Although he's a super-compassionate man himself, I could tell he just didn't quite get it. "They were playing!" I repeated, and he would say the right things, but still I felt as though I just wasn't communicating the full enormity of this reality. So I gave up, understanding that this was my journey and nobody else could be force-fed what I learned here. I tried to reinforce that over and over within myself, because at times I had such a strong desire to scream from the hilltops, to plead with those who had been like me, sleepwalking through life for decades at a time, to wake up.

CHAPTER TWENTY-NINE

The closer I came to Colorado, the colder and darker the skies became. Shellie was expecting me in Denver around dinner time, but I couldn't resist the slower route to my hometown of Limon. I wanted to get there through old, empty ranch roads, which to me felt sentimental and romantic. I crossed the state line and found myself weaving through abandoned highways, hauntingly beautiful ghost land, back country ranch land. I hadn't been there for a quarter of a century, but it felt so familiar.

An enormous coyote trotted through a field to the right of my vision, keeping his eye on us. Arya seemed riveted by his graceful stride. Although there are coyotes all over Minnesota, I had never actually spied one. How was that possible? This one was beautiful, so powerful he gave me chills. Snow was starting to fall, and the sun hung low in a slate grey sky. I drove on, trembling, feeling the reunion, this *homeness* of the Colorado range.

The storm clouds moved in and complete darkness arrived. I kept driving, nothing to see by the illumination of my headlights but field after field on either side of the empty two-lane highway, until I came to an abandoned farmhouse. A ghost structure it was, completely falling apart, with one dead, twisted tree in the middle of open land—it was so beautiful! Even the barren tree seemed sculpted by some master of fine art.

I stopped the car to give Arya a bathroom break. With wind softly moaning around us, we walked closer to the house. Arya was intent on finding the perfect spot to sniff, but I started to get a little creeped out. For the first time since leaving Minnesota, fear descended on me. I felt like something was watching us.

I wanted to go inside the house, mainly because it terrified me and that pissed me off. I wasn't willing to be jerked around by fear. But I chose not to step through the gaping threshold because I didn't want to bring Arya anywhere near where she could potentially step on a nail or something else equally dangerous. So I sat there on a decaying stump in the cold darkness, somehow not able to look away from this house skeleton, but not running away, because nothing was going to cheat me out of this moment. The fear just made my senses stronger, more refined. It was now pitch black, and the wind moaned deeply, like the subtle rumbling of a dog's warning growl, the kind a person should pay attention to. "I'm not afraid of you," I said into the darkness.

We slipped back into the car and headed down the empty highway, the final stretch to Limon. What once were just a few flakes of snow quickly transformed into a blizzard. The eastern plains of Colorado are open and flat with nothing to protect the road from the rampaging onslaught of blowing snow. Drifts started forming and my little car struggled to stay on the wind-ravaged road.

Clutching the steering wheel so tightly my knuckles were white, I crawled into Limon and stopped at the first hotel I found, which very well may have been the only hotel in a town this size. I checked us in for the night, after calling Shellie to tell her I'd done exactly what she told me not to—got stuck in the snowstorm. I'd stay in Limon overnight and make my way to her tomorrow.

"One person and one dog." I smiled at the lady behind the desk. She seemed cheerful and motherly, in her seventies perhaps. She probably owned this place. Shaking her head and clucking at me for driving in a blizzard, she gave her spiel about extra towels and blankets. This storm was forecast a full day in advance, she lectured. There was no excuse. Receiving the full force of her finger-wag actually made me feel good, like someone cared enough to curse me out for taking my own safety for granted.

But I was exhausted, besieged by so many conflicting thoughts and emotions. I felt a little afraid being here all alone with nothing but the storm and the ghosts of my childhood for company. But, of course, I had my beloved Arya.

I opened the door that matched the big plastic number attached to my old-fashioned aluminum key. I entered to the smell of stale cigarettes and musty carpeting. I turned on a buzzing fluorescent light, which cast a strange orange-yellow glow on the avocado and gold wallpaper. I wasn't expecting luxury for something like thirty bucks a night, but after two days on the road, I was hoping for something a little less murdery-feeling. I walked over to check out the bathroom, which happened to have a big bench built into the wall covered with red shag carpeting. Not sure within what era that was hip.

I passed a big wall mirror on my way back out, when Arya erupted into a barking rampage, completely unlike anything I'd ever heard from her before. When I turned around to see what she was reacting to, I found her staring straight at me. "What the hell, Arya?" I said, walking toward her to comfort her, I tracked her gaze to find it slightly behind me. So I turned again, caught her reflection in the mirror and could only surmise that she was furiously sounding an alarm *at my reflection* in the mirror.

"Arya, that's just a mirror! That's me." I tried to reason with her. Arya has had plenty of exposure to mirrors and reflections. Our bathroom wall at home was one giant mirror, and she frequently hung out in there with me as I got ready for work in the morning. I picked her up, found her trembling, and gently walked to the mirror. "See? That's just me." But as we got closer to it, and keeping her focus on my reflection, she went insane with bared teeth, hair standing on end. And she glanced at me as if to say, "Sorry to be contradictory, but *that is not you!*"

I didn't know what to do! She couldn't keep this up or I'd be sure to get a noise complaint—not that anyone else was staying there, of course. In my panic, I picked up a blanket folded at the end of the bed and secured it all around the top edge of the mirror, covering up the reflection. Arya immediately quieted. By this time, I was freaked out, tired, and emotionally overloaded. I washed my face and tried to get Arya comfortable. She seemed to calm down quickly as soon as the mirror stopped assaulting her senses. We went to bed, and despite the smell and the fear and the confusion, sleep came quickly with Arya sprawled all over me in her usual style.

I woke up at around 2:00 am, stared at the hotel digital alarm clock, and felt a little overwhelmed by what Arya had done a few hours earlier. Why did she react like that? It was scary and it made no sense. I found myself wondering if I had made the right decision to bring her.

Before I was even finished with the thought, the man's voice broke into my head and sharply broadcast into my left ear, "Arya is a *sentant* being. Be patient." My eyes shot open wide with the exhilaration of hearing the voice, and with those words a wash of understanding and gratitude came over me. I wasn't alone. My inner Zen master was here, assuring me of how critical Arya was to this journey. I kissed her on the temple as she snored in my ear. Whatever had happened was probably just a strange anomaly. I'm sure she was every bit as exhausted as I was.

I woke up in the morning feeling fortified from a good night's sleep, including the auditory wakeup call from whatever wise being tended to talk in my ear. *Sentant.* I had never heard that word before. It came encoded with an understanding; I knew he meant something like sentient or feeling. I found it fascinating that the voice used a word I wasn't familiar with. I looked it up online. *Sentant* was a French word for feeling, and another reference said it was an extinct version of sentient. If the voice was some inner aspect of me (I was open to all possibilities), wouldn't it use words that were a part of my vocabulary?

I felt thankful for Arya, but I didn't want to push it, so I left the mirror covered. I showered, blew dry my hair without a reflection, put no makeup on, and didn't even put in my contacts, choosing my old glasses instead. I threw my hair up in a clip, packed up the car, got Arya all settled in the back seat, *and then* came back into the room and took the blanket off the mirror. She seemed content and peppy, so whatever she had experienced the night before seemed not to have any lasting effects on her.

We took off, a bright sunshiny day for me to explore Limon for the first time in over two decades.

It was less powerful than I'd expected. In fact, I was a little blown away by how underwhelming it actually was. How could a place that held the entire start of my life have so little to say to me now? Things were so different from how I remembered them. To be fair, the town had been decimated by an F5 tornado a few years after we left and had never fully recovered. Many people never bothered to rebuild, but instead took the opportunity to collect their insurance money and move on.

I drove by the house I had grown up in, and of course it didn't feel the same. It was too normal.

It was just…a nice house.

It used to be a boarding school many years ago. My parents bought it for something crazy like $13,000 in 1972. The old lady who originally owned it died in the house. They removed her body, but they didn't remove her stuff. The house was sold as-is. I remember my mother carrying me through it when I was very young; I saw old jars and bottles on antique dresser tops—mostly a lot of junk, but there were a few treasures we kept. My parents bought the house because it was big enough to house their brood of five children; only two of us had to share a room. It also had an in-law apartment perfect for when my Gramma came to stay with us each summer.

It was totally worn down inside, but my mother was resourceful and had amazing carpentry skills. My father would go to work, and my mother would artfully and meticulously remodel each small section of the house. I so admired her ability to transform a dump into something beautiful, but I wanted her to work faster. She had a tendency to do a flurry of work and then nothing for months or even years at a time. I was too young to realize that crippling depression derails ambition. I also wasn't privy to the reality of our finances. At times it was difficult to feed five hungry children, so buying construction materials wasn't in the budget.

For many years we lived in this half torn-up house, a metaphor for my mother herself, and though I was very young, I still felt shame around it. But I loved that house, and every time the stars would align, and Mom would find the financial and emotional resources to keep going with the remodel, I would cheer her on like mad. Suddenly the dining room would be fully finished, with elegant wallpaper, a chair rail, and a new chandelier. Or my room would get a fresh look with white paneling and built-in shelves. A new breakfast nook would be constructed, and the laundry room would have some cheerful wallpaper and incredible cabinets built by my mother's hands. I was amazed by her, and so proud of that house's transformation.

Some of us loved the house, some of us hated it, but there was one thing we could agree on—the upstairs seemed to be haunted in a subtle kind of way. We said it was the old lady who died there, but she didn't act out all that much. Nothing manifested but a feeling that someone was watching us, peeking over our shoulders.

Here I was standing outside the only home that had ever felt like home to me. After we left Colorado, we moved too often—dumpy rental after dumpy rental—to ever put down roots again.

The warm sunshine was already melting the high drifts of snow from the blizzard the night before. I took pictures of the house to share with my siblings. It felt surreal to be here, gazing at this place so dear to me with new eyes. But when I looked at the images in my camera something caught my eye and I enlarged it digitally. In my mom's old room, the very room in which the old lady who ran the boarding house over half a century ago had died, was the outline of a ghostly face and a perfect bone white hand pressed against the window. At least some things stay the same. I like to think our old-lady ghost recognized me, as if she'd had a hand in raising me. Did the new residents feel her? I hoped they did, if she wanted them to.

CHAPTER THIRTY

*D*riving out of Limon and feeling nostalgic, I listened to a 70s station on my satellite radio. "Cover of the Rolling Stone" came on and I turned it up loud. Barreling down the highway, overlooking the rolling sea of ranch land ahead of me, I lost myself in peace. So many difficult memories to sort through, but I suddenly felt none of the darkness. Fun, silly, hilarious, adventurous, safe, comfortable, wondrous…I felt no pain. No memories of the sad or scary. No feelings of dread or emptiness or fear. Instead what came flooding back were memories of my inseparable best friend Shellie, adventuring, listening to cricket symphonies on summer nights, exploring dry creek beds, eating butter and sugar sandwiches, finding salamanders, playing with Beauregard our Cairn Terrier, and playing outside until it was so dark we couldn't see our hands in front of our faces.

Arriving in Denver later that afternoon, I had the joy of seeing Shellie for the first time in over twenty-five years. We reminisced about many memories from our childhood, and laughed until our stomachs hurt.

I couldn't stay long. My head wasn't in a socializing space and I had to head out, to keep driving. But as I left Shellie's and continued down the highway, the memories continued to flood into me: Mom playing records, patiently teaching me how to carefully place the needle on the spinning grooves of the vinyl; her singing, painting, and laughing with us kids; Mom and Dad playing cards with whichever neighbor would show up at our doorstep with a six pack of beer and a couple of kids; Dad hitting homeruns on his softball league team, teasing our friends, making them laugh so hard they'd cry.

Dad had a horribly dangerous career as an electrical lineman, and there weren't a lot of safeguards back then. He was constantly enduring work-related injuries, but they never dulled that sparkle in his eye at least in his younger years; he was always winking, always the life of the party. He was a jitterbug star, cutting up the dance floor to something like, "Cover of the Rolling Stone." I'd hope he'd pick me to dance with, hope he'd do that thing where I got to stand on his feet, and he'd dance me all over the room. I'd laugh to absolute exhaustion. I loved him so much. I felt everyone was jealous because he wasn't their dad.

As I drove down the Colorado highway, I felt no anger at either of them for tragically and repeatedly making the wrong choices. I wondered how they carried on, with five kids and so little money. They must have felt stuck in a life of barely keeping their heads above water. They sacrificed their dreams and life callings because they couldn't manifest them and also pay the bills. Over the years I had tried to forgive my mom for all the crying. She sat in dark rooms while all of us played outside. We tried to have a good time, tried to pretend we didn't know that she was inside, *just always crying*. There were times when I hated her for that, for making my life feel heavy with her inherited grief.

She wanted to devote her life to painting. That's all she wanted. I never faulted her for that. If I could have erased myself to give her a life as an artist, I would have.

I don't even know what my dad's dreams were. I tried to visualize what they could have been, and I got nothing. Just emptiness...drinking beer and sustaining another gruesome injury for the sake of supporting his family.

We didn't have much, but I would have done with much less if it meant they could have lived a more fulfilling life together. I found myself asking them to forgive themselves for the train wreck their lives turned out to be. I found myself peeling away the bad memories, like layers and layers of dirty clothes, and trying so hard to throw them away to make room for forgiveness. I sensed the truth, which was that they did the best they could with suffocated, deadened spirits passed on through multiple generations of shocking abuse. They could have found a way to get back on track. They should have found a way. But I was tired of faulting them. I was ready to release the anger, the resentment. I wanted so badly to forgive, to get rid of this 5,000-pound gorilla on my back.

It just wasn't that simple.

I could think the forgiveness; I just couldn't feel it yet.

I saw pronghorn antelope grazing in the fields and my heart burst. No matter how often I had seen them as a child, it had always been this exciting. It had been over twenty years, but here they were again, my old friends.

I kept driving, wiping away quiet tears that meandered

down my cheeks, feeling so strongly that there is no greater gift parents can give to a child than to live their own dreams, which frees the child to do the same. It wasn't lost on me that this is what I was trying to do for myself. Changing myself, changing my life, accepting simpler as better, and considering what that might even look like.

I had been driving for a few hours through the semiarid, desert shrubland of southeastern Colorado. I was in some kind of zone. Hundreds of miles evaporated into timelessness and before I knew it, I was crossing the city line of Trinidad, Colorado on the border of New Mexico. I rolled through the charming brick-lined streets, and passed the Victorian architecture and wrought iron streetlamps that felt like taking a step backwards in time. I felt myself perk up with a sudden infusion of energy. Trinidad was vibrant, buzzing with natural beauty, a small oasis in the southwestern frontier. It had a vibe of busy people going about their chosen life off the beaten path. It didn't take long to travel the full extent of the city limits.

"Watch for bears," the sign warned, as I cruised through great coniferous swaths of pinyon-juniper woodlands, surrounded by the majesty of the Sangre de Cristo mountain range, with the dramatic Spanish Peaks of the Rockies right behind me. My little car crawled up the steep incline as I ascended the mountain pass outside of Trinidad—Raton Pass, the very place Harry had warned me about when I was in Nebraska. This was my *gateway* and the source of Harry's strange advice to "be careful on this pass," that seemed to confound Lisa so much. I luxuriated in the glorious view of wild meadows at the base of Fisher's Peak, a towering volcanic mesa standing 9,600 feet above sea level. My car slowly progressed up the steep grade while tractor trailers limped along at fifteen miles per hour. I could do a maximum of thirty. I appreciated the slow speed because it allowed me to drink in the natural beauty all around me; it was truly magnificent. I reached the top and there was the enormous golden sign, "Welcome to the Land of Enchantment." I had reached New Mexico.

I'd forgotten it was called the land of enchantment! I felt it like a punch to the solar plexus, as if the sign had read, "Welcome, Enchanted One." As I rolled across the state line, I peered into the rearview mirror to glance at Arya, but instead I witnessed the endless expanse of the white-capped Rocky Mountains behind me. In a split second I felt them love me, wrap their arms around me and embrace me, a child of Colorado, born of the Rockies. My whole being expanded, my heart hurt from so much expansion as I felt Colorado release me and New Mexico take me in.

The second I crossed into New Mexico, I felt my reality reorganizing. Rusty gears started shifting, something dormant inside of me slowly creaked and then quickly whirred to life. The popping and snaps began in my head and, whoosh, euphoria flooded my senses. It felt like somebody took a wood plank from behind me and cracked me across the back with it as hard as they could. There was no pain, but I physically pitched forward into the steering wheel and gasped for air.

Arya began ferociously barking, so vigorously the car bounced. Not once in her life had she barked in the car—she'd always been a perfect passenger. My brain and I struggled to calm down and address what was going on with Arya. I asked her what could possibly be the matter, hoping to reassure her with the familiarity of my voice. Stealing a peek into the rearview mirror to see her, I realized she was staring directly at me.

This time, it was clear why.

It wasn't my face in the mirror's reflection. Somebody had replaced me. I was speechless as I watched her howl with fury at the dark-eyed man with the long grey braid who was staring back at me, looking just as shocked as I was. Everything slowed at this point, and I lost my hearing. I watched Arya, in slow motion, soundlessly lunging and charging the empty space between us. And then time started up again, and I took back control.

Stunned silence gave way to outrage and a sense of complete invasion. "Who the hell are *you?!*" I screamed. My reflection returned. Arya got quiet. I felt my internal infrastructure crumble like a rockslide, obliterating any sense of familiarity or knowing. My brain went wild, trying to comprehend what I had just seen, and then froze. I suddenly felt nothing. I went from careening down the highway in stunned rage to a state of stony autopilot. I was in psychological shock. Everything was quiet; nothing moved in my mind.

I wouldn't be making it to California. I was meant to be here, in New Mexico, to meet the man whose voice was in my ear, the man whose face was now mine. This is where my answers were. A deep trance overtook me. It was too powerful to resist. A voice told me to stop driving, to rest a minute.

I pulled over and parked. Still heading down Raton Pass, we were in a stretch of mountainous wilderness with wide, safe places to rest a car. By this time Arya had recovered from the shock of watching me wear a new face. She seemed comfortable at the moment. I got her out of the car to shake it off, but she seemed to need no recovery time. She sniffed, and peed, and bounced to the end of her leash and mumbled a muted "wruff" when a rabbit hopped by. I remembered the voice had told me she was *sentant*; I realized she had so much to teach me. Her recovery from intense emotion was nothing less than masterful. Like a dog who predicts seizures, she could sense when my energy was changing, but she didn't hold a grudge or dwell on the strangeness of it. She moved through, fluidly, moment by moment, knowing it was all natural. Her response helped to assure me that what I had just experienced wasn't necessarily the telltale signs of a mind unraveling. There was something happening that neither one of us could make sense of. But like Arya, I was being asked to roll with this, moment by moment. That was all I could do. I had to surrender to whatever was happening, because no matter how maddeningly inexplicable it seemed, I had the overwhelming sense that I was somehow being healed, being made whole through thousands of cracks in the glass of my soul.

So, I let Arya be my teacher. And I willingly entered the enchantment.

Part Six

TESTS, ALLIES, AND ENEMIES

"The door to God is the insecurity of not knowing anything. Bear the grace of that uncertainty and all wisdom will be yours."

~ Adyashanti

Even in our sleep, pain, which cannot forget,

falls drop by drop upon the heart,

until, in our own despair, against our will

comes wisdom through the awful grace of God.

~ Aeschylus

CHAPTER THIRTY-ONE

I have come to a realization: In our intact, everyday state of sanity, we are afforded the humane privilege of a filter. This filter is something like a set of sunglasses we never take off. Through their lenses, we see life as it makes sense to our perception. Not everyone wears the same set of sunglasses, but each pair allows only a certain amount of life, of truth, to enter the lenses on its way to our brain's processing center. We make sense of what's around us through this individualized pair of glasses—and everything seems "normal" to us— thanks to the structure of judgment, discernment, and worldview. When I crossed the border into New Mexico, my sunglasses were torn off the moment I saw the wrinkled brown man in place of my reflection. The shock of that caused me to dissociate, which felt something like being adrift in deep space or in the depths of an uncharted ocean.

In the process of this sudden shedding of my worldview, I lost the invisible protective covering that being a part of a society provides for us. What remained were raw nerves and unclassified senses, simultaneously wondrous and terrifying. The colors were brighter, the sounds were louder. I was seeing individual sunrays streaming through my windshield as if each were a living, breathing entity ready to share its cosmic secrets.

Radio waves were no different. The moody New Age music streaming through my satellite radio became nothing short of conversational. Suddenly every instrument, every melodious sequence was speaking directly to me, imploring me, encouraging me, warning me, providing clues to my next move, my next choice, as if my life depended upon its counsel. Every license plate from a passing car was a code, a signal. Every bumper sticker gave sage advice, sometimes mind-blowingly so, and through all of it there was a new sense that I had entered another dimension entirely.

I sensed I wasn't alone, that I was being watched. There was a war happening, a battle. I could see it. All the love of the world was battling all the fear of the world, and I was just one player in all of that. I sensed this battle happening all around us, with everyone on the planet enduring their own painful struggle. But somehow, when my filter was torn away, I could see it unfolding right in front of me. I could see every player involved, dark or light. I could feel fingers wrapped around my spine, working my sense of inner direction like a sail. I could hear the hissing from the darkness and see the laugh lines from the light's smile. I was being ripped in two. I thought I was all about the light; I wanted to be. But somehow, having the full gaze of the darkness felt pretty good too. I suddenly felt like the devil's pet, and the power of this attention was disturbingly compelling. When the devil himself looks you straight in the eye, who has the will to ignore him? I wanted to hear him explain himself. I wanted to know why he was so filled with hate, why he had overtaken my grandfather. I told him he'd never win with me; he'd never have me. I had too much of my Gramma in me. But I liked the attention. I felt close to the darkness, like I felt close to the light. I understood it as deeply as I understood an old family friend. I could have this conversation.

Wholeness suddenly took on a new meaning, a nondual understanding of connecting with all of me—the light and the dark. I knew of the darkness—the Void—but I had never been this close to it. From the moment I crossed the New Mexico state line, I felt it breathing down my neck. It spoke soothingly, wise and manipulative it was, elegant and smooth. The conversations came with no voice in my ear; it was a gradual knowing, like a dark, warm blanket gently draped over my head, hoping to dull my senses. There was nothing more than that. No dark actions, no dark thoughts. It was empty. The light wasn't fighting my introduction to the darkness. It was standing back, having every faith that I could come this close to the precipice without jumping in. When in balance, the light existed with the dark. They didn't try to change one another. It wasn't personal. Neither resented who the other was; there was mutual respect.

But *jumping in* to the abyss meant becoming the darkness. It meant leaving the light and losing all the love. I had a choice. In my mind I was already made of fairy dust. I thought I had made the choice long ago to be an agent of the light. But right now, in this fragmented state, finding wholeness meant I had to meet the light and the dark in a new way. I had to have a conversation with both. I told myself I was doing this for myself, my family, and humanity. I believed we were all being asked to have this internal conversation; right now, I was just doing my part.

Through all of this, the vestigial voice of my old perception was screaming loudly in the background. I had enough knowledge of psychology to be aware of the possibilities. And if I were to follow the principle of Occam's razor—when searching for an explanation, the simpler one is generally your best bet—then I was very simply and very clearly going insane. *Hearing voices*—check. But I had also studied enough to know the normalcy of hearing voices, depending upon what those voices are saying. Other cultural worldviews make room for this possibility much more so than the Eurocentric one, the foundation of western psychology. Even so, I ran through the possibilities in earnest and formed a checklist in my mind.

Delusions of persecution—check. You could certainly make the argument that this sensation of, "OMG the darkness is staring at me!" was a crazy version of me believing that some scary thing was out to get me. But I wasn't paranoid. It was simply an understanding that the universal forces of love and fear were real, and each of them seemed to have entire armies behind them.

Delusions of reference. This refers to the belief that everything has special meaning just for you: every sign is speaking directly to you, every billboard is a living breathing entity giving the next command. Songs on the radio are being sung directly to you, and conversations between strangers at the coffee shop are being had for your benefit———check! I fully believed that the universe, God, and my spirit guides were using any resource they could to help me through this massive brain reorganization. I was hearing what I needed to hear, seeing what I needed to see, reading what I needed to read, following the signs—to make it one step further through the disintegration of everything I had ever known, any order I had ever had the delusion of controlling. I truly believed the delusions of reference were my breadcrumbs, leading me back to myself.

Delusions of grandeur: Honestly, I think I was experiencing the opposite of this. I was being led to a humbler version of myself. Even though I felt that if I navigated this journey of horrors successfully that somehow humanity would benefit, I fully knew that each and every one of us would have to do the same, and currently were doing the same, and no two journeys would ever be alike. We'd have to do this for ourselves and for each other. While mine was an individual journey of profound discovery, I assumed everyone else was, had, or would be undergoing their own version on some level.

One of the scariest facets of hearing voices to those suffering from schizophrenia is that the voices can be cruel, demanding, insulting, dangerous, and even violent. Whomever or whatever was responsible for directly talking into my left ear was infinitely wise and kind. The voice talked about my own unbalanced ego. The voice kept me tethered. It was nurturing and reassuring. Sometimes he spoke with odd word choices that I would never use, such as sentant rather than sentient, though I knew exactly what he meant. The voice filled me with a feeling of love so deep it felt celestial. I had never felt such love.

Delusions of control. With schizophrenia, this can manifest as, "Aliens are controlling my movements. The CIA is broadcasting their thoughts into my head. I'm forcing my thoughts into somebody else's head in order to control them." No. There was that incident with the cashier in Nebraska, but I never thought that was my doing. I just recognized the convenience store clerk as being telepathic. Telepathy is something I have believed in my entire life, something my Gramma told me stories about. I did feel that I was channeling something like the collective consciousness, but channeling is also something that was a part of my worldview previous to this disintegration of my identity; and honestly, I think everyone channels to some degree. History is filled with the accounts of artists, scientists, musicians, and writers claiming to have received their seminal works from mysterious external sources.

So, my self-correcting jury was not entirely decided. Schizophrenia in my family? Check. That was a strike against me. But I still maintained the thought that maybe those family members, my aunt and uncle, were like me. Maybe they were privy to unexplained phenomena which, back in the 1950s and 60s, were harder to accept. Maybe some psychologists have such established sunglasses in their minds that any experience like this outside the spectrum of "normal" can only be classified as horribly broken. If my aunt and my uncle had been born wired a little differently, like me, and then tortured by a psychotic father who had clearly given himself entirely to the darkness, then of course their destinies would have taken an alternative path.

But despite the mixed feelings of broken mind vs. heroine's journey of the soul, I couldn't help but feel that I was somehow coming together rather than shattering. I felt hope for the first time in my life, delivered through the jagged holes in the windows of my psyche. I could literally see myself, kneeling over a massive pile of glass shards, somehow piecing them all together like an intricate puzzle. I felt like I was doing this for my horrifyingly broken lineage, including whatever cell belonged to me from my one alleged and precious drop of Cherokee blood.

But I couldn't keep up right now. Every new, wild, and unexplained experience was another softball thrown through the pane of my consciousness. If it continued, there'd be nothing left of my window to the world. I was desperately grasping for the solidity of my intact mind. But at the same time, I also welcomed what was happening as if my life depended on it.

I was convinced it did.

CHAPTER THIRTY-TWO

The sun was cascading through my side window. I drove with my right hand on the wheel while holding the tiny *cadejo* tile Lisa had given me in my left. Feeling my friend's love made me smile. I felt an invisible net of support waiting to catch me should I fall. I wasn't alone in this world.

And then I slammed my foot on the brake pedal.

None of my loving thoughts cushioned the sight before me, a hundred miles into New Mexico on the eastern frontier. I stopped breathing as I pulled my car over to the side of the road, parked and turned off the engine.

In the median strip of the four-lane highway stood a grotesque wax-like statue of a man, caught in midstride. There was no one else on the road at the time, so I easily walked across two lanes to get a closer look. He was there, immobile. A young Latino he was, maybe early to mid-twenties and very handsome, with an enormous backpack strapped to his shoulders as though he were trekking cross country. I walked around him, slowly taking in the spectacle of a human being frozen in time and space.

"What the hell." My stomach was turning. Was he dead? Could anyone else see him? Was he really there? I didn't reach out to touch him. I felt that would be an intrusion on his personal boundaries. Just then a car drove by. The wide-eyed driver didn't seem to look at anything but me, this strange woman in the median with mouth agape in horrified wonder, walking in a small circle.

I had no answers.

I ambled back across the empty highway. A low wind whispered while a tumbleweed beat me across, racing me like a playful puppy. I got back into the driver's seat. Arya was still napping in her backseat queen's lair. She woke up when I opened the door, one ear akimbo, stuck to the top of her head.

I slowly turned the ignition, still staring at the man in the median. "I wish he could talk," I said to Arya, who was now licking her paw, relishing the direct sun. I couldn't take my eyes off him. "I wish he could tell me what this is all about, why he's stuck here, frozen." I held my stomach, sick inside.

Shocked at the injustice of it, the cruelty, I unsnapped Finlay's collar adorning my rearview mirror, adjusted it as small as it would go, and snapped it around my ankle, still so big it slipped down over my shoe. I rolled up my jeans and kind of tucked them into the collar, so it would stay put. I turned the car on, closed Arya's window, put my car in drive and headed back onto the highway. A few cars were passing the frozen guy on the opposite side of the road, but nobody gave him a look. I stared at him, getting smaller and smaller in my rearview mirror. "I don't know what that was, Arya, but it feels sad and unfair." Arya, still basking in the late afternoon sunshine and moving wherever she could find its spotlight, seemed indifferent.

And then I heard, "Through the eyes of a child." It shocked me like a thunderclap in my left ear—the deep baritone voice of my clairaudient messenger, and I knew immediately what he meant. The Buddhist concept of *beginner's mind*—having an attitude of complete openness—was critical in my quest to get through this experience with my sanity intact. If I couldn't be open to the questions of the universe without trying to furiously wrestle meaning or a simplistic explanation out of each of these shocks, then I was sunk. My mind would pull apart like stretched taffy. My brain was already stressed enough. As Arya was teaching me, I had to roll through these insanity-inducing experiences with a shrug and a "Wow" and then get back to enjoying the sun and licking my paw.

But that was so hard to do.

I felt at this point my sanity could go either way. Whatever wisdom and knowledge were feeding me during this journey, I was fully aware that there was a stark-raving quality to my frame of mind, and I could either tiptoe my way through it with my psyche intact, or I could take a misstep in this field of mental landmines and never see my sanity again. I was fully aware that if I were witnessing someone behaving as I was, I'd wonder if they were a little nutty. But then I thought, that level of self-awareness must count for something, right? Insanity doesn't generally allow for this level of witnessing our own unraveling.

But what did I know? I was supposed to be seeing everything through the eyes of a child.

And even that kind of bothered me. The lingo. Was that biblical? Why couldn't the voice have referenced this concept

as beginner's mind? Zen Buddhism made me much more comfortable. *Through the eyes of a child*...it felt so...not me. But I could respect the wisdom. There was an element of surrender to that advice that felt freeing to me. If I didn't have to cling to understanding—dangling white-knuckled over the 1,000-foot abyss—a peace could take hold. Fascination could lead me through this, or madness would undo me.

I stopped at a gas station, and while the pump steadily fed fuel into my car, I wrote "surrender" in lip liner on my rearview mirror, to remind myself that understanding was no longer a necessary ingredient to this experience. "Let go," I said out loud, as I took a few slow, deep breaths. "More Zen, less Stark Raving, sweetheart." Hearing my own voice calmed me. My sanity depended upon it. I replaced the pump and gazed down at my foot while getting back in my car, remembering that I had Finlay's collar rolled up in my pant leg. No wonder the guy next to me was chuckling a little as he filled up his tank. "Buddy, if you had any idea how weird things are getting..." I muttered to myself as he drove away, and I returned to the road.

CHAPTER THIRTY-THREE

No longer wanting to hold my *cadejo* talisman while driving, I tucked it into my bra. Dog collar around my ankle, *cadejo* stuck to my breast, I was fully aware that I had jumped with both feet out of the realm of normalcy. But here I was, navigating a strange alternate reality for which I had no roadmap. I would wear my armor in whatever form I could find it. It didn't matter what anyone thought of me. All that mattered was that I kept going.

I was exhausted, and the sun was dropping, igniting the vast horizon in an explosive, painted swath of deep orange, yellow, and magenta. It took my breath away. I pulled off the highway and found a quiet residential road, so I could take Arya for a walk to stretch her legs. Sniffing every little wonder, she was the picture of contentment. If she had any idea her human mama was struggling to keep her head above water, she certainly didn't show it. Arya, like all dogs, seemed to be in a permanent state of *through the eyes of a child*. She was built

to adapt—a small Zen master from the moment she was born.

I found a hotel for us to settle into for the night and rented a room, then pulled my car around and lugged my bag up an outside flight of stairs. I put the electronic key card in the slot. Nothing. Tried it again. Nothing. After walking back to the lobby to get a functional one, I entered the room before Arya and immediately covered up the mirror with a bath towel, so as not to outrage her senses. Who knew if the old man was scheduled to show up again? I then went to fetch Arya, who was so tired she curled right up on the scratchy polyester bedspread and was snoring within minutes. I had to wake her up to remind her it was dinner time.

The digital clock stopped working. It started flashing random numbers in utter confusion. "It's 8:00, no it's 5:35, wait …it's 2:57…9:15…? Damn, I don't know!" It gave up and blinked 12:00, demoralized. I unplugged it, figuring it was broken. It wasn't something I needed, so I didn't give it a thought.

My hands felt electric. They hurt. I felt a current running through them; if I touched somebody, I thought I would injure them. I felt like a live wire literally and figuratively. Maybe I had just been spirit dead for so long, I'd forgotten what it felt like to be jumpstarted.

That night I wrote in my *Stark Raving Zen* blog:

> *I feel like a part of me is dying. But maybe that means the opposite. Maybe I'm evolving. The old me may be dying, but I welcome the new. I can see dead ones all around me, dead ones who fool themselves into believing they're living. Emptiness. We've lost our connection to instinct and nature. Do we care about others? It's too late for so many. I hope others find a way to break out, like I'm trying so hard to do. We'll make it.…Are you*

listening, Kristy? If you are, you'll know a life where you are the stuff that superheroes are made of. Natural abilities the animal kingdom understands. If you are not listening, and the simulated sounds of nature are enough for you; if you are content to gain material wealth at the destruction of your fellow man, wildlife, and the health of the planet, you'll be left behind. I'm sorry.

There was a strange discordance to that. As if halfway through, somebody else took over, responding to my original scattered thoughts. My words were starting to feel foreign, less like journaling and more like dictation. That stifling-a-yawn sensation that felt frustrating and euphoric was beginning to feel stronger. I went to bed feeling uneasy and nauseous, but Arya's effortless snoring was infectiously calming. In minutes I was out.

It felt like I had just closed my eyes when the television in the room came blasting on of its own accord. "Trust in the Lord!" the late-night evangelist crowed. I looked at my cell phone; it was 3:00 am. I'd been asleep for hours. I felt around for the remote, thinking the logical solution was that Arya had rolled over on it. But then I remembered I had never watched the television, so the remote wasn't near the bed. I found it across the room on the credenza. Another check in the weird-as-hell column.

I turned it off and unplugged it, just in case. I closed my eyes to return to sleep and found myself saying to anyone who was listening, "If you're trying to find ways to speak to me, can you please find another context? The language of evangelism doesn't work for me. *Trust in the Lord?*" With a weak snort, I drifted off into the blackness of night.

CHAPTER THIRTY-FOUR

Next morning, I tucked my *cadejo* talisman back into my bra and took Arya for a short walk. I clicked Finlay's collar around my ankle and once again bunched my jeans around it. It was a January morning and there was nothing but sun above me. The warmth on my face pacified me. The birds were chattering, and Arya was having the time of her life on this perpetual adventure, clearly loving my mental breakdown so far. We returned to the room to get ready to leave. Inserted the key. Nothing. Again. Off to get it reset; we finally made it back inside.

The bathroom had a large vanity and mirror inside it, with a door to the main room, so I could actually close myself in with the mirror this morning. Win/win. Arya didn't have to lose her mind and I could actually blow dry my hair and use some mascara. Up to now my appearance had been the farthest thing from my mind.

In the past I had been a slave to my looks. My friend's

husband jokingly referred to me as "Whiplash" because when I walked into a room, every head turned. I began to value myself for my beauty, using it as a shield, focusing on only that so I could bypass the connection to anything deeper.

But since leaving my job a month before and beginning this journey, I had forgotten that I was supposed to be attractive, that it was important to my ego identity. I forgot that I cared, that I even connected the concept of *attractive* with physical appearance. I became au naturel, with no use for hair dryers or eyeliner. Today I was okay with the eyeliner. As I gazed into the mirror my own reflection took my breath away. I was literally glowing. I felt a light emanating from inside of me. My face was radiant, like a newborn baby's. I stared at myself, gently touching my skin, not wanting to break this enchantment if that's what it was. "I'm *beautiful*," I whispered. For the first time in my life, my concept of inner beauty came from my spirit, not from the impossible demands of a distorted body image.

As I was walking to the car, my little glass *cadejo* tile worked its way out of my bra and down into my partially tucked-in shirt. I fished it out at my waist and tucked it securely inside the speedometer where it would be safe. I felt such contentment, as if I were in a constant meditative state. My mind was uncluttered and expansive.

We drove down the highway toward Santa Fe, and I was breathless at the beauty of this land. Towering red mesas, wide stretches of white-tipped indigo mountains, sage brush, orange clay, fragrant pinyon trees, all on a backdrop of the bluest, most magnificent sky I had ever seen. It was deep into winter, but the air was t-shirt warm and nothing seemed dead to me, or even asleep, compared to the barren, frozen, grey and white landscape of Minnesota. Everything felt alive, vibrant, interactive.

I pulled into a Santa Fe bank to use the cash machine. I was still aware of the need to care for myself and Arya, to handle logistics, to think ahead to the "what ifs," and I didn't want to find myself wandering the roads with no cash. I always made sure I had plenty of water too. But maps? It was impossible to read them. When I tried, my brain would turn to mush; a foggy haze would take over that made me feel nauseous and afraid. So I put the maps away. It didn't matter what route I was taking—nature itself would call me where I needed to be.

By now, every turn I took, every directional decision I made was determined by my gut feeling. Half the time I had no idea where I was, but I never felt lost. I was just here and would eventually be there, but beyond that I had no care. When I stepped out of the car to get to the cash machine, I got an immediate hit that I wanted nothing to do with Santa Fe. I recoiled at the energy, which felt painful. Nothing against one of the most beautiful cities on the planet; there were just too many people. I felt like a reverse porcupine, with every-body's quills suddenly stuck in me. I needed back roads, wide expanses of nothingness. I needed simplicity.

I'd like to say some miraculous directional compass took over where my brain stopped processing, but that would be a lie. Suddenly on this adventure I had no idea if I was driv-ing south or north, east or west. When often I thought I was driving in one direction I would be shocked to discover I had actually driven a hundred miles in the opposite. I was having one of those experiences today.

I glanced at a road sign that told me I was driving in the direction of Raton. I had just driven an hour back the way I had come last night. "Damn." I said out loud, as I scanned for a good place to turn around. But honestly, I wasn't all that disappointed. The view was so gorgeous, and I felt unflappable this morning. I was seeing names of things like "*Cañoncito at Apache Canyon*" which inexplicably made me cry, not with sadness, but with the strong sense that some critical thing was connecting with me, a knowing, a coming home.

I turned around and this time drove in my intended direction, south, back through Santa Fe, never stopping through Albuquerque, deep into the quietly beating heart of central New Mexico. The sunlight embraced me, the music on the radio serenaded me, the thump-thump of my tires on the highway seams lulled me into a state of trance—euphoric and comforting—as if somebody else had taken over and was deftly working my mind and movements. I felt a sense of assurance that I was being cared for. It allowed me to become a passenger, to rest, to take everything in as directed: *Through the eyes of a child.* My body was alert. I was still a good driver, but I had somehow become peacefully disconnected from the mundane. There was no boredom. Hours passed like seconds. My mind was in the hands of the universe, and my body became an agent of support for me, a chauffeur, lucidly escorting me as I gathered the experiences needed to put my pieces together.

After a couple of hundred miles I found myself in Valencia county, south of Albuquerque. The shades of orange across the landscape continued to stun me, and the energy was changing. It felt heavier, denser, though still beautiful. There was an ancient wounding here, a sadness.

I got the urge to explore a back road, which seemed more like a directive. It was only curiosity I felt when somebody else's hands—I could see them sharing the steering wheel with mine—took control and gently turned us right. There was no sense of danger, no fear. I found myself on a dirt road filled with deep, dry, orange potholes, ridged like rugged corduroy. My tires stirred up small peach dust clouds along the way, and I found myself navigating the divots with care, so as not to jostle Arya, who was now sitting up, alert and curious. I took it slowly, soaking up the amazing sights and the piquant, dusty, earthy smells all around me. There were a few houses scattered about—nice houses, with extensive adobe courtyard walls surrounding them, offering tiny glimpses of protected lives. I kept rolling, not much faster than ten miles per hour. My car was small with a low clearance, and I didn't want to cause any damage to our little chariot. Arya seemed to be thoroughly enjoying her view out the side window, quietly entranced by the beauty, as was I.

I had driven maybe a mile when I came to what seemed to be the end of the road. There was a house off to the left, behind a large wall with an elaborately sculpted iron gate. To the right was nothing but glorious desert landscape, with juniper, sage brush and sand, and a circle to turn around in. I stopped the car and thought this would be an excellent place to walk Arya, though I was a little concerned about the dangers of rattle snakes. Were they even out in the wintertime? Or were they curled up somewhere, sleeping the cold months off in a reptilian torpor? I didn't know but I wasn't taking any chances. I vowed to keep my eye out and stopped the car.

I changed my mind when I saw Arya intently staring at something through the back window. She stayed completely quiet as we watched two enormous canines emerge out of the desert. They walked in tandem, in complete synchrony, always within a foot of the other's side. One was howling with rage; I'd never heard such screams from a dog. The other made no sound—she was calm and peaceful, but unnaturally so— and had a strange, comical smile on her face, as though some illustrator had crudely drawn it. The smile never changed; she wore a mask frozen in place, a disturbing caricature.

They seemed to be the size of cows. And they were scaring me to a nonsensical degree. I glanced down at the *cadejo* tile leaning against my speedometer. I locked the doors and tried to turn the car around while they circled us.

I was suddenly shaking so hard I could barely hold onto the steering wheel. My whole body went rigid.

Cadejos are mythological creatures that travel in pairs. The lore says that one is good, to protect, and one is deeply, terrifyingly malevolent, there to kill. One is light, one is dark. One is love, one is fear. The benevolent one is present to keep the evil one from killing, but which one is light and which one is dark has nothing to do with their color, which varies depending upon the sighting. They appear in the form of very large shaggy dogs, but some claim to see goat's hooves for feet, and a flaming chain around the malevolent one's neck, indicating he's broken free from the gates of hell. If you are found by the satanic *cadejo*, without the protection of the life-giving twin, there is no hope for you. You will be torn apart and dragged to Lucifer, a most horrifying game of demonly fetch. The good *cadejo* tries hard to hold back the force of evil but is smaller and works strenuously to do so. The legend says, do not turn your backs on the *cadejos* or your sanity will be torn to shreds even if you survive the encounter.

These were my *cadejos*.

Outside my window the dark *cadejo* was shrieking, screaming, like a satanic banshee. The white one, mute, placed herself between the larger one and my car and continued with her otherworldly smile. She never blinked. One was life, one was death, hovering so close to my driver's side door.

I continued to drive slowly, my eyes transfixed on them. I tried to stay focused on the one with the smiling face. Arya remained stone silent. She couldn't take her eyes off them either, never once growling or barking, though her hair stood on end.

I managed to snap a picture of the *cadejos* while crawling along this broken road, driving so slowly I could take the photo and drive at the same time. The digital image was startling. The white dog had that crude grin on her face. The dark one had deep, black, empty pits for eyes and a howling sphere, like a gaping hole, for a mouth.

After a short distance, the *cadejos* stopped following. I drove on while staring at them through the rearview mirror, and Arya stood like a statue, gazing out the back window, maintaining eye contact. Neither one of us wanted to look away first. I was already holding onto sanity by a gossamer thread and Arya was no fool.

We dropped down into a canyon and turned a corner, losing our view along with our connection with the *cadejos*. "They were just dogs, right?" I was desperately asking Arya to make sense of this for me. But she wasn't answering, too busy existing in some strange blissed out state. She had her mouth open, panting. Her eyes were closed; she was breathing hard, face pointed to the heavens and wearing that white *cadejo*'s strange comedic smile. It wasn't hot in the car and she hadn't been active, so her physical state didn't make any sense.

I stopped the car and stepped out, no longer afraid, only

confounded and wonderstruck. Whatever dimension we had just wandered into, we were out of it now. I bent down and picked up a handful of orange earth, letting the silky grains slip through my fingers. I made Arya get out of the car and walk with me, to shake this experience out of our bones. She pranced in a kind of a daze, occasionally gazing up into the sky, her neck gracefully arched, still smiling. We walked around a little until I felt Arya was back in her body, acting herself, sniffing natural treasures on the path. I opened the door and she jumped onto her traveling throne of pillows and blankets.

"What the hell." I said, as I returned to the driver's seat. I stared at the speedometer. My *cadejo* talisman tile was gone. "It was just here," I said to nobody. I jumped back out of the car and frantically searched for it. Under my seat, under the floor mats, outside the car, just in case I had somehow dragged it out with me, though it was secured inside the speedometer, so I wasn't sure how that would be possible. I considered the possibility that someone stole it. But the doors were locked. And I was only a couple of hundred feet from the car, never out of sight. Nobody was around. I had an expensive DSLR camera with lenses, worth thousands of dollars, sitting right in the passenger seat, open and visible in its bag. Who would steal a tiny glass tile and leave a camera?

*Let it go, let it go, Kristy...*I leaned against a street sign right outside my car door. *Through the eyes of a child, through the eyes of a child...don't try to make sense of this.* I breathed deeply and intentionally, trying to get my mind to white-knuckle the edge of the cliff for just a little while longer. I cried then, really let loose, but no tears came. And they weren't sobs of sadness or fear, but complete awe, and divine gratitude, like I had just come face to face with an angel and had no idea how to handle that. All of it, the reality of everything, came flooding into me, out of me, and no matter what would end up taking place, I thanked God profusely for allowing me to experience things so outside the mundane, so incomprehensible to the human mind. All of this was worth it. The fear, the horror, the sadness, the complete inability to understand any of it.

My body began to shake uncontrollably again, teeth chattering, jaw clenched. My spine felt like it was ready to snap. I glanced up at the street sign. Las Mangas Trail. I got back into my car and shoved some crackers in my mouth, a cheap trick to stop the energy from coming too fast into my body. Las Mangas Trail.

"I wonder what Mangas is?" Taking one last look at the sign I took a few deep breaths, put the car into drive and pulled once more onto the New Mexico highway. I'd find us a place to stay overnight. I was looking forward to doing some research.

Part Seven

THE INNERMOST CAVE

"The real voyage of discovery consists not in seeking new landscapes, but in having new eyes."

~ Marcel Proust

"Barn's burnt down...now I can see the moon."

~ Mizuta Masahide

CHAPTER THIRTY-FIVE

The evening sun crept low along the horizon, igniting an inferno of color over the distant mountains. Broad brush-strokes of canary yellow lined the ridge, blending to gradations of tangerine, lavender, electric violet, and indigo—daylight's last stand. I'd never experienced these colors at twilight. For New Mexico it was just another Wednesday. The sunsets here were a part of its enchantment, and every human experience seemed bound by the spectrum of the sun's retreat.

I took my foot off the gas and coasted down the exit ramp, compelled by the blinking neon invitation from a local motel. I was in Los Lunas, making every decision based on nothing more than "feels good" or "doesn't feel good." My solar plexus relaxed. This place felt good.

I pulled into the empty parking lot and made my way to the lobby, anxious to get settled for the night and research my burning question—what does "Mangas" mean?

I zipped the key card through the electronic slider and

was met with the angry flashing red light. The key card was nonfunctional—again. I looked down at a disappointed Arya. "I'm sorry, Baby." She just looked up at me, eager for me to open the door. By now I had come to the conclusion that the electronic oddities happening to me in hotel rooms were a result of my changing nervous system. Could a body's own electrical system affect electronics? Weren't these key cards magnetic? I had no idea what was happening. The painful buzzing in my hands was nearly constant now, with tremors and muscle spasms happening whenever the channels came through. I found patience with all of it and just kept going through the motions to do what I had to do to get into my room for the evening. We trudged back to the lobby.

Key refreshed, we settled into our room, then immediately left again to allow Arya to stretch her legs. We took a walk around the neighborhood, which was brightly lit by incandescent streetlamps. Los Lunas was a busy little highway town bustling with travelers, gas stations, Starbucks, and drive-thru fast-food chains. I turned down a quiet street, trying to find some friendly greenery suitable for Arya's potty break. I saw nothing soft or green in this prickly desert town, but she did find an empty dirt lot to be an acceptable substitution.

It felt stabilizing to walk. I embraced my connection to the earth with each step, visualizing Mother Nature sending protective energy straight up from terra firma into the soles of my feet. I started to get that familiar tugging feeling, the buzzing, the sense of trying to suppress a yawn, and was compelled to turn down another quiet street, this one more residential. It was brightly illuminated, and everything felt perfectly safe. Normally I'd be a little anxious about wandering around in a strange neighborhood in a strange land particularly at night, but I felt none of that. I had just survived a visitation from Satan's house pet. What could I possibly be concerned about here?

I stepped up to a beautiful English cottage-style house; it looked a little out of place in this land of sand-colored adobe with painted turquoise doors to keep malevolent spirits out. This house had no garden, just a lot of carefully placed rocks and dirt, but in the window was a neon sign that read, "Psychic Services." Seemed like an excellent idea. I knocked on the door, eager to ask the psychic behind it what was happening to me. I was desperate for answers—answers from another living human being. Nobody responded. I stood there for half a minute and rang the doorbell. Nothing. After business hours perhaps, though the neon was still lit.

I hated to leave in case somebody was inside, but I didn't want to be a nuisance either. I stood under the bright porch light, pushed my hair behind my ears and dug through my little backpack purse to find a small notepad and a pen. I'd write him a message and leave my cell number, I reasoned. That way he could just phone me when he had a minute and maybe he'd agree to a phone session. But instead, I found myself writing a 1,000-word paragraph of nonsense! It poured out of me and was impossible to halt or censor—it was also wincingly embarrassing to read. Something about "I have returned." Why would he care? And—returned? I'd never been here before!

I blathered on: "Don't you worry, because all will be well shortly. Mother Nature is waking up, and she is going to right every wrong…" Blah, blah, blah, for another eight hundred words or so. Volcanically incoherent thoughts erupted out of me.

I skimmed through my written words when the feeling passed and thought, "No way am I leaving this; it'll scare somebody." But I had this sense that I had better not betray the trust of whatever or whomever had poured this stream of consciousness through me—it seemed like the divine feminine waxing poetic about making an epic comeback. I added my phone number, hoping somebody would call me back. (Of course, they didn't.) Then Arya and I made our way back to the busy street, and back to our hotel room.

My phone started buzzing. I slowed my pace so I could read it, squinting at the little screen in the dark. My sister had texted me something her husband had sensed on my behalf, testing out his own intuition by overriding his generally reserved, stoic demeanor to pass me a message. "Keep your eye on the horizon, think only of what is before you," he wrote.

I shrugged. "Well, it's a beautiful horizon," I mused, recalling the divinely painted sky I'd seen just a short while ago. I closed my eyes and inhaled his words. It was a simple sentiment which gave me a ton of peace. My lungs spontaneously expanded with a deep, calming breath. Each day's experiences had begun to pile on top of me. I felt like I was climbing a mountain, and my brother-in-law had just yelled down from the top, "Don't look down!" Supremely simple but critically important advice.

Keep my eyes on the horizon, think only of what is before me. His simple message became my mantra; it felt like a wildly generous gift from a guy who rarely said more than a few words to me at any one time. It also reminded me that I had family and friends following my journey, keeping an eye on me, spirit to spirit.

CHAPTER THIRTY-SIX

*F*ollowing Arya into the hotel room and locking the dead-bolt behind me, I closed my eyes and took a moment to lean my back against the smooth, cool door. Pressing my spine against that stable surface felt reassuring. I opened my eyes and saw another confused digital clock, flashing multiple times in succession—4:50, 7:29, 2:18. I unplugged it and the television too.

Arya was totally calm this time as she watched me walk back and forth in front of the large mirror. She was no longer responding to my reflection. Either the old man wasn't borrowing my face any longer, or he had become familiar to her by now. Exhausted, she sprawled out on the bed, her long limbs spanning half the surface. She groaned with contentment and fell fast asleep.

I spread lingonberry jam on crackers, a provision I had picked up near Santa Fe, and delighted in licking my fingers as I waited for my computer to power up. Nothing had ever tasted so good! It was like my taste buds had awakened from a thirty-year nap. "Where do lingonberries come from, Arya?" I asked. She ignored me, choosing not to open her eyes for our usual intelligent and inquisitive nonverbal dialogue. I wasn't all that interested in the answer as I googled the true million-dollar question: "What is Mangas?" I expected a Spanish adjective.

I stared in silence. Mangas wasn't a thing. Mangas was a *who*. Mangas Coloradas was a nineteenth-century Apache warrior from this location on the map. I opened an image and was hit by that jolt of electricity I had experienced weeks earlier when I'd stumbled upon the Fox Sisters. An ice-cold sensation poured down my spine while an electrical inferno erupted where my scalp had once been.

Mangas Coloradas was the voice in my ear. He was the reflection in the mirror. The dark-eyed man who had swapped faces with me, and had served as the guide in my dreams, the impatient director. He had called me to New Mexico, and I had found him. My heart rate doubled, and my forehead began to sweat. I wiped silent tears off my cheeks as I devoured information about the man in my head, the man who had parented me from the moment my mother died and my father disappeared into his alcoholic stupor.

Who was he? Why had I never heard about him? Initial sources referred to him as a murderous war criminal. I consumed about an hour's worth of reading, enough to know that he was a Mimbreño Apache chief who is credited with uniting all of the Apache tribes. The famed Cochise was his son-in-law.

I read on. He didn't seem murderous to me. He seemed to be a fierce warrior who fought back against the Mexicans and Europeans who had a tendency to systematically slaughter his people. My body shook and tensed up; my teeth began to chatter painfully. I was suddenly freezing.

I had Mangas Coloradas sharing my consciousness, even borrowing my face every now and then. But why? Why would a warrior who died in the 1800s have any interest in me? There was no doubt in my mind that his was the voice in my dreams. He was the slightly bored, strong-willed man in my left ear, forever offering me wise teachings on non-attachment, the sensate nature of dogs, my own spirit, the beginner's mind. How could this man have ever been a berserker on the battlefield? Maybe he had been. I'm sure he did what he had to. But I just couldn't see that being the full story, and certainly not what he was now.

"You learn only what they tell you," the voice chimed in. "And I can be in many places at once."

I understood.

He meant that I would never have any idea what truth was if my only resource was the written word in Wikipedia or American history textbooks. Traditional sources are oftentimes manipulative and just plain wrong as it pertains to the truth about indigenous America. I had to feel my way through these answers to get a comprehensive picture of who Mangas was, not look for someone to give them to me through a filter of their own choosing.

And I was to have no delusions. Mangas is a highly evolved spirit who pays attention to millions. This somehow didn't make me feel any less personally connected to him. But he wasn't *mine*.

I closed my eyes and felt my way into the truth of Mangas Coloradas. It wasn't hard. He was sharing my mind. I had become like a student driver in one of those adapted cars with two steering wheels. I saw no insanity in Mangas Coloradas. I felt no fear in my body. I saw a man desperately fighting to preserve his way of life, his innocent children, his land, his simple right to exist. It was heartbreaking. He, like everyone else at the time, did some terrible things. But what he and his people had to endure was inhuman and horrifying. I slipped deeper and found myself looking through the eyes of a man 150 years ago, a man and a tribe facing a genocidal onslaught. I felt the insanity of the situation, and faced down the energy of extinction moving toward me like a tidal wave I knew I could never escape. My body was paralyzed. The visions kept coming, horrible and intense, but I felt no emotion. I witnessed the truth, but my empathy had been unplugged. It was as I had once practiced in my astral travel to the Boston stabbing. Perhaps the empathic skill I had learned then was needed for this very moment in time.

Just then my cell rang. It was Aaron. Bad timing.

"Hello!" he said. I registered his voice, cheerful and strong, but I felt paralyzed with Mangas still in my head.

"Yes." I said.

"Yes? How are you?"

Silence.

"Kristy?" He asked.

"You're not talking to Kristy."

Now the silence was Aaron's.

"Okay, well, can you put Kristy on the phone?" Aaron wasn't all that polite about it—if this was a joke, he wasn't finding it funny—but Mangas obliged.

I felt myself slowly slip back into my own mind, like a hand working its way into a leather glove. It felt good, like I had just taken a rejuvenating power nap. I was holding the phone.

"Hello?" I asked.

"Kristy? What the hell?"

"Hi, Baby!" I gave him no recovery time, launching into a nonstop recount of the entire day's entrancing experiences: the *cadejos*, meeting Mangas. I babbled with such force he could barely take it in. While I was rattling on, he was busy googling Mangas Coloradas. Of course he went right to the *murderous psycho* version of the story.

"This guy's the voice in your head?" For the first time I could hear concern and fear in his voice. The world's most patient man had finally reached his limit. "Kristy. Do you have any idea who he is?! What his story is? You're telling me the voice in your head is a notorious killer?"

His choice of words hurt me, like he had punched me in the stomach.

"You can't believe everything you read, Aaron. You know that. There's way more to the story. That's just not true." I didn't know what else to say. I remained quiet.

More silence from Aaron. I could feel the wheels in his mind frantically turning. I could hear his thoughts, wondering if he was going to have to come down here and get me, for the first time losing faith that what I was going through was just a phase of regeneration. Maybe I wasn't recovering at all. Maybe I was losing my mind. Maybe he was losing me.

But then I started talking, calling up *sane Kristy*, softening him, feeling sorry for what I must be putting him through. God knows it was hard enough on *my* mind. I could understand how it must feel to an outsider, someone who loved me. I talked him down out of his panic feeling. As I explained more about the day, he felt his skin catch fire with the electricity of wonder. All his hair stood on end. It felt real; what I was going through felt important. He felt like he was coming alive again through my experience, something in him igniting when he hadn't even been aware the flame had been extinguished. He told me he had been reading random things, finding spiritual writers who seemed to be explaining to him what was happening to me, as if the universe was also guiding him through my madness. He was hearing reassurance in songs, like he was connecting to that sunglasses-off reality too—as were my friends and a couple of my family members. They were going through their own transformations, fueled by mine. As with any fire, standing too close was likely to get a person burned, but it was the best kind of fire, the life-giving, soul-reviving type. Rather than think me crazy, they were being pulled into a new place, quietly following along, wanting to believe me, loving me. Not understanding, but somehow trusting. They kept me alive with their undercurrent of acceptance, wonder, and support.

Throughout this journey I had been blogging every day's experiences, without trying to explain the events, just rambling about what insights I was having, sharing urgencies and insistence that we all come alive—right now—that we all start to care about the environment and each other, that we snap out of this spoon-fed material existence that was killing us and the world. We had to learn to trust, open our minds and hearts, and be authentic. We had to learn tolerance and spiritual freedom. We had to learn that killing the earth was killing us, that transforming our lives couldn't be done independently of our relationship with the planet. My writing was frenetic at this time, with an urgency that scared some. It was rabid and embarrassing, sometimes nonsensical, not unlike the crazed note I'd written to the psychic down the street in Los Lunas. But all of this seemed to be leading me to my purpose. And connecting to that purpose seemed to broadcast an underlying energy that made some kind of sense to my readers. They could feel it. Their unwavering love was also an anchor for me. They seemed transfixed by my story.

Having talked long enough to feel like I was in complete charge of my body and my mind once again, I told Aaron I loved him, and we said goodnight. I disconnected the call, turned off my computer and was hit with an exhaustion so intense I couldn't even take the time to remove my contact lenses. I crawled into bed fully clothed and turned off the light.

Before I was out, though, my phone screen lit up and began dialing itself. It was calling Ann, my best friend in Boston. I immediately hung it up, hoping I hadn't bothered her—it was two hours ahead of my time zone and way too late to be calling. After about five minutes the phone did it again. I turned it off, not even registering the strangeness of it.

It was dark and quiet. Out of my peripheral vision I could see someone playfully jumping on the second double bed in my room. Arya, as always, was right next to me but hadn't seemed to notice this ghostly ruckus. I opened my eyes just a crack, all that I could manage, being encased in my heavy tomb of exhaustion. It was Maggie Fox. Just a little girl she was, full of joy, bouncing up and down in a flouncy dress and braids. I lifted my head an inch. "Maggie, go to sleep, will you?" I threw a pillow at her. She blipped out of sight, but seconds later I found my phone slowly moving across the side table. I grabbed it and put it in the drawer. "I turned it off, Maggie. No phone calls. And I unplugged the TV, okay?" I was asleep in seconds.

Eight solid hours later, I woke up feeling rested and strong with a lightness and happiness at the memory of Maggie Fox bouncing on the bed the night before. As I opened the drawer on the bedside table to fetch my phone and charge it, I noticed that my notepad and pen had a bunch of scribbles on it. I turned on the light for a better view. My contacts were foggy from overnight wear, but I looked at the words closely. What was most disturbing was that I had written this seemingly overnight with absolutely no memory of doing so. Just words and fragments of phrases…. Were they even mine? Could Maggie write? "Apache," "my mind," "who am I?" "blue-grey," "Aaron's mom is a cat." Most of it perfectly legible, but some of it unreadable.

"Aaron's mom is a cat?" I stared at the collection of words, trying to connect the dots, but the meaning behind the scribbles and phrases remained a mystery. Like everything else on this journey so far, I resigned to accept them and be patient—to just stay in the moment. *Think only of what is before me.*

CHAPTER THIRTY-SEVEN

I got out of bed, threw the curtains open, and watched the New Mexico sun barge in without asking permission. Was it ever overcast here? I was trying not to let the word salad I had woken up to dampen my mood. If I wanted to gather evidence of my sanity, this had set me back a little. But honestly, by now I wasn't all that concerned with keeping track. I was so deeply into this experience that one foot in front of the other was the best I could do. I still felt a lot of love around me, and that kept me stable.

I wandered into the bathroom, brushed my teeth, rinsed my contacts (which hadn't gotten their proper rest the night before) and stepped into a hot shower. I hovered under the steaming water for a long time, letting the heat relax my muscles—until I began to feel stronger.

I grabbed a towel and thought about filling my growling stomach. A bagel with lingonberry jam sounded really good.

"You can't eat this morning," Mangas said abruptly in my

left ear. I winced and instinctively covered my ear. It startled me and hurt a little. It was too loud.

"What do you mean, I can't eat?" I argued. There was no answer, but the message was clear. I was scheduled to have some kind of cross-dimensional experience today, and I could not have food in my stomach to do so. My guidance wasn't an austerity test or punishment, it was simple logistics.

But I was hungry. And though my intuition told me to follow this simple decree, I ate half a bagel anyway. It was every bit as good as I imagined it would be. And within thirty seconds of having my last bite, I promptly puked it all up right in the bathroom sink while applying my mascara. No warning, no nausea, no queasy butterflies; the universe just stuck its finger down my throat and pounded me on the back. Drama free, but decisive.

So weird.

I didn't take it personally. Whenever I got a message so clear there was no interpretation to be made, it felt like a gift. "Okay. No food this morning. Got it." I'd had an intuition and I'd ignored it. I was learning.

On the road again, I made my way farther south, in the direction of Las Cruces. Meanwhile, the channeling became more intense. I kept pulling over in order to scribble the transmissions coming through. Reading them later, I had no idea what any of them meant—I couldn't even read some of them. This plan wasn't working. I decided to purchase a small voice recorder so I could capture the messages without worrying about pulling over or forgetting the words of the speaker who was borrowing my brain.

I stopped at the first place I could find, which happened to be a Walmart. Navigating my way around the giant parking lot, I found a rare spot in the shade and parked my car where Arya would remain comfortable. It was the middle of winter, but the sun was still hot, and I wasn't taking any chances.

I rolled down the windows some, stepped out of the car and walked toward the building. There was a man holding up a sign, but he was a distance away from me, and I couldn't read what it said. I tried to amble in a slightly modified direction to avoid contact, but the moment I chose to do that, I was struck by the familiar buzzing, that euphoric sensation taking over my brain. Somebody was trying to butt in again. I kept walking.

"He's a gatekeeper, Child. Here for you," said the voice in my left ear.

"That guy?" I pointed. "Is he guarding the gateway to homelessness? Of course he's here for me; that's probably where I'm headed." But I obediently changed course and headed straight for the guy with the cardboard sign. He stared at me as I approached.

As I got closer, I read his sign, which said, "Traveling a great distance." Nothing more. He was a middle-aged white guy, partially bald, clean. He wore shorts, a flannel shirt, and hiking boots. He had a large backpack resting by his feet, like the frozen statue guy up north had had. My gatekeeper looked like he could have been an accountant a month before, an accountant who had said, "Screw this!" and took off. Exactly like me.

I squinted through my sunglasses and dug into my purse. "I'm on a long journey myself," I said, as I handed him a twenty-dollar bill. Before he could engage me in conversation, I began to walk away. "Thank you!" he called out. I thought it only polite to have eye contact with the guy when I told him you're welcome, but in the time it took me to turn my head, he was gone. Poof. Disappeared.

I stood staring at the empty space he had occupied two seconds before. Had he ever been there? Or had I imagined him? If imagined, then who had I given my money to? I couldn't have imagined him! My heartbeat increased, but only slightly. My body was getting more comfortable with disappearing people.

I wandered into the store, still dumbstruck, and found that digital voice recorder. On the way out I chuckled at a tiny shirt designed for a Chihuahua. It said, "Fearless" in rhinestones. I made my way back to the car where I found Arya a little too anxious to see me. I had only been gone about ten minutes.

"Sorry, baby girl, but I apparently had to buy transportation somewhere. That guy was a gatekeeper. A gatekeeper." I stressed the word as if the emphasis would provide clarity for her. She looked at me blankly, and faked a yawn, which is what she does when she's a little embarrassed for me. "I know," I groaned, putting the key in the ignition. "I'm fully aware of how stupid that sounds." She perked her silky ears at me. I'd take all the reassurance I could get.

In that moment I felt renewed, energized, optimistic. I could have worn the Chihuahua shirt; I was fearless. I thought about the gatekeeper and said to nobody, "Okay, so, where did we buy entry to? Where's my gate?" I looked in my rearview mirror to see if Mangas was there. Nothing but my reflection, Arya—and now Maggie Fox politely sitting next to Arya, gazing out the side window with her hands folded on her lap. Words caught in my throat, but I stopped myself. I'd been about to ask her to put her seatbelt on. Arya curled up on top of her and went to sleep. Did she know Maggie was there? I couldn't tell.

Part Eight

THE ORDEAL

"Only to the extent that we expose ourselves over and over to annihilation can that which is indestructible in us be found."

~ Pema Chodron

And so long as you haven't experienced

this: to die and so to grow,

you are only a troubled guest

on the dark earth.

~ Johann Wolfgang von Goethe

CHAPTER THIRTY-EIGHT

*I*t was well into the evening, and I had no idea where I was. Blissfully not lost, though, because I had no destination. I had spent most of the day winding through dusty dirt roads, not really getting anywhere. In the darkness an enormous owl swooped right in front of my windshield; my headlights illuminated his flight while I instinctively ducked to brace for impact. He was beautiful, a Great Horned, and he cleared the battering ram of the glass just in time. My jaw relaxed. I released my iron grip on the steering wheel and exhaled the fear out of my bones. He'd definitely startled me. He seemed to be half the size of the car, but adrenaline is known to exaggerate.

It was time to stop for the night, and feeling ready to rest, I saw a sign for Socorro. Since narrowly missing the owl, I could not shake a strange feeling, a mix of welcome and dread. Something like, you belong here, but it won't be easy. I shook it off and kept driving, while the memory of my father replaced that of the owl. I couldn't get him out of my head.

❖❖❖❖❖

My father had died eighteen months earlier, and all I had felt at the time was enormous relief. A neighbor had found him sitting straight up in his chair, dead at his kitchen table, in a sick mockery of the life he had led for the previous twenty years. Clearly the Angel of Death has a dark sense of humor. The medical examiner told me it was coronary failure, an instantaneous death. It was how those in the medical exam industry all hoped to go, she had said. But she also found something about the death scene interesting.

"Was your dad a religious man?" she asked.

"Uh…not so much." Who really knew? My father didn't have much to say on the matter, but I did recall a conversation we'd had a few weeks before he died. He had brought it up.

"What do you think happens when a person dies?" he'd mumbled.

I pontificated some rambling thoughts, probably not going very deep into my own spiritual reserve to answer. The only way I could stand to be in the presence of this man who had inflicted so much injury on his own children was to encase myself in concrete. Once I sat down, I was usually only inter-ested in getting out of there. But on this particular day, Dad became something like a Taoist. He said he believed that when he died, he'd become sunlight or nourishment for the earth. He'd become one with everything.

I couldn't connect with the idea of my dad nourishing any-thing. For the past two decades he had done nothing but sit in his apartment, right there at the kitchen table from where he would eventually depart this life. A few years before he had nearly swilled himself into the grave directly. He got so drunk that he aspirated alcohol, which resulted in near-fatal pneumonia. The whole family gathered, but he somehow rallied, despite suffering severe delirium tremens from alcohol withdrawal. The doctors called it a full-blown medical miracle that he survived.

Dad swore he'd actually seen the Grim Reaper that time in the hospital; some big guy in a black hood had stood over his bed, telling him time was up. It scared him, but his scrappy Irish fortitude kicked in and he somehow punched and clawed his way back. He recovered and swore off alcohol for good. During his medical crisis, we were informed that he had emphysema and cirrhosis of the liver, and warned not to get too attached to having him around. He didn't stop smoking, however, and the "swearing-off-alcohol-for-good" thing didn't last either.

At the time of his near death, I was living in New England and thought I'd make a push for the A+ Daughter award. When Aaron and I moved back to Minnesota, I started taking care of Dad, which consisted of shampooing the seborrhea crust off his head, cleaning his assisted-living apartment, cooking for him, and taking him to doctor appointments—for which he was grateful. When I was done providing whatever service I could, I'd scram—I felt literally sick if I spent too much time in his presence.

A couple of years later, he was dead. That was that.

At the scene of my father's death, the coroner had found a small statue of Mother Mary teetering on the very edge of his refrigerator, pointed in the direction of where my dad was found dead in his chair. She had thought it a little spooky, like an omen.

Okay, I was open to the mystery. I hoped it was so. I hoped

Mary had been there to usher him to his healing place.

I used to dream that my father was a demon. He'd chase me, hunting me down in cars or on foot. I would hide behind some flimsy barrier, feeling no protection at all against this man I had loved so fiercely as a child. In the dreams he had no eyes, just open sockets with flames burning within, like the evil *cadejo*.

When was the exact moment I stopped loving my father? When did the laughing, sparkly eyed, dancing Irishman that I had loved like crazy morph into the drunken devil who gave in to the darkness, like my maternal grandfather had?

The moment I stopped loving my father was likely the first time I claimed my space and my body by screaming at him to stop leering at me and grabbing my ass whenever I walked past. From the time I was about twelve years old, when the alcoholism completely enveloped him, living with my father was like walking a gauntlet between two rows of snarling, lunging, ravenous Rottweilers, chained but straining. I prayed I'd make it through intact. I grew up walking a tragically straight line, fearing those chains would break at any time, vowing I'd kill that man with my bare hands if he ever forgot his boundaries and came one step closer with that alcohol-hazy look in his eyes.

Yes, that was it. The moment I stopped loving my father was the moment he stopped protecting me and became something I needed protection from. But that protection never came. Because my only other parent was a mother too preoccupied with her own brokenness, sitting in some dark room, crying.

When he died, I felt released from my shackles.

I found Socorro. I got some sleep.

CHAPTER THIRTY-NINE

The next morning, I woke up to one sentence written on the hotel note pad beside my bed. It was practically illegible, but I could just make out, "Go to the origin, the origin of where Mother Nature began to die." The words shook me awake.

I felt miserable, as though I had gotten no rest at all.

I was no longer searching for the "crazy" or the "sane" Kristy; I had no sense at all of what description fit. My experience was becoming more wander, and less wonder. I had no boundaries, no borders; I felt as though I had no physical form, that I was invisible. Could people even see me, or was I like the statue man in the median strip, invisible to all but a select few?

As I drove away, I felt like breathing was superfluous, as if I no longer needed oxygen. I tried to hold my breath for extended periods of time, just to test it. I wanted to be the oxygen itself, to not have to inhale or exhale, but to simply disappear into the atmosphere. I found, however disappointingly, that oxygen was still a necessity. I gasped as I released my pent-up carbon dioxide and took an enormous recovery breath. Whatever the state of my transformation, I wasn't ready for no-oxygen living yet.

I drove through the Bosque del Apache, a national wildlife preserve, listened to my ethereal music and followed the sunrays at their entry point through my windshield, each one piercing the glass without effort. What power, light. The rays felt alive, they seemed to bubble, providing me with effervescent energy. My spine straightened.

My hands started tingling and burning and my back muscles began to spasm as I sat taller. I got that euphoric rush. Somehow, I hit the correct button on my digital recorder, heard it whir to life. It collected words that poured out of me so fast I never would have been able to record them on paper. I felt as though I was being filled with a nourishing and energizing elixir, sparkling sunshine itself. The words relieved my hands, relaxed my spine, and filled me with love and wonder. I believed Mother Nature herself spoke through me as a silky voice said, "Come alive, Child. Stay awake, and I will always be able to connect with you. I'll always find you. Now is the time when Nature will start looking for those she knows are listening. She needs all of those who can hear this message to stay awake, stay alive, feel her love, and love her in return. She will find you. She will spare you."

Spare me?

As I processed her words, I scanned the beauty all around me. It was like some fairy realm. The colors should not have been this vibrant in January. I stopped the car to take it all in. The buzzing in my head returned, deafeningly loud, and my vision began to blur. I played the recording over and over while I shook my head, closed my eyes tight, and rode the wave of energy overtaking me.

When I opened my eyes, there were flowers blooming everywhere. Wasn't this unusual for the middle of winter? I wasn't familiar with New Mexico. Had all these blooms been here when I'd closed my eyes? Wait—many of these flowers were not even native to the desert. I was looking at botany from all over the world—plant life I had seen in Hawaii and Florida: tropical plants, flowering vines, colors so psychedelic they burned my eyes. Waves of energy and light permeated my body. I looked to Arya for confirmation of my awe-inspiring vision but received none. Whatever was happening was clearly not interesting to her; she remained fast asleep, which was odd since I had stopped the car. She would usually be eager to get out and explore. The soil began to sprout flowers faster than my eyes could track, until the whole horizon was covered in a million colors of flashy neon and soft pastel. Mother Nature had gone gloriously insane, right along with me. More words came through. "Remember this, when you find yourself at the place where Mother Nature began to die. Remember this. Hold on to this, my sweet love."

And with that, it was gone. I put my hand on my chest to slow my breathing and quiet my galloping heart. Tears poured down my cheeks, and I started a weird mix of laughing and sobbing simultaneously, which felt like the only response my body had for miracles. My face lifted toward the sun, and I cried out in gratitude to anyone or anything responsible for showing me what I had just seen. By then Arya had awakened and was licking my face from the back seat. She wanted to be closer to me, seemed desperate to do so. I let her crawl up into the driver's seat with me, and she tried to fit in my lap, but her thirty-pound frame was too large for that. She was asking me if I was okay. I thought I was. I put her leash on and we climbed out of the car. I needed to walk.

"This is what *Alice in Wonderland* must have felt like," I said to Arya as she trotted next to me down the empty road. I felt enveloped in delight. I found a big rock to sit on and let the sun beat down on us while I took in the cool air. We rested there for over an hour until I felt like moving again. The colors had normalized, and the tropical flowers had disappeared, but their energetic signature remained seared into my consciousness. I couldn't stop smiling. Whatever dread I had felt upon waking this morning had faded.

Back on the highway, I spotted a road sign. "Truth or Consequences" in seventy miles. "Truth or Consequences. *Seriously?*" I smiled, feeling a definite date with destiny in a town so aptly named for this wild journey. I took a deep breath to clear my mind and headed in that direction.

My vision was sparkly. Everything seemed polished like a diamond. I wondered if these colors were the colors everyone else was seeing. Everything was so beautiful. The neon oranges, the electric blue sky—they were otherworldly. I had no desire to be in the northern part of the state, famous for its flamboyant beauty. I was drawn to southern New Mexico, with its barren strength: vast, empty, and lonely. I wanted sand and sky, nothing else. I felt the land respond to this desire, suddenly fanning its feathers like a peacock.

As I drove, I listened to my music and I absorbed the deep peace of Arya now sitting in the passenger seat after demanding closer proximity. I normally wouldn't have allowed this, because it's a dangerous position in a car for a dog, but I didn't know how to contend with her insistence. It seemed like she knew something I didn't. She wouldn't take no for an answer, so, front seat it was. I passed a billboard that said "FAITH" in giant block letters and felt so full, so certain that forces I couldn't explain were watching over us. It was all true. Arya was untouchable. She would be fine.

I pulled into a rest area and parked the car. It was time to make a new throne for Arya. I pushed the front passenger seat as far back as it could possibly go while tipping it near flat into a sleeping position. I transferred Arya's pillows and blankets to her new front seat. She grabbed her red Teletubby from the back, punched it around with her feet until it was positioned just so, curled up with her chin on her toy's face, and released a long, slow, exaggerated groan of victory. "Don't get used to this Arya. This is a special occasion. When we make it out of this state, you're returning to the back seat. Front seat in New Mexico only." I wagged my finger at her, only to be completely ignored.

I had known days ago that I wasn't going to California as I'd originally planned, so it was about time I informed Delilah, who was expecting me. I had never given her a specific arrival date in any case, since I wanted to be slow and leisurely about the drive. Right then, though, I could barely stomach the thought of having a conversation with anyone, especially when I had to deliver disappointing news. My mind was falling apart in New Mexico, getting ready to be reconstructed into something entirely new. All of the pieces of me were scattered across this desert land, and something or someone, like some giant kid playing with Legos, was putting me back together only to dismantle me again, then on to a new creation, a new aspect of me, over and over again. I was driven by something I couldn't understand, taken by some force I couldn't see—I'd never been more tired or confused. All of this made every-day conversation nearly impossible. But I had hope, the hope that someday things would make sense to me, that I'd find my bearings again. For the first time in my life, despite all this madness, I felt a healing happening. And that healing was being delivered by spirits and history in a landscape of orange and blue.

There were very few answers here, though, at least not the kind of answers my logical mind craved. The sense was of an energy, an energy that communicated through vague concepts like surrender and trust. I was being asked to *feel* my way through this and not try to comprehend it with my mind. I was being asked to become *sentant*, to communicate with my instincts, to learn directly from nature.

I did bite the bullet, then, and called my friend in California to tell her of my change of plans. I wouldn't be coming to see her after all. New Mexico was my only destination. She was disappointed, but she understood. She said, "Kristy, you're on a powerful vision quest. When you're done with this, you're going to need to rest for a very long time. Please don't push yourself. Be careful." I promised her I would, though the promise felt empty. I would be pushed as far as the spirits felt I needed to be pushed. I appreciated her concern, I said, and I vowed to do the best I could, given the circumstances.

CHAPTER FORTY

I took the exit to Truth or Consequences, feeling certain this town had something to teach me. My brain felt foreign to me. I almost constantly felt as though something was trying to pull at it, to take control. I was being carried to deeply hidden locations in my psyche, to places and things my spirit needed to see to become whole again. A force was trying to take over my mind, but it felt safe. I felt cared for, which is something I hadn't felt since my mother's violent end in that hospital room twenty years earlier. So, I allowed it. I simply went where I was told, with no struggle.

It was a small place, and it didn't take me long to find where this force was sending me: The Geronimo Springs Museum—a tiny institution of history in the middle of nowhere. I felt like an excited ten-year-old pulling into Disneyland.

I parked the car in the shade and walked Arya in the gorgeous sunny afternoon. Sixty-five degrees and not a cloud in the sky. I found a tiny labyrinth and walked it with Arya; I believed it was a gateway for her. I considered this her spiritual journey as much as mine, although more likely I was just projecting my own experience on her. We walked across a tiny bridge within the labyrinth. Arya looked at me like I was a bit of a nut, but she politely accommodated me, walked her gateway, and finished the labyrinth. She stretched, underwhelmed. I took her back to the car, rolled all the windows down a few inches and entered the tiny museum.

The moment I crossed the threshold I felt someone else take over my consciousness, that hand-in-the-glove sensation. I froze just inside the doorway. I could see through my eyes, but nothing else in my body felt like it was mine. A pretty middle-aged woman with blonde hair pulled back into a knot smiled while making her way over to me, her only visitor. "Welcome!" she said, a little too enthusiastically, but nevertheless sincerely. "Where are you from?"

"Minnesota," I replied. I tried to smile but my facial features felt leaden.

"*Min-nee-soh-tah!*" she said, long and slow. "A long way from home!" People think it's great to speak the accent.

I took her to the door, opened it and pointed to my car. "With my dog." I said, but Arya wasn't visible, curled up sleeping I guessed. "You'll just have to believe me. She's in there."

"Well, I believe you! Come inside and I'll show you around. We have an incredible exhibit on Mangas Coloradas!"

Mang...? "What?!" A jolt of electricity shot through me. I'm sure she thought it was weird that I said it so forcefully, like maybe I was mocking her with sarcasm. My hands ignited, pulsing with a painful shockwave. I felt like I couldn't bend my fingers and wanted to run, not walk, to the exhibit. She literally held me back, her fingers wrapped completely around my small arm, holding me in place. It felt nice and calmed me down. I was meant to be here. But then my head started to spin, and I began to question everything. Maybe I was just a damn lunatic. Was I making all of this up? I had followed the breadcrumbs all over New Mexico to learn more about Mangas, about myself. Were the breadcrumbs random? Was it all piecing together because I was forcing it? *Was any of this true?*

The museum lady started talking again, and her voice brought me back to center. She asked me why I was there. She seemed honestly interested.

"We're on kind of a vision quest." I felt sheepish using the term my friend had just shared.

She straightened, became more focused, less superficial. "Tell me."

"Well, I just quit my job, declared goodbye to the career I've known for twenty years, and now I seem to be drifting, just going where New Mexico tells me to go."

"I'm honored New Mexico called you here. I did exactly as you did many years ago. I took off by myself on a motorcycle journey. It changed my life. It brought me here. I feel a real kinship with your journey. I believe in you."

Her words cut right through me. The doubt faded. Tears collected in my eyes. I turned away, pretended to look at something else, so she wouldn't see. What was it with all this *crying?* My stoic, emotionally repressed self had no idea what to do with all these tears.

"Forgive me," she said. "I suffered a traumatic brain injury a long time ago, so my communication might be a little strained at times." Her communication was perfect. I told her so.

"It's just that every now and then when I search for a word, it's not there. So, bear with me, but I want to tell you a little about our exhibit and then I'll let you roam."

I wandered a foot to the left and grabbed a book from a shelf with a title that jumped out at me, *Mangas Coloradas*. I smiled and showed it to her.

She said, "You'll find the truth in there. Traditional histories have not been truthful about much of the indigenous past. They will tell you that Mangas Coloradas was a psychopath, a ruthless killer, a heinous criminal. It's not true. He was a warrior, yes, but he was also innocent. In the end he did what the white men asked him to. He surrendered himself for the sake of his tribe. He tried to do the only thing he felt he could do to keep his people safe. He chose to stop the fighting; the most powerful warrior in Apache history chose peace. Those who ultimately did what they did to him—torturing him, killing him, beheading him, betraying him the very night he turned himself in, not even allowing for a proper burial—they've found themselves in the darkest corner of hell, those people. They boiled his head so they could play with his skull. And yet the Indians were the barbarians?!" She suddenly caught herself and looked stunned.

She held her hand over her mouth to stop what seemed to be pouring out of her. "I'm so sorry!" she said. "I'm being overbearing. Oh my God! It's the brain injury." She shook her head, embarrassed, clenched her fists. She took a deep breath. "Let's just wander into the next room. We'll see the exhibit, okay?" Eyes wide, mesmerized, I quietly followed her.

She pointed to the paintings, over a hundred years old. They were of Mangas Coloradas in various scenes. Her back was to me and we both stared in silence. When she turned around, I felt an energy pierce me. "These were painted in real time. The artist created them while actually watching Mangas do these things. He was an artist historian." She was getting worked up, oddly intense. I nodded my head in rapt attention.

"It's just that what you're seeing is real. This is all real! You're seeing reality. What you're experiencing is all real, Child! It's real." I thought she was going to grab my arms and shake me. She looked a little distressed, as though she couldn't control what was coming out of her mouth, or the intensity of it. I silently nodded, barely breathing. Mangas called me Child. I didn't want to break this spell, whatever it was, I was drinking up her words like life-giving elixir.

There were messages between the words. What I heard was this: All of the craziness I was experiencing—had experienced over the past decades—all of the otherworldly curiosities, the faces in the mirrors, the *cadejos*, the electronic anomalies, the flower explosion, the astral traveling, the visions, the voices, they were all real. I wasn't crazy. I had somehow wandered through a doorway that for me seemed to have been the border of New Mexico, and the land of enchantment became all too literal. And here was some stranger, imploring me to accept all of it as truth. The woman started to apologize again. "I'm sorry," she said. "I have a brain injury," she said for the third or fourth time. "I'm not quite the master of myself today."

"Thank you so much," I said. I felt that in less than five minutes this woman had effectively validated my entire existence.

She turned to go back to her station at the front of the museum, smiling kindly, but still seeming a little lost and confused.

"Really, you don't know how much I appreciate your words, your truth, your delivery. You've given me a real gift here."

I grabbed her hand and squeezed it a little, reassuring her. Peaceful again, she clicked back into her original jovial self, telling me to take my time, get a good gander at everything and not to forget to shop the beautiful native jewelry. She left me alone with the real-time paintings of Mangas Coloradas. I sat on a bench and absorbed each one, getting to know this man who seemed to be living inside my head. Feeling no fear around him, I found the truth—that he was a man of integrity, depth, loyalty, fierceness, bravery and generosity. A man who was ultimately destroyed at the hands of the true madmen, the victorious white history writers who could tell whatever stories they liked with the expectation that we would believe them. Wasn't that convenient for everybody? Unless you happened to be indigenous.

The voice erupted into my left ear again, deep and strong, "It's about learning to choose the truth for yourself, learning what is right for you, based on instinct. It's about letting your experience guide you, not doing what others tell you is right or wrong." My hands felt explosive, so painful I thought my skin would burst. My own history was being rewritten. I had gaping holes where my identity had been. Someone was taking a sledgehammer to my frozen façade and I had no idea what would happen when it finally shattered. Would there be a brand new me, waiting to emerge, or would I just fall in shards, my psyche not able to adjust to this new world all at once?

I took a break and walked outside to check on Arya. The car was still in the shade. She was not visible, which meant she was still sleeping, and there was a cool breeze. She was content, or she'd be at the window imploring me to get back in the driver's seat. I returned to finish my exploration and entered another part of the museum that had artifacts behind glass cases. It was a dark maze of rooms with never-ending treasures. I felt compelled to look at every single one.

Until I found it.

Within one of the glass displays, I found a final gift. I gasped, involuntarily holding my breath as I read the description. It was a simple and very blurry photograph of a woman. In that moment I understood the why of Mangas Coloradas and his choice to be my earpiece for so many years. It was clear to me as I stared at her framed picture that this blurry image was me. Time disappeared, past and present merged, and we were the same person.

This was not a belief that "in a past life" I had been Lozen, the historical female Apache warrior. I meant right now. Psychologically, although she had lived a hundred and fifty years before, *I believed I was Lozen* right there and then in the museum. I don't know why or how, I simply had a definitive understanding that we were the same person, that our feet concurrently stood in the same place, in two different time lines. I felt complete unity with her, as if she were looking through my eyes, and breathing through my lungs.

Staring at that grainy black and white image, I marveled that Lozen looked exactly like me, when in fact her face was barely visible in the photograph. Reading her history below this only photograph ever taken of her explained everything. She was loved by Mangas Coloradas. She held a mysterious power whereby she could sense danger by holding up her hands. If they tingled, there was some threat ahead. She was a healer, a fierce warrior, one of the only females allowed in battle, but she was also a gifted midwife, lovingly delivering the babies of the tribe, though she never wanted children of her own. She kept the other warriors safe with her precognitive abilities. When her hands tingled, she advised them to go another direction, or to prepare for what was coming. She was a perfect ambassador of the Divine Feminine.

I held my hands in front of my face, seeing them as Lozen's hands, feeling the painful electricity coursing through them.

In the end, Lozen had to choose between her warriors and a baby being born. There were serious complications with a birth she attended, so she decided to stay back and help deliver, which meant sending the scouting party out on their own. Without her abilities to navigate impending danger, the party of men was ambushed, and her beloved brother Victorio was killed. She blamed herself. She told herself that had she not held back to deliver that baby, her brother would still be alive. Her tribe would still be undefeated.

Who can say what would have transpired had Lozen been scouting that day? But what did happen was that the warriors were overpowered. The tribe was eventually captured and transported to Florida and then Alabama, a humid mosquito-infested hell to her, indigenous as she was to the desert. Heartbroken, eventually Lozen died of tuberculosis.

I, with all of my being, believed I was staring at an image of myself in that glass case. It was why I was born never wanting children. It was why my hands tingled. It was why I'd always been precognitive. It was why Mangas was with me. It was why I had come back to New Mexico. It was why I felt at home here. It was why I cried when I saw the word Apache. It even explained my chronic cough—Lozen's tuberculosis—which spontaneously resolved the moment I entered New Mexico. My identity somehow got tangled up with Lozen's, and two dimensions collided. Suddenly I even understood why I loathed humidity so much.

I ran to the front of the museum and gave the angel lady a hug goodbye after buying an armful of books: *Apache Voices*, interviews from the 1800s; *Mangas Coloradas*, his biography; *Bless Me Ultima*, a classic New Mexico story that somehow made me feel safe; and finally, an astonishingly revelatory book, *The Day the Sun Rose Twice: The Story of the Trinity Site Nuclear Explosion on July 16, 1945*—the first atomic bomb detonation, which took place on July 16, my birthday in this current lifetime. The waves just kept crashing, every one of my life's mysteries was coming to fruition. Trinity...the word that had been with me ever since my friend Harry had mentioned it in my dream of the dystopian hellscape. And then I recalled the words I had mysteriously written last night, only a short time before channeling Mother Nature while the psychedelic flowers exploded all over the beautiful *Bosque del Apache*...something about "the place the earth began to die." Could that be a reference to the first detonation of the atomic bomb, which had occurred a short distance from here? I was astounded and bewildered by all of these pieces so rapidly coming together. I was finding so many answers in this one, beguiling place.

I was so mesmerized by my experiences here in the Geronimo Springs Museum that I couldn't think about death or dying right now. I was buoyed by the magic and all that had transpired within it. I left the museum, woke Arya up and got her out of the car, encouraged her to drink some water—always the Egyptian desert princess, she refused—and then walked a few blocks just to move a little before driving. A car passed by with a bumper sticker that said, "Believe." I wiped silent tears from my cheeks. I did believe. I truly did.

I believed all of it. And for that moment, I also believed in myself. I knew this journey wasn't a manifestation of insanity. It was a return to sanity—perhaps an introduction to it—from an insane world.

It was late in the afternoon, and I needed to move on. I stopped in front of a store window. A beautiful bronze statue of an owl stared at me through the glass. I recalled the owl that almost hit my windshield the night before and took a moment to thank him for the visitation before heading back.

Sitting in my parked car, I smiled at my new stack of books. I picked up *Bless Me Ultima* and buried my nose within its opened pages to inhale that inky new book smell. Why had I been drawn to it? I leafed through, stopping at a page near the end, and read a couple of lines:

> *"I went to Tenorio's side and carefully picked up Ultima's owl. I had prayed that it would be alive, but the blood had almost stopped flowing. Death was carrying it away in its cart."*

I put down the book. "*What* is with the owls?" I said slowly, staring out the window, trying to get a feel for what was in the air.

I had looked up the totem medicine of Owl in the past twenty-four hours which, by one definition, was a harbinger of death. I didn't like the implications of that, so I tried not to understand Owl at this point. Must be more talk about the origin of Mother Nature dying, I reasoned.

CHAPTER FORTY-ONE

I meandered out of town, my heart full, feeling so confident, as if the small percentage of my brain still holding out for the "she's crazy" version of the story had been all but flushed out. I found my truth in Truth or Consequences. I found validation there. My tattered mind told me I had found *proof* there; the possibility of delusion never registered. I played the words, "This is real, Child," over and over in my head; they covered me like a weighted blanket, soothing and healing.

In a few minutes' time, I found myself on a breathtaking stretch of road, driving through vast canyons, towering mountain ranges and prickly pear cactus. I breathed it all in, deeply and purposefully, with gratitude and a Buddha smile. There was so much life in this high-desert paradise. In my state of Truth or Consequences euphoria, I marveled that everything had a shadow. I saw the shadow as a kind of partner to that which cast it, an agreement they would never break. As the night overcame the daylight, I fantasized that the sage, the

sandstone, and the cactus would pull their shadows closer, holding them tight, rocking them to sleep. In the morning they'd all spring to life again, together, and the shadows would be allowed to wander a bit.

I was the only car on the road for a while until the highway sliced through a narrow canyon. It was beautiful in the canyon—a deep, dark, expansive crevice breaking up the sunlight, forming shapes and symbols. I stopped the car, turned it off, and got out, leaving Arya inside. I just wanted to soak this up for a second, the beauty, the coolness, the silence of this deep cavern. The sun in New Mexico is relentless; it felt good to hide from its gaze. As I scanned the high cliff walls, I saw an enormous cave opening about fifty feet above the road. It just happened to be the perfect shape of an owl. There it was, a black hole in the sheer granite surface, cookie cutter clear. Incredible. Owl was not going to let me rest. I took it in, thanking it—*was I supposed to thank it?*—and after a long pause in contemplation, I got back in the car, feeling a little unsettled. I wish I knew what it was that Owl was trying to tell me.

I left the darkness of the canyon and drove a while. Then I slowed the car and squinted to see more clearly what was out there. Wax-like statues of human bodies, like the one I'd seen in northeastern New Mexico on the median, seemed to be scattered across the landscape. But this time, not all of them were frozen. Some moved with deliberate intent, emerging from the sand looking perfectly intact, amiable, and certain of where they were going. There had to be a hundred of them. I didn't even blink. I just watched them, curious, wondering why they were so active now. Or was it that I was just seeing them now, and they'd always been there? And why were some

frozen and some moving? I went into a half trance as someone moved in to share my consciousness. Eager for answers, I handed over seamlessly. I was getting so much better at this.

I knew he was with me now, so I asked Mangas about the people. What made them frozen?

He replied that there were some people who, when they died, were so injured or ashamed that they felt they had no right to move on. Not able to accept light or love, they remained in a permanent state of self-punishment and loathing, stuck, unable to move forward. Many living people are also in this state, this self-imprisonment. I thought about my frozen father sitting at the kitchen table for decades. I thought about myself.

It all felt so horrific. "What can we do? How can we help them?" I couldn't accept their chosen state of frozenness. I couldn't face my own.

"It's theirs, Child. Heal yourself. When we heal ourselves we can't help but to heal others."

I couldn't accept that. It was always about control for me. Something that wasn't so clear to me was my own savior complex. I wanted to save everyone from their own pain, while repressing my own.

Since I was not one to accept or dialogue with pain, I thought it was worth a shot to keep exploring.

"Archangel Michael, is there anything you can do to help? Will they ever love themselves?" These were, of course, questions I needed to ask myself, but projection is the great deflector.

I heard no response, but I felt satisfied in the asking. I peeked in the rearview mirror and saw Mangas sitting back there next to Maggie Fox, who had also appeared. She innocently tried to put her hand on his knee. He removed it while shaking his head. I'm not sure if the head shake was for me and my questions to the archangel or for Maggie and her inability to respect the stolid Apache's boundaries.

There was very little sun left as I drove into the mountainous Gila National Forest, with its towering Ponderosa pines and soaring vistas. With no idea where I was going, it was a gift just to come across a completely different ecosystem, to be able to feel grateful for the opportunity to wander into this great beast of a wilderness.

The sun was long down by now, and the darkness descended heavily upon me as we passed a sign for Silver City. I thought about the owl cave and the black canyon walls and was relieved to see the sparkling city lights that finally flickered into view. Coming down off the mountain I pulled into the first hotel I found and checked into a room with the usual preambles. It was a nice room, but I couldn't shake a sick feeling. I felt on high alert, and all my senses were stuck in a painful overdrive. Everything was too bright, too loud. I could hear a conversation all the way down the hall, freakishly clear, as though it were taking place inside my room. What was happening?

Invaded and exposed, I could do nothing to stop this violent auditory and visual assault. I stood suffering, enduring, helpless.

CHAPTER FORTY-TWO

*I*t was late. As I turned on the light to the bathroom, I heard something hissing. Following the origin of the sound, I found the toilet water boiling.

Boiling. I could have cooked spaghetti in that water.

I flushed it. Still boiled. I shut the lid, too exhausted to analyze it. We were in hot springs country, so it must be that, I told myself. I thought about calling the front desk, "Should my toilet water be boiling?" but was just too tired. I accepted it as perfectly normal because that was most convenient. I crawled into bed.

Arya was in the double bed next to mine. Strange. She *always* wanted to curl up next to me. I tried to coax her over. Then I tried to join her in her chosen bed, and she promptly jumped the carpeted canyon to the other bed. She must have needed her space that night. I turned out the light and made some attempt to sleep in spite of the fact that every noise was now an assault on my senses. My hearing felt painfully acute. I had a new appreciation for what domestic animals must experience with our incessant noise pollution. I put my head on the pillow while a dark blanket of fear descended over me. I felt death all around me, could hear its ragged breathing, could sense its hands around my neck.

A new group of people started making noise down the hall. I could hear every word. Each time someone spoke, it felt like I had one hand immersed in a bucket of ice water while the other was exploring the depth of an electrical socket with an aluminum bread knife. I received intense power surges, as if I was standing an inch from a highway lane allowing eighteen-wheelers to blast by me at one hundred miles per hour. These surges only lasted a second or two, and then everything was still, the air thick and suffocating, fear the only constant.

I think I could have electrocuted someone, I had so much energy coursing through my hands. I had the ears of a highly attuned animal. When I'd hear something, I'd freeze and raise my head an inch from the pillow, sensing the danger. Something inside of me screamed, "Pay attention! Listen!"

"Pay attention to what?! What am I listening for?" I pleaded.

My body was shaking so violently I thought my spine would snap. Why was everyone screaming? I tried to cover my ears, tortured by my own senses.

Hours passed, and the noises in the hallway finally stopped. In the silence I started to see things. I noticed movement on the walls; a human-sized something with lizard-like grippers on its hands and feet slowly crawled. More of them appeared. At times the traffic traveling around my walls was so thick they'd bump into each other, slithering over one another. I sobbed into my pillow, desperate for daylight. Time became cruel and refused to move. Every second felt like an excruciating eternity.

"Stop this. Stop it. Stop all of this!" I cried into my pillow as I reached the threshold of my sanity.

Then the buzzing returned, so loud I thought it would break my eardrums. I held my hands to my ears, crying out loud. In the darkness I could make out Arya's sleeping form on the next bed, oblivious to my distress. My spine straightened, my muscles became rigid with spasms, the freezing cold sensation coursed down my spinal column. Then silence. No more buzzing.

No longer was I in that hotel room, crawling with death.

I was in a cave with smooth, white stone walls. There was a circular opening in the cave ceiling, like a chimney, allowing moon-rays to filter down into a spotlight, casting enough illumination for me to see Mangas standing with me in the lunar circle. Mad with relief, I hugged that giant like I'd never let go.

"Are you ready for this, Child?" Mangas broke my hug and held me at arm's length, staring into my eyes. He seemed genuinely upset, sad for me, sick for what was about to transpire.

"Am I ready for what?" I had no energy left to give him or the spirit world. I was spent, empty, in total surrender. If death had offered me respite from what I had just experienced in that hotel room, I would have chosen it. At the very least, I wanted to go home, to be done with all of this, to be curled up in the arms of my beloved.

Mangas illuminated a torch that was as bright as sunlight. I gasped as I looked around the enormous cave. Then my relief turned to horror.

"Stay in the moon's circle, Child. Stay right where you stand; don't take a step. If you break the moon's perimeter,

I'm powerless to help you."

As far as I could see, there were small humanoid creatures crawling, like those around my hotel room walls. In Mangas's light I could see them now. Over my head, skirting the moon's opening, on every side of me, they dragged themselves. Having never seen the sun, they were bright white, blind, feeling their way toward me, stopping only at the moon's protective barrier. Guttural sounds like those of thick, boiling liquid came from their throats. Their eyes were cloudy, like clotted cream. The air felt unbreathable, smelled sulfurous. I clung to Mangas. My mouth agape, I couldn't think.

One of them spoke in a croaking groan.

"Please let me in." He blindly felt along the perimeter of the moon beam, gentle and careful. "I'm so tired of suffering. Please let me in."

Another one spoke.

"I don't want to hurt anymore. I'm so tired of hurting. I know you can help. Please let me in."

They were a mass of limbs and spines, each vertebra visible, climbing over one another. I absorbed their pain, in all its heartbreaking and excruciating waves. My legs weakened, so Mangas held me up, kept me standing.

"Why are you showing me this?!" I screamed at him.

"Because it's here," he said quietly. "Pain and suffering will always be here. It's a part of nature. It's a part of your history, a part of you. But it can't define you, Child. You have to make your choice." One lone tear made its way down his cheek.

"But we have to do something!" I screamed.

"If you leave this perimeter, Child, you cannot undo the consequences of your choice. You have to understand the reality of limits. It's not up to you to eradicate the world of its pain all at once. This will become your greatest teaching; your refusal to grasp it will be your undoing. You will have to focus on yourself first, heal yourself. There is no shame in saying no to this. There is no shame in walking away, in choosing another path."

"But there's room in here for two or three of them!" I pointed to the space inside the moon's embrace. I couldn't heed his warning; I was wild with grief. "We can do what we can! Even if it's not all of them!"

"No, sweet Child. No. If you open this perimeter, you will have to die. It's inherent in the path you will have chosen." He said this quietly, knowing my nature. He knew why I was taken here to begin with. He knew this was a test I couldn't refuse, a date with destiny I could not reschedule. That made it no less horrific.

I paused, looking into his deep black pupils dilated with pain. I made my choice. There was no question. Nowhere within me was the ability to say no to this path I was committed to–healing myself, assisting others. I had waited my entire life for this.

I threw my hand out to grab the one closest to me, breaking the moon's protective perimeter to the instantaneous shrieks of a million blind demons of tragedy, pain, and fear. Mangas immediately vanished with the broken barrier.

I heard a man's deep voice wailing, sobbing, over the din of animal screams and shrieks as the beings climbed on top of me, overcame me, grasping, clawing, each one having to touch me, tear me, receive a piece of me. The spiritual pain turned to physical pain, like in the astral traveling experience of my past, where I had felt the stabbing. Then I'd been a witness, separated to some extent from the experience, but this time there was no protection from the emotional pain. Great handfuls of flesh were torn from my muscles, muscles were torn from their tendons and ligaments, my marrow was sucked out of my shattered bones. My ribs were now in another's mouth, and every part of me was dismembered while I screamed as long as I could scream, while I still had the facial features required to do so, before they ripped my jawbone from my skull. I felt every broken nerve, every artery severed, each organ being ingested by these creatures who had only wanted respite from the pain, who only wanted me to heal them. I became the pain. And then I was consumed by it. Completely consumed.

And after I was annihilated, when there was nothing left of me, when the last drop of my blood was licked clean from the smooth white stone, when I had become the empty void of the now moonless night, I returned.

CHAPTER FORTY-THREE

The sun illuminated the room, forcing its way through the heavy hotel curtains. I slowly opened my eyes to find that Arya had jumped from her bed to mine and was busy licking dried tears from my face. I felt no guiding presence—no Maggie, no Mangas, no Archangel Michael, no God. I curled up into a fetal position and relaxed into the emptiness. Maybe I was dead. I was unable to think—paralyzed with exhaustion.

Arya jumped off the bed and shook herself awake. She wanted to go outside and refused to leave me alone. She implored me, poking at me with her nose. "Come on. Get up. You have to get up." Pulling at my covers, she continued to lick at my face. "You have to move," she insisted.

What was left of my caregiving instincts sparked, and I was able to pull myself upright, then out of the bed. Arya needed me. I found my way into some clothes and twisted my unbrushed hair into a ponytail. The toilet water was no longer boiling.

I had to get out of this place. I shoved my jammies in

my bag, clicked on Arya's leash and bolted out the door. My urgency was too much for her. She froze in the hallway, refusing to move, frightened and confused by my sudden explosive energy. I pulled on her leash too hard. Arya didn't make a sound, but I felt horrible. I calmed myself. "I have to leave this room, Arya. Please. Let's get out of here, okay?"

With my brief explanation she got a little spring in her step like, "Oh, hey, okay, I get it!" and we jogged out the side door into the blinding sun. After walking Arya for a bit, we jumped in the car and drove ten minutes before I stopped and pulled over to the side of the road. I put my head on the steering wheel and sobbed. If it hadn't been for Arya, I'd still be back there in the fetal position. I probably would have remained there until Aaron could have somehow arrived to take me home, a shattered version of my former self. But Arya needed me, and that was the glue I needed.

I drove out of Silver City, feeling no life in anything. I couldn't feel Mother Nature, nor could I feel any form of love or comfort. I wasn't thinking about the miracles of the previous day, or the vast spiritual journey I was on, or Mangas Coloradas. I was zombified but kept my hands on the wheel and numbly drove. I was about as far south as a person could get in New Mexico, and when we reached Las Cruces my intention was to drive north. Taking in the view of the Organ Mountains, with sharp plates resembling the back of a stegosaurus, I thought I was headed in the right direction, but quickly found myself at the USA/Mexico border patrol. "What the hell?" I mumbled. I was obviously still driving south.

I pulled up to the post and a gregarious twenty-something Hispanic man looked out the window. "Where are you going, young lady?"

I smiled weakly. "Honestly, I thought I was driving north," I said.

"North? You must be a real blonde." He winked, speaking way too loudly. I stared at him blankly; I had no idea what he was talking about. I was a brunette. At least I was born a brunette. Ten years earlier I began having my hair dyed lighter to cover the premature grey that seemed to be dominating. I must have forgotten that minor detail because his classification of me as blonde made absolutely no sense to me.

I wasn't in the mood for this, but I thought it best to keep it light. My story did sound a little strange, even though it was true. "You are most definitely driving south, as you can tell by the proximity to Me-xi-co." He elongated each syllable, theatrically pointing in the direction of the border with two hands and then he winked again. He smiled and leaned a little out the gatehouse window, looking at me closely. "But seriously, what are you doing down here?" he asked, "with Minnesota plates?"

"Well, to tell you the truth, I'm just driving around New Mexico. I live in Minnesota, I just quit my job, and I came here to wander and clear my head." Thinking about the freak show of horrors I had endured the night before, the head-clearing project now seemed as big a failure as my navigational skills. I was forcing myself to be conversational, which was the last thing I wanted to be. When we were small children, Shellie, my best friend from Colorado, once told a tall tale in which a shark bit her into several pieces and the family taped her back together with scotch tape. That's how I was feeling right about then.

"Just driving around? Your husband lets you do that? If I

were your husband, I would not allow you such a long leash. You're too beautiful to be straying." This remark was followed by a third wink—I was getting real tired of the winks. "No, honestly, I think that's cool. Nobody does that anymore, just gets in their car and drives. I love it that you're doing that. I just think for your own safety, you'd better learn to read a map. Comprende?"

"Yes sir," I gave him what I thought he wanted to hear, and I nervously twirled my scraggly ponytail in my finger. I still hadn't brushed my hair. "Can I turn around here?" I just wanted to get the hell out.

I found my way out of the border checkpoint.

I was done with New Mexico. I was done with all of this. I had awakened from a week-long trance, thanks to the razor-sharp pain of a million lost souls, and was now wondering how in the hell I was going to get home when all of my energy reserves were gone. I had experienced a kind of portal through a doorway at Truth or Consequences (the spirits do have a sense of humor)—the truth I'd found miraculous, and the consequences had nearly killed me. The Angel of Death was now perched on my shoulder, casting a sightless darkness over me. I was encased in concrete, could sense nothing. No intuition, no feeling as though I was being lovingly held and guided. It was as if I had somehow made a wrong turn and had been completely abandoned in the process. I thought of the choice I had made, despite the warnings of Mangas. He had made it clear, however, that it was my choice. I unquestionably made it and got annihilated in the process. Was it possible to choose wrong? I still understood none of this. Was it game over for me? Had my own stubborn defiance defeated me? Was I dead? How could I know?

What I did know, now that I had walked through Hell, was that the Owl could not have tried any harder to forewarn me. There was just so much I didn't know. I had no context for any of this. And if I had previously been walking the precipice, I was now wandering the abyss.

I was so thirsty. I could feel the crenation of my cells from lack of water. The desert was greedy for any hydration it could take from me; soon my body would be reduced to nothing more than a resource, a sponge it could suck dry. Telling the desert I needed to keep what little hydration I had was not an option. It just took what it wanted.

God, yes! I was seeing a pattern in this: never knowing my limits, never knowing my boundaries, running into every burning building, believing every problem was mine to fix, even at the expense of another's dignity. I remember my brother Scott once asking me, "Who made you the captain of everyone's ship?" I loathed that about me.

I was so tired of the silence. Looking into the rearview mirror, there was no Maggie Fox, no Mangas. There were no energy bursts, no electrical currents in my hands, no feelings of euphoria.

I felt like I had been driving forever at this point, and now the pavement had curiously turned to gravel. Where the hell were we? A herd of black cows ambled in front of us, so I slowed and then stopped. I wanted to get out of the car, to pet them, but realized how stupid that sounded. I knew nothing about cows and didn't want to scare them. I rolled down my window, sharing eye contact with a particularly brave one who approached. That felt like enough connection. I felt a little thankful that I hadn't eaten beef since I had seen those baby cows playing in Nebraska, like somehow this cow could sense that and find comfort in it. They moved off the road, and for the first time in a few days, I took out my map. If it had been struggling before, by now my inner navigational system was completely broken. I looked at all the squiggly lines and had no ability to make heads or tails of them. I didn't even clearly understand directions. It was as if this was the first time I had ever tried to process the concept of geographical lines, and I was not getting it. I saw a symbol of arrows with N, S, E, and W but had no idea what it meant—it was like trying to read Sanskrit for the first time. My brain was broken.

Trying not to panic, I folded up the map and gently put it back into the glove box; it was of no use to me. I reassured myself that my nervous system had simply blown a fuse. That was all. "We'll stick to paved roads," I said to Arya as though this was a brilliant and viable plan. I stopped in front of the highway, looking left and right. "*Why don't signs tell you anything?*" Knowing full well they told you plenty if your brain happened to be working, I held my face in my hands and suddenly felt a surge of intense anger. "Why am I so lost?!" I yelled, pounding the steering wheel with both hands, and feeling utterly abandoned. Arya sat up in her seat and stared at me. I needed to be strong for her. I needed to hold it together. I took a deep breath and turned left on the highway, knowing I had a fifty percent chance of getting it right.

The sudden return of the familiar voice in my ear startled me, "It's dead here, Child," as I drove past a sign that read, "White Sands Missile Range (Not Open To The Public)." My hair stood on end, remembering Mother Nature's words twenty-four hours earlier. White Sands, "where the earth began to die," where that very first atomic bomb had been detonated on July 16, the month and day of my birth, but twenty-four years before I was born.

And then I had a vision, a momentary glimpse, of me as a young Japanese girl, melted to a crimson puddle with the detonation of the atomic bomb in Nagasaki. I recalled my history, being plagued from the very beginning by an irrational obsession with the idea of nuclear holocaust, which was baffling to my parents. As a result of my reaction, they would allow no mention of nuclear energy in my presence. Here at the perimeter of that first test detonation, I realized humanity shared it all. What we do to another, we do to ourselves. What we do to the earth, we do to ourselves.

I screamed "Stop!" and grabbed my head in my hands, refusing to allow this to overtake me; I already felt too vulnerable. I broke the Japanese slideshow and forced it out.

Mother Nature had prepared me; she also provided me with an escape out of this hell. She told me she hoped the flowers would bring me through the darkness. She told me to recall that glorious moment at the *Bosque del Apache*. I closed my eyes, connected to it, felt its magic. Mangas was still with me. It was enough to cause another spark.

I pulled my car over and found some shade beneath an accommodating grove of gnarled pecan trees. I took out my phone and called Aaron. His voice was a lit candle, leading me back from the dead. I told him how dark I was feeling and what had happened to me the night before. I told him I was empty, lost, alone. I told him where I was and how Mangas had finally spoken to me again, telling me "It's dead here." I told him how I suddenly couldn't understand any detail of a simple road map. I told him I had been reduced to a molten puddle of biological waste when we drove past the Trinity site. I told him about the strange power surges I had been feeling up until this morning. I said I'd just be moving along and suddenly I'd feel a strange snap, crackle, pop.

I stopped, aware of how dumb that sounded. "Did I just say…snap, crackle, pop?" My lips formed an embarrassed half smile.

Aaron replied, immediately coming clean. "Yes," he said, a little nervously. "Probably because someone just gave me a Rice Krispy bar. I was thinking about it while you were talking."

My brain froze, pausing to recalculate. The absurdity of a Rice Krispy bar battling for my husband's attention through the intensity of what I had just told him—being torn apart, dying, irradiated, melted—set off a chain reaction within me. I could feel him freeze a little, bracing for my anger, but it had the exact opposite effect on me. I felt lighter as I had a vision of a valiant little Rice Krispy bar beating back the demons. All this dukkha, the suffering of life, I thought to myself…it's all an illusion, no more powerful than a Rice Krispy bar.

And then all the pain released its grip on me. I exploded into laughter and felt an enormous relief. The blood was pumping through my veins again. Aaron took over.

He assured me he had heard everything I told him and held me in a loving embrace over the phone. He told me he had been reading a lot to try to cope with what was happening to me, desperate to find answers, feeling so helpless. The books he was reading all said the same thing, that in order to fully see our world's reality, in order to reach an absolute state of sanity, one must experience for themselves a period of perceived insanity. He believed in me. He felt that by following with me along my journey, somehow he was coming alive too. He said he'd spoken to Shari, one of my best friends, who'd called him the night before worried about me. He told her he didn't know what was happening to me, that he had no answers, but he felt it was bigger than all of us. He also somehow sensed it was going to be okay, that it was somehow healing me.

All of what he was saying brought me back to life. I felt my blood warm and gathered the strength to evict the Angel of Death from my aura.

And then Aaron looked at a map for me, to help me get a sense for exactly where I was. "Mangas said it was dead there?" he asked.

"Yes," I replied.

"Well, according to the map, you're right in the middle of what's called the *Jornada del Muerto*."

I knew enough Spanish to know the meaning of that. The original, historical translation of this route, *Jornada del Muerto*, meant journey of the dead.

Head-to-toe goose bumps.

"Baby," I said, "I'm coming home." I had walked through enough fire. I asked New Mexico to please release me, and it granted my request. Having agreed that I had died to its satisfaction, that my mind had been demolished enough to let the light in, to heal, to become whole, to meet my destiny…"The Land of Enchantment" let me go.

Part Nine

THE REWARD

"I swear to you there are divine things more beautiful than words can tell."

~ Walt Whitman

"If you bring forth what is within you, what you bring forth will save you. If you do not bring forth what is within you, what you do not bring forth will destroy you."

~ Jesus

CHAPTER FORTY-FOUR

I was plugged back into life. As I passed through the *Jornada del Muerto*, I felt the spirits returning to me and fell into a trance-like state while I drove, feeling in near-constant channel. The hours felt like seconds as I drove along, my mind downloading voice upon voice saying variations of the same thing. The messages were so clear now, not just cryptic sentences here and there but entire lectures, diatribes by voices not familiar to me. I felt light, transparent, like I was a pure radio wave receiver, or perhaps the wave itself. It wasn't important to me who the voices belonged to. They were wise and loving.

These channeled lectures had one theme: we were in trouble. If each of us didn't pass through our own individual *Jornada del Muerto* to find a new way of being, interconnected with all of Earth's inhabitants, we would continue to suffer. Love would show us the way. Each of us was being asked to transcend the illusions, inner and outer, to find truth in a world that seemed to have lost it centuries ago.

What was happening to me, as fantastic as it seemed, wasn't unique, they said. Millions of others were undertaking their own journeys, each as unique as a fingerprint. No two journeys were identical, but they all had a central theme: become true, become whole, become love, become one with the earth.

Those who could feel their way to a new version of sanity—a version that included caring for ourselves, for each other, for our planet—would thrive. The voices were saying that love was the fiercest warrior.

It seemed to me that we were trying to find our way back to a balance of the sacred masculine, long ago mortally wounded and turned toxic with unchecked power, and to the sacred feminine, beaten into submission for too many thousands of years. One was never meant to be subservient to the other. Becoming a part of Nature, becoming interconnected with all beings, depends on our own relationship between our inner masculine and feminine, an achievement of that perfect dance between logic and intuition, perfectly embodied by Lozen. This is why it was so important for me to free myself, and express myself more intuitively, in order to restore my own balance. Long ago, intuition—an expression of the divine feminine—came to terrify the masculine and became a crime punishable by death. The Fox sisters, and millions more, died as a result. They chose to guide me, as a baby in my crib, as one advocate among countless billions, to help restore the balance as a pathway to healing humanity's evolution. We all had a job to do. This was mine; my glorious purpose that had stalked me since the beginning of time.

My inexplicable connection to Lozen was a strong enough thread to connect me to Mangas Coloradas, another spirit warrior of the Light, who chose to mentor me through the spirit realm. I was not his only student. He is responsible for teaching many.

The channels shared a prediction: As humanity attempts to restore the feminine balance, we will become more connected to empathy, more connected to the Big Picture (our own survival, both as individuals and as the collective humanity) and less connected to greed and materialism.

For those who cannot make the leap, who will not come alive to the interconnection of all beings, suffering will occur because a purely material outlook will become harder and harder for this world to support. The voices told me that across the globe resources were waning, financial systems were changing and those entrenched in the material wouldn't be able to adjust to this new world—which would become less about blindly amassing wealth and more about creating global stability through the sharing of resources, including intellectual resources.

And this wasn't something forecasted to happen in some far-off future, it was already happening, and it would continue to escalate. There were dark forces (greed and fear) battling light forces (altruism and love), in a herculean struggle for balance. Invisible to the majority, I had somehow found my way into this hidden dimension and had watched the battle become more and more visible inside of me, as it had already become and would become for millions of others. I was not alone. Old paradigm battling new, inside of me and across the planet, this was a civil war of titanic forces. We weren't just ants in the face of unchecked power, either. We could directly influence the outcome one way or the other. Whether or not our life on the earth would be saved or destroyed was our choice.

I heard common threads within the messages from all of

the invisible voices, my favorite being, "You know nothing." It was a beginner's mind concept to keep me rooted in the moment. I wasn't supposed to be agonizing over understanding all of this on a cognitive level. I was meant to feel my way through. As I had been told from the start, "Through the eyes of a child," was the only way I would survive this intact. I was to question everything I had ever been told, to take nothing at face value just because it was written in a history book. "The history books are being rewritten" was a repeated addendum. Truth would find a way to reveal itself; full disclosure was coming.

I was told I'd find my truth in my heart and in my instincts. I was to search my inner reserves for self-love and unconditional self-acceptance. That didn't mean I couldn't legitimately learn from my mistakes, but I was being asked to resist the knee-jerk tendency to immediately label things as "good" or "bad." Much of what happens in our world isn't so black or white.

I was told that, for me, opening to the truth would feel like being ripped apart by bare hands, which is exactly what had happened to me the night before in that demon cave. So, I asked, that was all about opening to the truth? The reality of who I really am? Complete annihilation occurred in service to the emergence of my soul-self?

And now, Mangas and Maggie had returned, visible again in my rearview mirror. Small Maggie was sitting behind me, scooted forward, with her hands on each of my shoulders, resting her chin on the back of my seat, gazing out the windshield. Mangas was sitting across from her, his back to the passenger door, behind Arya's front-seat perch. Angled sideways, his long legs barely fit in the car. I asked him why he didn't change places with Maggie, since I had Arya's seat pushed way back, but he didn't answer, like it was a foolish question. It absolutely was. He seemed comfortable. Ghosts don't feel cramped.

Mangas seemed relieved that some other voices were piping through my ear. He stayed quiet and watched the scenery. I knew he could hear the voices too, and that he disagreed with nothing.

I kept thinking about the night before, but I was also afraid to let the memory back into my consciousness. In the end I felt too strongly compelled to resist the questions.

"Mangas?" I looked back at him through the rearview mirror.

He nodded, still staring straight ahead out Maggie's side window.

"So, if what I experienced last night was about me finding my identity, why couldn't you have prepared me?"

"I could not have prewarned you about that particular experience, because it would have been a game to you, Child. It was not a game."

I sighed, understanding. Being seriously averse to pain, I would never have chosen to play. I would have found a way to deny it, but it would have been like placing my hands over the mouth of a volcano, foolishly hoping to prevent an eruption.

Mangas heard my thoughts and raised one eyebrow in agreement.

I remembered asking my podiatrist years ago why I had to have both feet operated on at the same time. Both of my big toes needed to be broken and realigned. His totally honest response was, "Because it's such a painful procedure, you'd never come back for the second surgery." True that. I understood completely.

Mangas continued, "But the bigger truth is, I have been

preparing you for this."

I could acknowledge the truth of that. I thought through my history to all the fantastic experiences I'd had, each one providing a key detail for my survival on this very journey. Empathic pain, empathic ecstasy, paranormal sensory experiences, direct communication with my own soul…each experience had strengthened and stretched my mind just enough to build the right amount of flexibility to get through this. If I hadn't had a lifetime of the unexplained, my mind would have shattered by now.

I was silent for several miles, listening to the road seams beneath my tires. But I needed to say more.

"Mangas, I could hear you sobbing. When it happened." I glanced in the rearview mirror, trying to gauge his response.

"Child, not everyone survives such an awakening," he said. "I feared you were not properly prepared. I did what I could knowing it could be no other way. This is such a thing your human elders traditionally prepare you for. You had none of that. I feared what I had done wasn't enough, that you were blind, mostly ignorant." He said it factually, stoically. "Your culture does a terrible job of initiating its people." He grimaced and snorted in disgust, shaking his head. I grimaced too. I felt like I had no culture.

He paused, eyes closed, face pointed to the sun. "I had no precognition. Your grandfather attempted his own initiation. Many do. But your grandfather failed. He broke, went insane, and in turn broke his children. But you were ready, Child. If you had not been, you would have permanently lost your mind. Long ago, you made the choice. You knew you had to do this. If you were to be initiated, you had to reach out to the lost souls, to temporarily break your protection. You could have died, but you did not. A small part of me wanted you to choose less risk. A part of me wanted you to choose another destiny, to reject the truth, if only to selfishly keep you safe, and comfortably numb. I was afraid for you. But it has never been your desire to choose the safe path, Child. Your own soul warned you of that, years ago. Your own soul helped you prepare for this."

I put a hand on my heart, quieting myself, feeling the painful enormity of the experience bubble up in my throat.

"Mangas."

"Yes, Child," with kindness in his voice, still gazing out the window.

"Will I ever heal from that? Will I ever recover?" The horror of it was so vivid in my mind I thought I'd never be able to unsee the memory of it, unfeel the pain, unsense the horror. An involuntary shudder broke through me.

He reached over and put his hand on my shoulder. Maggie was now slumped against the car door, watching the formidable spirit. "Yes, you will, Child. Yes, you will." He patted my head, his huge hand gently grasping it like a softball, giving it a little shake. "You already are." He growled at me, warrior to warrior.

"Mangas?"

He sighed, as if to say our time for talking was over.

"Just one more."

He nodded.

"Why are you so huge? Is your appearance just a metaphor? I mean, aren't Apache men typically pretty compact? What kind of Apache is, like, seven feet tall?"

"Well, let me introduce myself. I'm Mangas Coloradas," he said sarcastically, holding his hand out to fake a handshake.

"Read your history books, Child! I was born a giant." He pointed to the pile of books below Arya, on the floor of the passenger seat. I had not yet cracked the biography that I'd purchased in the museum. He continued to gaze, a little bored, out the side window, as if his guarding of me was a karmic assignment, but he was tiring of the heavy Earth plane. I was somehow happy to think of Mangas as a busy spirit, a teacher of thousands. It felt like I had a soul family out there.

"I thought I wasn't supposed to trust the history books?" I asked him, only a little serious.

"If it's complimentary, you have my permission to believe it." He winked at me, with a sudden deep eruption of laughter. I jumped, startled, having never experienced his gregarious side before. He slapped his knee. "Seriously Child, are you not seeing me with your own two eyes? Isn't that what this journey is all about for you? Why do you doubt what you see? Always doubting yourself." He shook his head again, reminding me of the voice in the dream twenty years ago, the one that said, "This is your dream! Just drive!"

I remembered that moment in Truth or Consequences when I read the bumper sticker that said, "Believe," and I did believe in myself. I smiled.

Satisfied, I gently smoothed the silky hair on top of Arya's beautiful little head as her chin rested on her Teletubby. I thought about how easily human beings are influenced and what a handy tool the television is for doing just that. *And now back to our original programming...* I tried to see my own programming, and all of my previous thoughts, destructive to me, that I had to work on undoing.

Arya groaned, burying her chin deeper into her stuffed toy's belly. Arya had nothing to undo.

CHAPTER FORTY-FIVE

As I drove, a feeling of contentment settled over me. I felt safe, protected from the memory of last night, and the exhaustion of the past week. I felt a kind of healing enchantment. The blessing of this numbness was keeping me from feeling the dread, the fear, and the maddening dismemberment of the night before.

I remembered what Mangas had told me yesterday, in the Gila National Forest. I had asked him if spirits were sad after their physical incarnation died. Were they sad, watching their loved ones struggle in their absence?

"Not so much," he replied. "Spirits retain some of their senses, but emotion, specifically the tendency to drown in it, is a human trait. Animals feel every emotion we do, but they understand emotions like the breeze on their face—feelings come, they go. Humans can't seem to disidentify with theirs. Spirits just shine bright with love and hope their cherished ones can feel it. They try to help but many humans are too closed off to open to their assistance."

As I drove, I decided that I would try to disidentify with the horror I'd experienced just a few hours ago. I breathed deeply and shook myself a little to calm the muscle tremors and the spinal pain that would occur when Mangas talked a lot. I peeked into the rearview mirror to find that both Mangas and Maggie had disappeared. I liked to think that they could sense when my physical discomfort was too great in their presence, so they would scram to give me relief. I also wondered where they went when they left me.

The day had evaporated like dew and the sun was planning its retirement. North of Santa Fe now, I stopped in a tiny village called Valencia and remembered the *cadejos* of Valencia county, same name but hundreds of miles apart. I smiled and closed my eyes in gratitude. Valencia...orange...my favorite color would from now on be orange. As terrifying as that meeting with the *cadejos* had been—it seemed like a lifetime ago—I could only process it through the lens of a miracle. It filled me with powerful waves of sacredness, as if on that day I had met Love Incarnate. The one with the smile, she had protected me physically and even now guarded my memories. I could think of nothing else but her when the *cadejos* came to mind. "That's how powerful love is," I said to Arya as I kissed her on the head.

So here I was, once again in a particularly orange place, stunned by the towering tangerine mesas, ponderosa pines and junipers, made even more breathtaking by the turquoise sky, which sparkled like a bejeweled crown on the land. I had one of those impulses to head off the beaten path, so I drove down a well-worn dirt road. Arya woke up when the cadence of the wheels changed. She looked out the window and then at me as if to say, "We're seriously doing this right now?" I remembered my promise to stick to paved roads but just couldn't stop the call to explore. I waved my hand and told her it would be fine.

Before long I hit the end of the road, which was punctuated by a lavish property filled with whimsically painted doorways—it was all very bright and welcoming. There was no building, just twenty or so solidly placed frames with doors that opened and closed, randomly planted around the property with no walls attached to them. There was a sign explaining that these were artistic gateways, that strangers were free to walk through them; they were a welcome to anyone who happened to find them. "You and your strange sorcery, New Mexico." I smiled and shook my head.

The place was completely empty. I parked and hopped out of the car with Arya on her leash and proceeded to walk through every frame. With each door I opened, each gateway Arya and I walked through, and each door I closed behind us, I fell deeper and deeper in love with the enchantment of New Mexico—even though so often over the past few days I had felt she was trying to kill me (or at the very least, scrape all the sanity out of my mind, carefully searching for every last morsel, like an orangutan cleaning out a coconut).

New Mexico was alive in a way I had never sensed in any other place before. I'd lived in Texas, Minnesota, Colorado, and New Hampshire. I had visited every US state with the exceptions of Alaska and Alabama, but I had never experienced the spirit of a place in such an animated, conversational, interactive, and personal way as in New Mexico. It has been said that New Mexico stokes an artist to create, to write, to paint, to compose. New Mexico did more for me—it made me want to live.

As much as I loved it, I still wanted to get the hell out for now. I was tired and had reached my limit exactly one dismemberment ago. After the previous night's experience, I had nothing left. I tried not to think about it; I tried not to think about anything. The spirit's gentle words, "You know nothing" played over and over, emptying my mind, mollifying me like a Beethoven sonata.

I focused on the gateways then, so beautiful. Arya and I completed the entire set, weaving in and out, opening and closing doors. Then we scrambled up a high, craggy hill made of orange rocks, red clay, and gnarled juniper trees. We arrived at the top and I gasped at the view. The nobility of the Sangre de Cristo mountain range, the brilliance of the otherworldly blue sky, towering pines, sweet fragrant sage, and the earth below my feet in one hundred shades of bright, muted, and deep orange. Was this real? Or was Mother Nature just painting with her psychedelic brush again? I had a feeling this was the everyday beauty of New Mexico.

A raucous cloud of cerulean emerged from overhead—a flock of mountain bluebirds—they descended into the junipers all around us, searching for a satisfying lunch of bitter berries. They didn't seem to mind us one bit, sharing their space generously.

Still feeling gooey inside from being torn apart the night before, I didn't yet fully trust what was real and what was spirit-enhanced, so I stopped trying to decipher the difference and rested on a large slab of sunbaked granite, feeling exquisitely reptilian. The scents and the breeze perfectly complimented each other, like an old couple who delighted in finishing each other's sentences. They welcomed us, crazy or sane, with a love that didn't discriminate.

After spending a good while in its company, I thanked the land, said my goodbye, and we made our way down the rocks. I was determined to finish this journey, to exit "The Land of Enchantment" tonight. I was shooting for the less volatile energy of Colorado for bedtime.

As we made our way back to the tiny trusty station wagon sparkling emerald green in the sun, I passed a sweet little empty house on the property which had a for sale sign in the yard. I fantasized about living here. Not possible, I knew. But I couldn't leave without thanking whomever had made this place possible. I'd write them a note. I tucked Arya into her seat and dug around my bag for a paper and pen.

What was supposed to be a nice gesture of gratitude turned once again into a nonsensical word salad, like the rambling garbage I had left on the psychic's doorstep days ago in southern New Mexico. I stared at the words being written on the page as though they were magically appearing, and I was just a witness. Again, something about "I'm back! Mother Nature is waking up, no worries, she'll find you..." blah blah blah. I couldn't stop the pen from dancing all over the paper. I felt compelled to leave it, even though it embarrassed me, because once again I somehow felt it wasn't mine to censor. I signed it Stark Raving Zen and hoped it wouldn't scare its recipient. I said a last goodbye to the whimsical doorways and pulled out of the property, grateful to find my way easily back to the highway.

I recognized the landmarks this time and turned onto the road facing what I believed to be north. I passed a sign for Denver, and my whole body breathed a sigh of relief; I was heading in the right direction. In a couple of hours I'd be safely across the state line. I tried to see if I could feel my sanity returning, but I didn't think I was the best judge. I just kept driving, hearing the words, "You know nothing" gently encouraging me to let go and just be. One mile at a time, I was on my way home.

I took in my final sensory fill of New Mexico by soaking in the wilderness landscape of Raton in the northeastern corner of the state. The mesa tops kneeling below the foothills of the Rockies were so glorious they made my eyes water. I smiled when I remembered driving through here a week ago, calling my husband to tell him we'd live here someday. "Um, no we won't" was his short reply, after googling the tiny mountain town in the middle of nowhere.

"Thank you, New Mexico, thank you," I said as I crossed into Colorado. We'd made it. A few miles across the state line, our car rolled into the city limits of Trinidad, and I tried to judge if I felt any different. I was so exhausted I couldn't sense much of anything at this point, but as far as I could tell, everything felt the same.

CHAPTER FORTY-SIX

I found an elegant hotel with a beautiful bronze sculpture of a bull elk out front. It felt safe, so I turned into the driveway. Arya and I walked through the gorgeous wilderness surroundings, then I checked us in and left her in the hotel room. I was starving and wanted so badly to sit in a comfortable place to eat something delicious. I had been isolated for the past week, preferring to be nowhere in proximity to other people, and had just grabbed a protein bar here or there to eat in the seclusion of my car or hotel room. But now, I wanted to hear human voices rather than spirit ones. I wanted to feel the company of those who currently had a pulse.

I walked down the bright hallway into the lobby and found my way to the restaurant, which was nice enough but completely empty. So much for company. I picked a booth and perused the menu, which was filled with meat, meat, and a side of meat choices. I didn't care, I'd find something. I was so hungry, it didn't matter what I ate.

The waiter looked like a character from a greasy spoon on a movie set. He smiled as he ambled to my table wearing all white, with a white chef's hat and a white kitchen apron around his waist. He asked me with exaggerated cheer if I'd had ample time to choose.

"Yes," I said. "I'll have a Reuben sandwich with fries. No corned beef please."

He paused. His pen, all ready to write down my desires, refused to document such a request. "Okay now, you said, a Reuben with no *meat?*" He was squinting.

"That's right." I folded up my menu, ready to hand it to him.

He blinked, his brain not computing. "But that would be…" he paused to visualize the thing, "that would be a grilled cheese with sauerkraut?" His squint had morphed to full-blown disgust and confusion.

"And thousand island dressing, with pumpernickel bread." I added. He was still frozen. "Look, just make me a Reuben sandwich, but leave the corned beef off. Okay?" I was trying to make this simple while being as congenial as possible.

"Whatever you say, lady!" He marched to the kitchen, yelling loudly as he banged through the swinging doors, "Dan, you are not going to believe this one!"

Never before had there been such excitement in Trinidad, Colorado, than when the lady attempted to order a meatless sandwich. It tasted lovely, and afterward, I made my way down the long hallway to my room, so tired I leaned against the wall while I walked.

When I arrived, Arya was quiet, which was a relief. I didn't know if she'd protest being left alone after being attached to my hip over the past several days. I put my electronic key into the slot. Blinking red. I tried it again. Still blinking red. By now Arya had heard me out there and was at the door, pawing at it, as if to say, "Get in here! I can't believe you left me alone!" I honestly felt that if I had to walk that enormous distance all the way back down to the lobby, I'd collapse right in the hallway and have an involuntary snooze on the freshly vacuumed verdigris carpet. Arya was going nuts now, digging at the door, whining, feeling teased.

I closed my eyes and put my hands on the door, leaning my forehead against the cool wood. "Arya, if you want me in there so bad, can you please just open this door?"

"Is…is somebody not letting you in there?"

I jumped a little. A beautiful Latina, one of the housekeepers, was standing next to me. She looked tentative, like she didn't know if she should interrupt. She must have just come around the corner, and who knows what she heard me say. It seemed my internal realities and my external realities were not exactly congruent, if I could judge by my thoughts versus my written words.

"My dog, Arya is in there." I tried to laugh. Of course, by now Arya was silent as a stone, probably trying to assess the second voice with me. "What's not letting me in is a demagnetized room key." I showed her the useless plastic card and tried to form a pout. My muscles were so tired I could barely smile, reversing it was even harder.

She laughed then, fumbling in her pocket. "I can let you in." She found her master entry key and I allowed her to take my place in front of the magnetic reader. She opened the door and Arya jumped all over me. That was proof enough to her that I belonged there. I thanked her profusely and watched her walk down the hall, expecting her to disappear at any moment, but she was apparently the real deal. How could I know anymore?

I don't think I'd ever experienced a more satisfactory room in all my life. This place was more expensive than my newly unemployed self felt comfortable with, but I knew I deserved it. I felt so ready to rest as the horrors of the night before became more distant. It felt peaceful here, welcoming. I would have paid any price for that.

I fed Arya her dinner and got ready for bed. It was only around eight o'clock, but I couldn't keep my eyes open, and Arya was sound asleep five minutes after she finished eating. I forced myself to stay up another hour so I could take her for one last potty break.

For the first time in my life I took the Bible out of the bed-side table drawer and put it next to me, just as a precaution, in case any other demons were inclined to crawl across my walls. I tried to shake that vision out of my head, not having any intention to undergo another *Jornada Del Muerto*. By this point, I felt that if I didn't get some sleep I'd go mad. I reminded myself that the demon hotel room was five hundred miles south. That relaxed me some.

I walked Arya in the dark, returning quickly and crawling into my bed after taking a long hot shower. Finally comfortable, I lay there in relaxed bliss and shortly after closing my eyes was met with the familiar cicadas, buzzing, and tingling. There was nothing to fight. It felt right.

CHAPTER FORTY-SEVEN

I traveled to the scene of a small, nineteenth century country church. People were dressed in very modest, puritanical attire. Not a smile to be seen—what a cold, austere environment. I was hovering over them as I had done in thousands of other visions throughout my lifetime. *Look at them,* I said to myself, *do they know what joy is?* Slowly, all heads turned to stare at me suspended above. The women wore their hair like strange hats, similar to the Fox sisters. *They can see me!* I thought, unafraid but bewildered. They pointed to me and shouted, "Evil thing! Demon!"

I was amused rather than afraid. It seemed such a primitive response. I smiled and hovered higher, safely out of their reach. "Be gone!" they screamed, and I rose still higher. I pitied them for being so filled with fear and wondered why it was that in a house of God, they so easily processed any unusual experience as the work of the devil. It didn't feel like they were giving God much credit. It was an honest question, an anthropological fascination. I kept watching as their forms became smaller and smaller while their anger became more and more demonstrative—it was like watching a swarm of furious bees.

I was no longer controlling my trajectory, caught in a tractor beam pulled by something above. Ecstasy suddenly filled me so intensely that I gasped. I closed my eyes, overwhelmed by the sensation, and began slowly rotating to face a new direction. The voices of the churchgoers were muted now, and my ears were filled with the loud buzzing familiar to me from my astral travels. I opened my eyes and looked straight into the church's massive stained-glass mandala window with a center image of Jesus with his arms outstretched. The window became vast, stretching on for what seemed like miles in every direction. I was an ant, miniscule by comparison now hurtling toward the window. *This is going to hurt.* I winced but I couldn't close my eyes.

If ever there was a gateway to be navigated, I suddenly knew this was the only one that mattered. I understood what was happening and realized it wasn't about pain. It was my reward for having teetered on the precipice of life and death for the past week, with my head exploding from the many teachings, and then filling with my own truths delivered by a team of angelic characters pulling for me to win my own battle of the Self. If the Darkness had directed the show last night, tonight the Light was taking the lead. I had been immersed in all of it over the past seven days, and in this very moment some ethereal gatekeeper was saying, "God will see you now."

Moments before I crashed through the glass, I found myself complaining, *Why does it have to be Jesus?* If I had to crash through a window of universal truth, couldn't the Buddha be the gatekeeper? Jesus all too often came with people like those in the church below—joyless, filled with cruelty, fear, hate, and rage. Jesus had betrayed me twenty years ago.

And then no more whining.

I crashed through the glass into deep space while the awesome sound of a cosmic gateway shattering reverberated throughout the universe. With every shard of broken glass floating away in slow motion, another one of my nerve endings exploded in screaming euphoric ecstasy. Every second felt like a glorious eternity. My whole body responded in what the feeble limits of a human mind could only describe as orgasmic, with every cell screaming in ecstasy. The constant torrent of pleasure was nearly too much for me to endure. I screamed until my throat went hoarse, while every remnant of pain was cast out of me through a process of cleansing so intense, I thought my physical form would break apart, leaving me to return to stardust in the blackness. If that had been my fate, I would have welcomed it. Perhaps we've evolved away from harboring this much joy, replacing our ecstasy receptors with those that process fear and suspicion, hate and pain. The chance to experience this intoxicating rapture was worth any price, including my own glorious destruction if that were to follow.

There were colors…colors I had no description for. Colors I don't believe my retinas have the cones and rods to make sense of. Millions of vivid colors moved and vibrated, like lightning shooting through me. Also, sounds I couldn't possibly repeat with the vocal anatomy I had been given. By now I was crying and laughing and screaming hysterically—all of it at once—in the face of so much love and awe. I was being shown all the beauty of the universe, in the language of color and sound and vibration. It was all energy, pure energy.

In my ecstasy I screamed out, "Who are you? Are you Jesus? Are you Buddha?"

Then everything came to a standstill. Time froze. I hovered there in the silent heavens, drifting. I caught my breath, and my heart rate began to normalize after the onslaught of indescribable pleasure. The stars sparkled in the blackness as they witnessed the Divine flexing its muscles and showing a tiny human what the gods are made of. I floated, limp and exhausted, taking in the enormity of the moment, feeling the cosmos inside of me, permeating my cells—I was immortal. And then, through the darkness, a voice filled with the power of a thousand voices transposed into one gave me my answer.

"I am Everything. All."

With that came a torrent of understanding: every story, every prophet, every ascended master, every version of every religious tome ever written, was simply a cultural variation of the same energy source.

I wept. I wept at my own foolishness, at the thought of rejecting Jesus because I had endured too much pain, accepting Buddha with some kind of delusion that the two were somehow on different teams just because some priest years ago had told me so.

For thousands of years people had killed each other because each believed their version of the same god was better, stronger, more just. Wars were fought and are still fought over story books. People died and are still dying because of so much human ignorance.

Then I was shown an alternative; what could happen if we combined our resources rather than warring over them. An entire planet aligned with love, no boundaries, no borders. I was shown visions of humankind sharing assets, discovering the key to quantum physics, able to bounce back and forth between dimensions with nothing but the power of our minds. Collaborative inclusion had to be the law of the land if we were to ever overcome our war consciousness. War consciousness was killing us.

I downloaded all of it and woke up with a start.

I was back in the hotel room.

The moment my eyes registered where I was, Mangas's deep voice said loudly into my left ear, "You carry the seed."

I just lay there, stunned and blinking. I couldn't move.

I looked at the clock. Ten hours had passed, but it seemed like no more than a few seconds. My face was saturated with tears. The covers were kicked off the bed and my back ached from arching it. I wiped my face and took a few deep breaths. Arya was resting upright next to me, staring peacefully at me, despite the blankets being all over the room. What could she have told me? What had she witnessed? I hugged her, feeling so much love for her, for the entire world, for myself. I was love. The room was otherwise empty, but I had never felt so supported. I had never felt so safe.

And then I sat up. "Wait." I said, smoothing my tousled hair. "I carry the…what?"

CHAPTER FORTY-EIGHT

I made the decision to stay in Trinidad for one more night. I needed to pause in this glorious experience. And I needed more recovery time before I made my way to Nebraska, my final stop before pushing on for home in Minnesota. I would stay in bed, write, talk to Aaron, walk Arya, lay my hands on the earth and let Mother Nature anchor me. I visited a health food store and bought some cashews, apples, granola, almond milk, sugar snap peas and dark chocolate. I remained in my bed most of the day, trying to recuperate as best I could, while reveling in the experience of the night before.

I drifted in and out of a midday nap and woke to the sounds of Arya pouncing around the room, having the time of her life. She was wrestling with someone, play-growling. Still half asleep, out of the corner of my eye I watched as she played so hard that she was panting. She seemed to be wrestling with another Saluki, some canine specter who had punched through the veil to connect with her. I opened my eyes and looked at them, a little shocked that Arya seemed to have her own little ghosts to keep her company. But suddenly her friend disappeared, and Arya stopped and looked around confused and a little disappointed. I smiled at her sweetness and promptly fell right back into a deep, regenerative sleep.

I woke up to my laptop indicating I'd received a new message. It was my husband, responding to something I didn't remember sending. I put my face in my hands, tired of having no memory or control over my humiliating communications. I read my original words, something about telling him to NOT cross the streams, Baby: "Do not cross the energy streams or it could be super dangerous!" I winced, embarrassed by the lunacy.

He replied, "I won't, Baby! Please don't worry about me!" Somehow, that was the best response. I let him know I was okay and shut down my computer.

God, I loved him.

I found a trail and walked Arya for a few miles, absorbing the crisp, thin air and rugged beauty of Trinidad. Arya was wiped out from her ghost-dog play, so we returned to our room and she curled up for a snooze. I snacked on my cashews and read a little, feeling my internal battery recharging, slowly filling up with the power I needed to take another step.

Just before darkness overtook daylight, I found Arya intently staring out the window. I saw nothing, but her gaze was unbreakable. There was something fascinating to her, just outside. I tried to focus on what she was seeing and finally found it. The feline face of a bobcat at the edge of the woods stared directly into our window.

I went outside to the back of the property where the bobcat crouched high on a rock ledge. She was a good forty feet away from me, and I felt compelled to go closer. Despite my moving toward her, she remained perched, compact and muscled, staring me in the eye. She was small, maybe three times the size of an average house cat and regal as a queen. So beautiful. I started downloading her silent transmission, holding on to every precious word.

The feline species, typically in the form of the house cat, has long been believed to be a guardian of the spirit realm. This Bobcat was telling me that I needed her. She let me understand that I'd be calling on her protection sooner than I knew. She asked that I be strong and to not discount the dark energy, which was not to be fought or destroyed or battled because to do so meant aligning with it as a partner. Hate never conquers hate, she said. It becomes it.

The dark energy wants only to be recognized, honored, and left alone. It has its own definition of what it believes to be love, she told me, but its illusory form of love is destruction, total ownership and mindless consumption. The Bobcat reminded me that no dark energy can touch us if we don't directly invite it in. Once we open that door it is extremely difficult to ask it to leave, and it oftentimes overtakes us. Right now, there is so much light opening up in the world, the darkness needs to fortify itself, insidiously asking for admittance to anyone who will allow it, actively seeking to challenge those who are working to shine brighter. There is only one way to overcome the darkness, and that is to illuminate it with love. More hate is an incendiary to Hate. "Possession" is real, she informed me, often invited in through feelings of justified vengeance and spite.

Most importantly, she said, we are not to judge the dark energy, because judgment is the universal key by which darkness opens any fortified door. Humans aren't built to judge. We're terrible at it, frequently getting it wrong based on our own projections and constantly changing perceptions. She ended by telling me to call on her. To not hesitate. I would need her soon.

Our gaze finally broke and the Bobcat silently turned, retreating back into the hills. My trance faded as I made my way back to my hotel room, but I still felt stunned and numb. I was exhausted; my need for sleep was a bottomless pit.

I had another ten-hour night, this time gifted with no dreams or visions, only the quiet stillness of deep space.

Part Ten

THE ROAD BACK

"I shall tell you a secret my friend. Do not wait for the last judgment. It takes place every day."

~Albert Camus

"Healing is not forcing the sun to shine but letting go of that which blocks the light."

~ Stephen and Ondrea Levine

CHAPTER FORTY-NINE

After two nights of regenerative healing, it was time to say goodbye to the protective, stoic strength of Colorado and head to Nebraska. If I got an early start, I could reach Harry and Lisa's place in Lincoln by evening, so I packed up the car, took Arya for a sunrise walk and found my place behind the wheel. It was just me and my sweet girl; the spirits had been quiet since I crossed the New Mexico state line. Colorado doesn't lend itself to opening to the spirit realm, its patriarchal masculine energy having no need for such foolishness (or so I told myself). I felt restrained in the granite embrace of the Colorado Rockies. I didn't care that it held me a little too tightly. I felt safe.

I stood in the parking lot, gazing south toward the mountain pass to New Mexico. Wrapping my arms around myself, I felt a sickening wave at the memory of my dismantling in Silver City. I exhaled the dark memory out of my lungs, and felt the strength of my limbs, rubbing my arms to remind myself I was still here, still in one piece. I forced myself to remember Mother Nature's psychedelic flower explosion and the physical sensation of meeting God, of awakening to the message, "You carry the seed." After all I'd endured over the past week, I tried to block the irrational fear that I had literally been impregnated by the cosmos. My mind, as stretched and as unformed as it had become, was utterly confused in the face of all that I had experienced. But I shuddered and waved away the thought.

I also understood that the human mind was easily diverted to simple, basal symbolism in the face of the Divine. What I had experienced in that Trinidad hotel room wasn't human; it wasn't of this Earth. There was no language, no reference, for what I had experienced. I had zero understanding of it. I vaguely recalled a biblical story, something like, when the angel spoke, humans exploded in proximity. If that was anything like my experience, I'm sure they went with smiles on their faces.

I said goodbye to New Mexico, certain I'd be back soon, regardless of the horrors I'd experienced. The beauty there far exceeded anything I could have ever imagined. I knew all of what I had endured was a coming home, a welcome back spoken in the only language New Mexico knows. Survive her or not, she'll never censor herself, never tame herself to fit our comfort level. New Mexico almost killed me, but in the face of what she'd shown me, what she gave to me—a direct path to myself—the rest of the world would never be enough, would never feel like home. "The Land of Enchantment" had infected me, like a glorious virus for which there was no cure.

I had the sense I'd never see the physical forms of Mangas or Maggie again. They had done their job, bringing me through this enchantment alive. Now they'd take their place in the ethers, watching silently, guiding me through dreams—Mangas slightly stoic, Maggie impish and innocent—keeping me connected to my own beating heart. I had the sense that each Fox sister somehow lived within each of my three oldest, dearest friends on Earth. I could see their original characteristics—reverent, doting, and skeptical— currently being played out by each one of my best friends—Shari, Ann, and Heidi—all of them steadfastly in my life for thirty to forty years. Nothing could break those bonds. The Fox sisters would always be with me.

I didn't feel insane. What I felt was closer to sane than I had perhaps ever felt, despite all the nonsense that came with a temporarily disordered mind: the confusion, the word salad writings, the inability to read a map or sense direction. What I felt was the possibility that I had been insane all my life, fitting perfectly into the mold of the American worker, being pulled apart on a daily basis but blending into my surroundings so effectively I forgot to be myself. I felt for a moment that insanity was so prevalent in the United States that we had no way of judging our sanity any longer. If we played the game, we were all right. If we didn't—perhaps because it was the actual game that was insane, not the player—we were labeled as sick, unwell, crazy.

I remembered the words of Mangas, "See the truth with your own eyes, Child." But that was so hard to do with societal filters so firmly affixed. I had to remove those filters and allow myself to see what was truly before me—just as I had seen Mangas as my own true reflection in my rearview mirror.

I drove out of Trinidad, thanking it for providing two days of healing respite. I slowed way down as two magnificent bull elk meandered out of the wilderness and dropped their massively antlered heads down low to nibble on some sweet winter grass. Of all the mind-bending experiences, there is still nothing more magical to me than the royalty of Mother Nature in the form of her spectacular animal kingdom.

I drove for hours, deep in trance. Finding my way into the Colorado Springs city limits, I was suddenly overcome with sentiment, the days of my childhood once again permeating me with memories of day trips to the Garden of the Gods. The sign for the park was right in front of me, staring me in the face, and I couldn't resist taking the exit. I had hours more to drive and was already scheduled to arrive late into the evening, but I was compelled to stop.

Entering the red rocks, my heart opened wide with child-like excitement. I felt so emotional, so connected to my father. Open road adventure was what he lived for. I was only now realizing that this was when I saw him fully alive, his deep blue Irish eyes sparkling at the start of any long road trip. I loved him so much in those days.

Arya and I strolled into the dramatic rock formations of the Garden; gravity-defying boulders that teetered on the verge of collapse but had maintained their balance for thousands of years. "How do they do that? When will they fall?" I remembered the questions I'd asked as a young girl. It was dead silent among the formations now; I had the park to myself on this early February weekday afternoon. I felt good. Strong. Grateful.

As I walked, I thought about my *Stark Raving Zen* writings, posted while I was in New Mexico. I had been blogging my experience—a highly truncated version, just bits and pieces—feeling uncomfortable and embarrassed by each day's entry.

But like the insane letters written to various people on the road, I did not delete these entries because I felt I owed it to the experience to be real, even if my poor attempt to articulate it sounded ridiculous. They weren't my words, I told myself. I was Stark Raving Zen, dictating for Mother Nature, with a creative feminine voice pouring through me. The words, intense and angry, were not meant to be censored. But how humiliating for a perfectionist! I wasn't doing a good job of translating. I had forgotten how to think, how to write, how to formulate sentences. I didn't yet know how to speak without urgency, without filling up with fear or hate or judgment, without becoming the darkness, as the Bobcat had warned.

I felt a presence with me then, heard a new voice, delicate and gentle. He told me that embarrassment was not a wise expenditure of energy, that my identity wasn't dependent on how I presented myself to the world. In fact, my identity didn't actually exist. It was a mirage. If I could connect with the Buddha Light inside of me, I would find that nothing was constant.

Hello, Zen Master.

I became incredibly still so I could catch every word.

He said that Mother Nature didn't lament the fact that she sometimes wipes out entire populations based on her mood— her hurricanes and tornadoes, her earthquakes and fires. She just wakes up the next day, unapologetic, focusing on whatever her mood happens to be and nothing else. "Mother Nature lives without the hindrance of regret," he told me. She doesn't look back. Her motives are never punishing or malevolent.

I felt a deep peace with his words. People would perceive who I was based on their own established worldview, landing on some version of my identity that worked for them; their perceptions were out of my hands. Those who judged me based on my odd, passionate, super-crazy writings throughout this experience would probably never know me. That was entirely their choice. Nothing I could do about it. No use being emotional about it. Plus, how could I possibly fault them? I was absolutely odd, passionate, and super crazy right now.

As I continued to walk, immersed in the natural beauty of the Garden of the Gods, I processed the wisdom of the last several days. Right now, I had complete clarity. I felt so much love for my broken siblings and my deeply flawed parents. I visualized myself sweeping up the shards that had once been our family, and though I couldn't make us whole again, I could at least collect them in a heap, so we could be together in our brokenness.

I didn't want this whole journey to be only for my benefit. If I was being shown these fantastic things, I wanted to share them. Crazy or not, maybe my experience would give one person the courage to jump over their own precipice, to experience their own transformation. I had no regrets over my attempts to articulate this experience.

After nearly an hour in this paradise, it was time to push through to Nebraska. Arya was tired and hot; she felt happy to curl up in the front seat next to me. I gained such peace from her presence that I allowed her to remain in the front seat with me, "But only until we get home, Arya. Don't get used to this," I lectured, fully aware that my reasoning was flawed. Unless a dog is in a secure kennel, which Arya never tolerated, even the backseat isn't all that safe. I just needed her close. And honestly, of all the things to fear on this journey, Arya's well-being was clearly untouchable. She must have had her own army of protective spirits guarding her. She was and would remain happy, healthy, and safe.

My shaking had stopped. The feelings of intense euphoria had passed, replaced by quiet contentment. No spirits in my back seat. No voices in my ear. As I passed through Colorado, I felt relief at that. My body needed the break and I was more than okay with the quiet. I'd be processing the experiences of the past several days for perhaps the rest of my life, and if I died tomorrow, I'd leave complete, having experienced more than I could have ever considered possible through this fantastic dimension—torn open by some form of insanity, or perhaps a coming home to sanity, which was without a doubt the best gift of my life so far. Was it over? I felt so…solid, but not in a paralyzing kind of way. It was a sensation of wholeness.

Was I healed? I knew better than to ask the incessant questions of the mind, and instead allowed my need for understanding to drift, focusing on the trajectory and velocity of my car hurtling north up the Colorado highway. I had been well coached.

I listened to my music, scratched Arya behind her silky-smooth white ears, and felt the reassuring hum of tires on asphalt. I was going to be okay. Wasn't I?

And then I quietly passed over the Colorado state line.

The energy of Nebraska hit me like a baseball bat to the gut.

I literally gasped, causing Arya to jump up, ears alert, trying to gauge where this was going. She'd had a couple of days off but was now back on duty.

I looked at her, sick with dread, and said, "I'm sorry Arya." It was happening again. I tried to calm my pounding heart but knew I had no other option than to drive into it.

CHAPTER FIFTY

I had been on the road for hours by now, and the sun was fading. An energetic sickness had settled over me. It was too quiet. My face turned grey, mirroring the deeply overcast sky; a storm was rolling in. All I could do was keep driving in a bid to outrun the rapidly descending darkness. My despair grew more intense as the muted sun dropped toward the horizon where it could be of no support. As my dread deepened, my energy bottomed out. I became a heavy stone; my chest felt so dense it took concentrated effort to inhale and exhale. There was a thick, sour, feedlot stench in the air. I no longer had delusions that I didn't need oxygen, but I was wishing it was true.

It was around six o'clock, with another three-or-four-hours' drive to get to Lincoln. I wasn't going to make it. I pulled off the highway to a nice-looking chain hotel in the middle of nowhere. I phoned my friends and told them I wouldn't be staying with them tonight—I was just too exhausted—and I got out of the car to check in.

It was empty. Not another car in the parking lot. It felt wrong.

A nice older East Indian couple met me in the lobby. They felt sweet, but haunted…tragic. I tried to bring some light to them; I smiled a lot and acted cheerful even though I felt as though a dark hole would open up and swallow me at any minute. The tiny woman slid me a key and tried to smile, her doleful eyes connecting with mine for only a fleeting second. Her energy felt captive. "I hope you'll be comfortable here," she said with a melodious accent and a charming side head bob, then she lowered her eyes as though it was a boastful request. The husband, I presumed, continued to do his paperwork, head down, only glancing up to give me a warm smile as I took the key.

I walked to my ground level corner room with an outside entrance and listened to my feet crunch on the frozen gravel driveway. It was so cold. The place felt desolate, devoid of life, with air heavy and damp. I opened the door for Arya and attached her leash. She pulled me over to a small pond, horribly neglected and littered with what seemed like a year's worth of dog waste. I wrinkled my nose. "Disgusting," I mumbled to Arya, pulling her away. I walked away from the property down a dirt farm road behind the hotel to allow Arya a little exercise, then forced her back to the hotel room. She was literally dragging her feet like a tiny stubborn mule, refusing to move forward. I figured she just wanted a walk and promised a lengthier one as soon as we settled into our room.

Upon opening the door, I heard a loud buzzing sound in the stagnant air. I opened the curtain to find a dozen black flies maddeningly beating themselves against the window, desperate to get out. I didn't even sit on the bed, just threw my bags on the floor and went to use the bathroom, tortured by a strange obsessive-compulsive thought forced into my consciousness—*eating spider sandwiches on white bread.*

I held my head in my hands. "What the actual *hell.*" I said to nobody. I was so tired and didn't think it would be possible to get back in the car in this state of exhaustion. But this room felt way too close to the experience of demons crawling the walls, and I was certain that I would not survive another experience like Silver City's. I brought the Bible out of the drawer…it gave me no relief.

Arya and I left the room to see if I could walk off my feelings of doom; heading down the gravel farm road, we heard geese in the slate skies overhead. My dread increased exponentially. I remembered the Bobcat's warning, "Don't discount the darkness. Call on me should you need me."

So I asked her through the honking geese to help me decide. Was this place dangerous? Or am I just exhausted? Should I continue north to Lincoln? Was I just being paranoid? I really shouldn't be driving when I'm this tired, I pleaded with her. I could detect no clear answer. I couldn't hear anything but the geese.

And then I heard her say, "Listen to the geese."

I paused before I looked up in the sky. I thought, "Show me a sign, my winged friends. Any sign." I turned around and craned my neck upward and found their answer. Their formation was not in the shape of a V but a startlingly perfect line drawing of an arrow, pointed toward home. Hundreds of geese formed a divine directive, telling me in no uncertain terms, "Get the hell out of here." I gaped at the huge arrow over me, stunned at its unambiguous clarity.

Suddenly I was filled with panic, wild with it, and ran back to the room as fast as I could, fumbling with my old-fashioned aluminum key, throwing Arya in the car. Grabbing my bags and leaving no wrinkle on the rented bed, I drove back to the lobby to check myself out. I forgot to put the Bible back in the drawer. "I'm not afraid of you," I said through gritted teeth, as I shut my car door. "Come near me; I'll tear you to pieces!" I had no idea who might be listening.

I ran into the lobby and stalled just inside the door, blocked with the sensation of getting punched in the chest. The smaller diminutive couple was nowhere to be seen and in their place was some younger man, just in to work the night shift. Moments ago, I had declared my courage, but this man made me a liar. Without a smile, his eyes empty and dead, I told myself he was being worked by some demonic overlord, a prisoner in his own body. Something ancient was inside of him, passed down through thousands of lifetimes. Nobility of the most evil, staring at me through this body that had clearly been overtaken, consumed, years before. Was I projecting? Was any of this real? I felt my grandfather's presence here, my mother's torturer, the dark rot, the shame of my entire maternal history. I felt my father's alcoholism, the demonic fire burning in those empty eye sockets. The murderous *cadejo*...

I could barely use my voice.

I put the key on the counter as I held my phone. I waved it at him.

"Bad news!" I lied, forcing my words while smiling sheepishly. "I just received a phone call. I've had a family emergency. I need to drive immediately back to Minneapolis." I explained to him. "I haven't even sat on the bed, so I'd love it if you could credit me the night that I've paid for, but I understand if you can't."

He stared at me in silence. Still no smile.

"How about if you look at the room," I said, trying to maintain my cool, "and then just make your decision. Your call. Either way, I've got to go." I smiled at him, calling on the Bobcat's wisdom—humans make horrible judges—just walk away, don't align with fear. Moments ago, I had done just that, provoking it, even threatening it, shaking my fist with "justified spite." I clearly had mastered nothing yet and felt my life force draining. I remembered the channeled words, "You know nothing." I tried to empty my mind.

He remained frozen, staring. I glanced out the window, trying to remain casual in the awkward frozenness, and saw Arya standing up in the front of the car, staring in the lobby window, wide-eyed, as if to say, "Finish your business! Get out of there!"

I had slid the key toward him, my arm outstretched but still fumbling with it, tapping it on the counter, an annoying cadence to settle my nerves, waiting for him to respond, to say something. "Here's the key," I said, holding it out to him. He reached out fast and unexpectedly, a spider's movement, slapping his hand over mine presumably to stop my tapping, pressing down on it with the key underneath. He held it there, staring me in the eye.

I swallowed hard, a cartoonish gulp which I hoped he hadn't noticed. Then time froze and a strange slide show of images began running through my mind, one after another, horrific images of dead children, being used, thrown away and buried in shallow graves. Children being trafficked, abused, killed, all over the world, disposable and innocent, being extinguished by so many dark forces, too many to count.

It was the energy of Darkness itself, of all the horrific things for which humanity is collectively responsible. I tried to force back the tears that were welling up in the corners of my eyes, and then they retreated by their own volition as my terror turned to rage. I visualized tearing my hand out from under his—how dare he touch me—matching his spider-like speed, and grabbing him around the throat, squeezing the life out of this man who felt it was okay to frighten me, squeezing the life out of the ancient inhabitant that lived behind his eyes, who could be found in my lineage too.

"*I know nothing,*" I said silently inside my head. My rage retreated.

He withdrew his hand and spoke in a slightly southern accent, breaking the major motion picture of horrors. He tucked his chin-length dishwater blond hair behind his ear. "I'll do that. I'll look at the room. I'll credit your card if it hasn't been used." I left the key, drawing back my hand, the anger quiet, cycling back to fear. I smiled too much, backing out of the lobby, saying "Thank you!" without taking my eyes off him. I literally ran to my car, watching Arya nervously shift from paw to paw, crouching and straightening and then crouching again, as if to say, "Hurry, hurry! Get in!"

I threw the car in drive, immediately locked the doors. It was not yet entirely dark, and I didn't think to put my headlights on, I was so desperate to leave that driveway. I put my foot on the gas and punched it, drove twenty feet and then jammed on the breaks. Something was in front of me. A raccoon? I strained to see. Why was it moving so slow? Was it hurt? I squinted my eyes. It wasn't a raccoon.

In front of us was something I couldn't identify, now close enough for a better view. It slowly slumped and wriggled across the gravel driveway. Black, greasy, the height of a smallish coyote, it couldn't walk very efficiently due to incredibly short back limbs and grotesquely elongated front limbs, which resulted in a bat-like gait, horribly awkward. Speed was physically impossible, but I got the impression that outrunning anything was not a concept it concerned itself with. Its face was sort of feline, with crooked features disturbingly misplaced. Jagged teeth protruded from the jawline at all angles, like a barracuda. It stopped its slow ambulation with a slump, pausing to turn its head, slow as a sloth, to gaze directly into my face. And though my headlights were off, with nothing to reflect, its eyes glowed bright red.

"Are you seeing this?!" I frantically asked Arya while I threw on the headlights. She stared right at it. Fully illuminated now, it was even more grotesque in the light. I couldn't move, I couldn't speak.

I couldn't breathe. Arya, watching its every move, seemed to be holding her breath too. "Don't judge it. Don't despise it. Have compassion. Don't fear it. Just respect it." I recited out loud, so as not to align with it, trying to learn, guided by the wisdom of the Bobcat. I heard her voice, "Fear has no inherent qualities. It's just the absence of Light." The creature slowly broke my gaze, seemingly unaffected by the bright lights, taking what seemed like forever to turn its head forward and continue its monstrous ambulation into the Nebraska darkness. As soon as it was off the path, I punched the gas, my tiny station wagon fishtailing, spitting gravel and dust behind us.

CHAPTER FIFTY-ONE

With the vision of who-knows-what-the-hell we had just seen, I was wild. All I could think of was getting back to Minnesota. There was no way I was going to Lincoln; I didn't want to risk dragging demonic beings anywhere near my friends. There was only one solution and that was to somehow make it back to Minnesota tonight. If I could make it to the very southern edge, if I could just cross the border, I knew I'd be all right in the loving embrace of my own state. I had about eight hours to go, with too much adrenaline to feel the luxury of tiredness, so I pushed through, a frenzied thing, pursued.

My sanity evaporated as the atmosphere exploded around me. I tried to grasp what was happening. Was I hallucinating? Mammoth deities erupted across the night, bursting through the darkness, warring across the Nebraska and Iowa skies. In the pitch blackness I could see them clearly, fighting to the death, a clash between Light and Dark, attempting to restore the balance. My car hurtled up the highway while I narrowly missed their gigantic toes, and they roared, tearing at each other in hand-to-hand mortal combat in the clouds. They were everywhere—swinging, punching, clawing, stabbing—unavoidably, completely visible even in the darkness. I clutched my chest as I felt the war permeate me. I felt their hammers and claws inside of me.

An industry smokestack attacked me, the plumes of toxic smoke changing direction and defying physics to blow down and to the left, filling my lungs with thick, poisonous air. I couldn't breathe. I screamed for help, and a wind goddess hammered through to my defense, shrieking and pulverizing the smoke plume so my car could safely pass. I was terrorized. I felt like I was navigating an ancient battlefield. And I had never been in so much pain. My bones felt like they would snap, energy coursed through me so fast and hard that my skeleton, my cells, couldn't assimilate it. Every muscle screamed, my skin burned, my skull felt the beating of the war hammers.

Meanwhile, Arya slept so peacefully I couldn't help but gain strength from her. She confused me. How could she sleep through this? I tried to connect to the peaceful whatever that Arya was embodying. Her attitude assured me I could survive this, that everything would eventually be okay. If she was aware of the war, it was certainly a different experience for her, or she had so much faith that we'd persevere she thought nothing of catching a few Z's. It was late by now, far past her bedtime. Her chin rested comfortably on her stuffed toy and while the forces of Light and Dark were wrestling for victory, I wrapped her little blanket around her, trying desperately to live vicariously through her functional mind.

Around two in the morning, I cried in triumph when we

crossed the state line of Minnesota, straight into a blinding snowstorm. On the two-way rural highway, the middle yellow line quickly became invisible, and the drifts on the side of the road encroached farther and farther inward creating a single lane, straight down the center. I started to cry. My exhaustion suddenly hit me hard; I had now been on the road for nearly twenty hours straight. I felt so alone and afraid. I'd lived long enough in Minnesota to respect the power of a winter storm, and recalled too many "people-found-dead-in-car" stories. I did not have a four-wheel drive vehicle, and the fury of the blowing snow on the open plains was maniacal. There was no one else on the road—I couldn't even see farm lights in the distance—and I had zero cell service. I couldn't have asked for a worse scenario.

Hundreds of miles away in Lincoln, Nebraska, Harry paced around his back porch, unable to sleep. An unsettling presence had permeated his dreams, and he needed a moment of fresh air. I had told him nothing of my recent experiences when I called earlier to say that I wouldn't be seeing them in Lincoln, but despite this he was now feeling my need for help. It was well after midnight, and he felt an intrusion, like he wasn't alone. He stopped to listen. Something felt wrong. He shot back into the house, bolting the door. He closed his eyes, feeling sick, feeling dread, afraid that wherever I was, I wasn't going to make it.

Part Eleven

RESURRECTION

"Who prays for Satan? Who, in eighteen centuries, has had the common humanity to pray for the one sinner that needed it most?"

~ Mark Twain

"Go ahead, light your candles and burn your incense and ring your bells and call out to God, but watch out, because God will come and He will put you on His anvil and fire up His forge and heat you and beat you until He turns brass into pure gold."

~ Sant Keshavadas

CHAPTER FIFTY-TWO

The snowstorm pounded the exterior of my car, closing in on the road and pulverizing my hope for safe passage. "You too Minnesota? You too?!" Rather than calculate a strategy to get out of this bind, my brain could only curl up in a fetal position, too exhausted to move its gears. I turned off my satellite radio and found a local FM station. "Winter storm advisory, stay off the roads, temperatures well below zero, life-threatening windchill, visibility zero." Did I actually make it all the way through the past week of angels and demons, mythological creatures come to life, sanity or insanity, a psychic opening so intense it felt like being ripped apart, meeting Unity Source, God incarnate, enduring the steely gaze of Darkness, Titans in the sky in hand-to-hand mortal combat... only to perish in a Minnesota snowstorm? I was so exhausted and afraid. I started to sob. I put my hazard lights on and stopped the car on the empty and embattled highway.

I rested my head against the steering wheel. The asphalt was now barely visible due to the deeply drifting snow, but I had nothing left. I was paralyzed. My stomach hurt, I couldn't recall when I had eaten last, and I was now near twenty-four hours with no sleep. The tears kept coming, my body wracking to keep up with them, and then my spine stiffened, and the familiar buzz of the cicadas came back to me. I stopped crying, comforted by the release of oxytocin that accompanied the buzz, knowing I was about to be transported somewhere else, away from this terror, into the loving arms of Mangas or some other spirit tearing into the third dimension to reach me, bare hands ripping and shredding this heavy, dense reality that seemed so intent on killing me.

I opened my eyes and was no longer in Minnesota. In fact, I was outside of my body entirely. I was back in southern New Mexico, watching my physical form from above, as Arya and I drove through a narrow canyon, with towering orange rock walls and blue sky above me. I could feel the sun's intensity.

My car was a speck on the road, viewing it up here from the eagle's eye position, and I dropped down lower to get a peek inside the windshield. I looked so happy. There was no sign of fear, just a peaceful Me sharing blue corn chips with her dog.

One for me, one for her, I was watching myself have a conversation with Arya, though I could hear no sound. Arya seemed to be tracking my words, drooling a little, blissed out by the promise of the next corn chip. The beauty was astonishing. Enormous carved canyon walls, silent, proud and towering, replaced the Minnesota snow drifts that had been encroaching upon us just moments ago. Viewing myself this way, I calmed, remembering I had felt this joy recently, knowing for the first time in my life how rare and good a deep level of peace could feel. I hovered there, now eye level, moving in perfect rhythm with the car, not wanting to lose sight of Myself, my whole, healed, radiant Self.

Then something caught my attention. I adjusted my gaze slightly upward and gasped. I was eye to eye with a being three times the size of my car upon which he gracefully perched. Magnificent, this winged creature was, shining golden in the New Mexico sunlight. He had dark skin, taut muscles, and black hair tucked a little messy behind his ears. His eyes glowed when I met his gaze. I was stunned by his winged form, so shockingly beautiful.

Archangel Michael, my beloved celestial warrior, built to guard the honor of heaven, built to mercilessly illuminate the darkness, crouched here before me, in the flesh.

I said a weak "hello," while I hovered in the still, calm air, and suddenly felt intensely bashful.

His words ignited my cells with a sparkling diamond light, renewing my body, gluing together my broken, fragmented mind, lighting my spirit from flickering extinction to raging inferno. He said, "Kristy. All you have to do is ask." He stared at me intently, his eyes piercing. And then he smiled with one corner of his mouth, confident verging on cocky. He gave one sharp nod.

And with that, I was back in the pitch-black darkness of the stormy Minnesota night. The snow was still raging, but I had new eyes, filled with an energy that felt as powerful as the sun itself. There was a blinding brightness behind them, like my brain had turned into a star, a brightness that remained even when I closed my eyes. I wiped the tears away, focused through my overworked contact lenses, gripped the wheel, and pushed on. Glancing down at Arya, I saw she was still fast asleep; she seemed drugged, protected from any fear or stress. I wondered if she had asked too, I wondered if animals were better at asking.

And then I did it. I cried into the night, "Archangel Michael, Beloved Universe, God, Mangas, every one of my helping spirits ever assigned to assist me in the name of my highest consciousness, please be here with me. I need you. I need your help. I'm so scared, and so tired. Help me drive! Please help us to get home! Please. I can't do this alone anymore. I can't be alone."

My car found tracks. I became a passenger, and somebody else took the wheel. The fear fell away, my exhaustion lifted, and through the blizzard I held the wheel another effortless hour, slow and steady, into the cherished embrace of Worthington, southern Minnesota. We were here in this small city, where humans gathered to keep one another safe.

CHAPTER FIFTY-THREE

I pulled into the first hotel I could find, with the time now deep into the middle of the night, not having any intention of pushing through this blizzard another three hours to get home. I felt protected and hopeful, like maybe, just maybe, I'd live through this. I had to wake up the person on duty; this I could tell by the rings around her eyes and her hair smashed against the left side of her head. She was alarmed that there was a traveler on the road in this weather and felt relieved to be of service.

"Do you allow dogs?" I asked her. "I have mine with me," I explained, using my thumb to point over my shoulder in the direction of the car.

"Of course we do, honey! What are you doing out in this at three o'clock in the morning?! Were you driving from somewhere? Thank God you made it!" Her words comforted me. I felt Archangel Michael behind me, standing twelve feet tall, polite and patient, ducked head and tucked wings barely squeezing through the door. I assumed she couldn't see him.

The woman behind the counter got my room key ready. "That'll be eighty dollars, sweetheart. I'm so glad you're safe now."

I smiled and fumbled for my debit card. I fumbled some more, digging deep within my small purse, removing items onto the counter to give my eyes a better view. Where was my card? I felt a panic welling up within me. It wasn't here. I remembered filling my tank up with gas in my advanced state of frenzy, the Gods across the Iowa sky still battling, just a few hours ago. I could almost see my card still lying there, resting on top the aluminum tank where I recall putting it while I maneuvered the gas pump. Oh. My. God.

"I lost my debit card!" I said to the nice lady, feeling like I was going to burst into tears.

She looked sick. "Is there someone you could call? Someone to help you?"

It was so late, I feared Aaron wouldn't hear the phone. I realized I hadn't even told him I was on the road. He thought I was still at the hotel in Nebraska! I dialed him with no luck. Nobody would hear the phone at this hour.

"I'm so sorry," She said, mortified. I looked out the window at the blinding snow. For the life of me, I don't know why I didn't just use another credit card that I had in my purse, because I had a couple. I had lost my mind miles ago, and reasoning was not something I had control of by now. I told myself I was meant to push on, to experience an extension of this never-ending personal nightmare.

I apologized for wasting the nice lady's time, for waking her up. She looked torn, like she was on the verge of saying, "Oh damn, just stay here! I can't let you return to that,"—the life-threatening storm outside—but capitalism prevailed, and she allowed me to wander back out into the night, shell-shocked at having come so close to being allowed to rest, only to be denied by my own neglectful misstep and a brain that wasn't entirely working.

I once again took my place behind the wheel, heartbroken and stunned, my spirit battered. Another three hours on the road felt like an eternity of horrors. Arya barely lifted her head, one ear was stuck, folded inside out, covering the top of her dainty little skull like a bad toupee. She stood up, arched her back in a cat-like stretch, circled around to find a new sleeping position. I tucked her stuffed toy under her chin and felt nourished by her relaxed groan of contentment.

If it weren't for her, I honestly think I'd be dead.

"We are meant to keep going, Arya. For whatever reason, we can't stop." I pulled back out onto the road, brightly lit with ample streetlights, and made our final push for home, three hours to the north. I was so close. I felt numb now, quietly insane, having far surpassed the exhaustion level to expend energy on luxuries like emotion. I was a peaceful shell of a human, navigating through the snow, with thoughts of my own bed, of being held by Aaron, giving my precious Finlay a big smooch on his black satin head, all of this love pulling me forward.

As I drove, I thought more about Archangel Michael. I wondered how it would feel to be such a powerful warrior, who feared nothing. I wonder what his place was in the titanic battle in the sky, no longer visible to me since I'd driven beyond the slaughter. I wondered why I was told to never align with the darkness by hating it, while Titans warred, and Michael incinerated injustice with his flaming sword. I said my new mantra out loud then, "You know nothing," in an attempt to answer my own question. I knew it wasn't that simple, the concept of black or white, good or bad. I guessed humans had their role to play in the universe, and to be all-knowing just wasn't a part of it.

And maybe it was all just me. Maybe the entire titanic war was my own broken pieces fighting amongst themselves.

CHAPTER FIFTY-FOUR

The snow was quieting, and the adrenaline had given me a second wind. I wondered what Michael would say about the hotel in Nebraska, about the man I'd experienced behind the counter there, and the terrifying creature that inhabited the grounds? I was trying to get better at asking, so I did.

I replayed the slideshow of visual horrors I had watched when the spider-guy slammed his hand over mine, scaring me to rage. Recalling it, I received a feeling so intense…sadness, pity, pain beyond comprehension. And I knew that this pain was one part of my own heritage. A movie of fear itself, the entity of Evil, symbolized by suffering children and the white demons who dragged themselves across my walls, too common to the human experience across so many cultures including my own. Innocent people, through hundreds of cycles of samsara, stuck in a pattern of pain, fleeing but never escaping, eventually becoming the pain itself. For millions of people across the planet this was reality.

I would never understand, but I knew one thing: hate wasn't the path through this war for me, empathy was, including empathy for myself and for my family.

I thought about my own lineage, which featured the dark players of suicide, murder, rape, insanity, sexual, physical, and psychological abuse, indigenous genocide—both victims and perpetrators. I thought of my mother's father, and my father. Also victims of neglect and abuse, did they do the best they could through their own unspeakable suffering? In my family it had always been a mortal sin to even consider my grandfather's suffering, to evaluate his motives for any reason other than to label him evil. I understood the wounds he inflicted, I really did. But suddenly only one question mattered to me: When would this cycle stop? When would the gaping wounds heal? When would I gather the strength to love through all the wrongs, the crimes, and the pain…to just keep loving? When would I earn the right to liberate myself from the heavy weight of past abuse? When could I release from my shoulders the crippling burdens of these two broken men who tore through their families like sledgehammer-wielding Titans marching across the midnight sky? And from their wives, so broken that they couldn't keep their own children safe.

Something opened inside of me. I wept into the black night, sobbing, wailing, howling unrecognizable feral sounds—were these my sounds? A dam broke, a dam that I had spent years carefully constructing, and a lifetime of deeply repressed agony washed out of me, the tears scrubbing my soul clean.

I prayed for that man back at the hotel then, and the lovely sad Indian couple too. I prayed for Satan himself, a fallen angel. I prayed for my own healing. I prayed for my lineage, seven generations forward and seven generations back. And I prayed for the dark slumped creature that crawled across the Nebraska driveway. I visualized holding it in my arms, loving it, stroking its greasy fur, cheek to cheek…asking Illumination to take its pain away. I thanked whoever was listening that Arya was safe and comfortable, that I was alive, that no matter what I had endured throughout my life, I finally had the strength to say "no more" to the pain and suffering. I thanked God, not having any preconceptions or ideas of what God actually was, that I had just enough access to insanity or magic to feel invisible things to keep me going. I prayed for the other superpowers of humanity's heritage—the joy, the laughter, the compassion, the empathy, and the love. I asked them to be my supreme teachers from this day forward, instead of the pain.

I thought about my own heritage—Welsh, Irish, Cherokee, German—and how they had historically warred with each other. Had I inherited that war, carrying it around inside of me? Had my grandfather? And my father too? I'd never know how much or little of my blood belonged to the Cherokee; because the truth had been shrouded in lies for so long, I saw no way to access it. For painful, frustrating reasons unknown to me, my one little spark of American Indian blood had spread like an inferno within me, dominating my DNA, burning my force-fed European identity to smoke and ash. And I was left to serve it silently and invisibly, asking for nothing in return, belonging to nothing, feeling outside of European or indigenous ancestry. I have nothing to show for my Native identity but a passion that drives me, a knowing deep within me, a worldview I was born with, passable physical features and an oral history built of whispers and lies. I never pretended to belong, because I never would. I had become comfortable with my role, belonging to no tribe, a wolf with no pack, crouching in the darkness, accepting the nothingness, just beyond the heat and the light of the campfire, waiting for another scrap of learning, anything to validate the confusion of my existence. I'd spent my entire life trying to form an identity. With the indigenous genocide from which most modern nations were born, how many hurt like I did?

The only world I felt I truly belonged to was the spirit realm.

An hour passed and the snow continued to lessen. Things got quiet. Without the blizzard-induced adrenaline, my exhaustion finally hit me like a granite wall. After over twenty-four hours of being on the road without sleep, I shut down.

I was still in farming country, and there wasn't a lot to be found here. I knew that without panic as an ingredient, I was now in danger of falling asleep at the wheel, so I looked for a place to safely pull over. I found a bright light in the distance and followed it to find a streetlight illuminating what appeared to be a parking lot. I drove in that general direction. It was a church, and it felt right, so I pulled into the lot and parked right underneath the brightness of the lamp. There had been less snow here, but the temperatures were still life-threateningly cold, well below zero degrees, so I didn't dare turn off my car. I had plenty of gas, so I left us idling, kept the radio low, and leaned back my seat—hoping to get a little rest, sufficient to carry me the relatively short distance home, now only about two hours away. Arya hadn't stirred; she still snored peacefully next to me. Within what had to be seconds, I was safe in the arms of sleep, rejuvenation covering me like a soft, warm blanket.

A couple of hours later, the sun nudged me awake. James

Taylor was crooning "You've Got a Friend" through my radio. Arya had finally awakened, and was standing up, licking my face. I listened to the words, "...just call out my name..." stunned by the synchronicity, remembering the big angel's directive only a short while ago.

Tears fell like a waterfall, tears of relief, of happiness, feeling Archangel Michael, feeling the Bobcat, feeling Mangas and the multiple angels who had worked overtime to keep me alive. I felt Oneness after so many years of disconnection, hearing loud and clear the message of protection through James Taylor's voice. The streetlight under which I rested was now asleep itself, no longer glowing since the sun rose. My car continued to gently idle, having stayed awake and vigilant long enough for me to get a couple of hours of rest. I felt so grateful for my car that had also kept us safe, unfailingly reliable through the Minnesota stormy night. It too had kept us alive. I put my hand on the dashboard and thanked it.

The knock on my side window jolted me. A man with concern in his eyes, bundled up like an Inuit, was peering in at me. I rolled my window down, feeling energized and light. A vision popped into my head of a road sign reading, "You are now leaving Hell's city limits. We hope you enjoyed your stay!"

"Are you okay? Do you need anything, Miss?" This grey-haired man with a thick Minnesota accent had arrived to begin his workday at the church.

"I'm good! I just slept here for the past couple of hours! Thank you." I smiled, feeling like he was an angel who had permitted me to rest at Heaven's gate. I felt none of my usual disdain for organized religion; only gratitude. "I'm totally rested, and I'll be on my way back home now."

"Well, okay then!" he said, in an accent straight out of

Fargo, "but hold up just a sec, will you?" He started toward his car, parked right behind mine. He darted away, jumped into his front seat and fumbled with something. In a few seconds, he returned with a fresh glazed bakery donut, folded in wax paper. I grabbed it maybe a little too forcefully, not realizing how hungry I was. I gushed my thanks to him, and he wandered toward the church, waving me home, a man sweet with goodness.

I ate my donut and shook Arya's bowl at her. It had been filled with kibble for her to snack out of whenever she felt like it. She hadn't eaten much over the past day either, not unusual for a young Saluki on an adventure. This morning she ate, after I gave her the tiniest bite of glazed donut, which helped her remember that she too had an empty stomach. We walked a brief distance—it was too cold for anything substantial—and allowed Arya to quickly stretch her legs before her paws froze.

With joy in my heart, I called Aaron, already at work for the day, to let him know I was two hours from home, I was okay, and had spent the tail end of the night in a parking lot. He had no idea I had left the hotel in Nebraska and was infuriated to hear that I had driven through the night's blizzard. He calmed after he realized how happy he was that I was almost home and perfectly safe after all. After chatting a little while I asked him to check our bank account, just curious, to see if the man at the Nebraska hotel had credited my room charge. Apparently he had not.

"You devil," I mumbled to myself. But I truly didn't care. I pulled on to the highway and made my way home.

Part Twelve

RETURN WITH THE ELIXIR

"This place where you are right now, God circled on a map for you."

~ Hafiz

"There is not one big cosmic meaning for all, there is only the meaning we each give to our life, an individual meaning, an individual plot, like an individual novel, a book for each person."

~ Anais Nin

CHAPTER FIFTY-FIVE

My driveway felt like the gates of Heaven. I rejoiced at the grey and overcast Minnesota sky. There was a sheet of ice below my feet when I stepped out of the car, but I didn't care. I could have knelt on the tundra and kissed it.

I stood in the early morning light, pausing to soak it all in, with Arya now out of the car beside me. She shook the long drive out of her bones and began shifting from foot to foot, prancing in place, ears pinned back, a combination of being cold and feeling the joy of home. I closed my eyes and tried to breathe in the icy February air, my nostrils not so welcoming to the brutal temperature—they were literally sticking together in a gesture of no entry. I unlocked the front door and was greeted by Finlay, ninety pounds of long-legged hound leaping all over me in celebratory hysteria. He checked Arya all over, sniffing and licking her while she stood frozen, and endured this inspection, waiting for his approval before she, at a quarter of his size, tried in vain to tackle him, but so happy to be in his company once again.

I led Fin and Arya to the snowy backyard to run off their excitement, then moved the car into the garage, leaving everything that wouldn't freeze in the vehicle, too exhausted to even consider sorting it or moving it. The dogs came back inside, and I barely made it up the short flight of stairs to the bedroom. A hot shower washed the hell of the past thirty hours off my exhausted body, restoring me back to life. Without even drying my hair I crawled into my bed and slipped immediately into a deep, dreamless sleep where no angels or demons dared contact me.

At around eight o'clock in the evening I woke to find Aaron quietly looking in on me, not wanting to disturb my rest. Both Arya and Finlay were sleeping next to me on the bed, a cozy arrangement given the size of Finlay, but it felt perfect to me, safe. I gathered enough energy to throw my legs over the side of the bed, standing to hug Aaron, kissing him hello, thrilled to see him. The dogs danced on the bed covers with excitement. Aaron wanted to bring me something to eat, but I couldn't possibly think of putting anything in my stomach. I crawled back into bed and immediately fell back into a comatose state, not waking or even moving until about ten o'clock the next morning. I slept for nearly twenty-four-hours.

I awoke alone. It was black in my room, with the darkening shades doing their duty, creating a cave-like hibernation spot. All that sleep and I still felt as though I could barely lift my eyelids. In the liminal state between wake and dream, I felt disembodied. Lying on my side, my hand was on my pillow next to my face and I gasped when I saw it. Slowly turning to my back, I found myself lifting the appendage to eye level where I could study it, bending and straightening my fingers, spreading my digits apart, horrified at this thing attached to my arm, and without having any idea what use it could be put to. It was ugly, like a tarantula. The contemplation of it completely exhausted me. Tears welled, and the weight of the past ten days crushed me.

What had happened? What was I? Who had I become?

In that moment, I was given a choice. I can't explain the choice; it wasn't through a voice in my ear or a channeled arc of current coursing along my spine. It was a simple knowing that slipped over me like a silent wave of dense fog. This knowing informed me that it was my choice to stay or go. If I wanted to exit this dimension right now, there was a doorway in front of me that would open wide at my bidding. There would be no negative or positive repercussion for my choice, but I needed to decide in this moment. "You can stay, or you can go, your choice, make it now. Here's the door."

Without hesitation I chose to stay.

I believe that had I chosen not to, had I said "Game over, I didn't sign up for this, it's all a little too intense for me," that doorway would have opened, I would have stepped through, and Aaron would have found me dead in our bed, autopsy revealing no explanation.

I forced myself to get up, brush my teeth, eat something, and call Aaron to tell him I was awake. But then I crawled right back into bed and slept until around six-thirty that evening when Aaron once again came home. Careful not to wake me, he peered through the door, saw I was asleep and quietly stepped away, leaving the door open just a crack. But I felt the light illuminating through the hallway, and I really wanted to jump out of bed and into his arms, fully connecting for the first time since I came home.

There was only one problem. I couldn't move.

Before I had a chance to panic and process what was taking place, my body, flat like a plank, started to elevate off the bed. I felt like I had raised a few inches; I was floating. Was I still asleep, experiencing some version of gentle, subdued astral travel? I once again remembered Michael imploring me to ask.

Why am I floating? I thought, knowing I wouldn't have to speak out loud.

Because we're carrying you, four different angel voices replied in perfect unison. There were two on each side of me.

Why can't I move? I asked.

Because your body is regenerating, they replied.

Why can't I seem to wake up?

Because there is much healing to do, the angels answered.

I can't feel anything. Why am I so numb?

Because for right now, Child, you've felt enough. And with that, I was lowered to my bed and came awake, still on my back, staring at the ceiling. All feeling and movement came back to my body and Aaron slowly opened the door.

"Hi, Baby," he whispered. "Are you awake?"

I sat up. "I think so," I smiled. "Is this a dream?" I asked.

"Nope. I'm right here." He smiled, crawled into bed, arms enfolding me, holding me to his chest. With every beat of his heart, I could feel mine getting stronger. "I cancelled your lost debit card. No worries. They're sending a new one." His mundane update anchored me, helping me feel a little more *normal.*

I felt like a soggy butterfly just out of the chrysalis, so vulnerable that an encouraging pat on the back or the slightest punch on the shoulder might turn me back to goo. Aaron told me that my friends had been trying to call me, that he'd taken messages. He told them I couldn't speak just now as I was resting after my long journey. Aaron had no idea of the full scope of what I had experienced over the last couple of days, receiving only a few sentences here or there. I didn't know how to verbalize most of it, and I didn't want to scare him.

And so I continued to rest. I tried to be patient while my dismantling was slowly reversed, and my pieces were put elegantly back together.

CHAPTER FIFTY-SIX

*I*t would be weeks before I could be in the presence of people again, and I could speak to only a few on the phone. My lifelong friends, Ann and Shari, eased my rattled psyche, and I could be face-to-face with my sister Jill, who had become a powerful source of healing support for me. She tried to stay open to what was happening inside me, really tried to understand it. I was still sounding pretty crazy if pushed. I asked her not to try to figure anything out, to just allow me this temporary insanity, if that's how she needed to see it, without trying to wrestle logic out of it. Nothing associated with this whole experience had anything remotely to do with logic, I was pretty sure of that.

It was also weeks before I could be in the presence of negative energy. I couldn't watch television or read the news or be around people making small talk, which was often some form of complaint or gossip. It wasn't that it was simply unpleasant or disturbing for me, I would spontaneously vomit when exposed to it. It would happen with absolutely no warning, no physical symptoms as in "caution, treading too close to"—no, just a sudden minor eruption with no feelings of nausea whatsoever, as had happened to me in the hotel room when I had ignored Mangas and had eaten that bagel.

I couldn't leave the house for weeks and spent most of that time sleeping. Twelve hours a night with an additional long nap during the day wasn't unusual. My brain just could not handle much of anything and had to shut itself down frequently. I had no desire to see a psychologist or medical doctor. I just instinctively knew that everything was unfolding by design.

When I was awake, I was content and peaceful. I had a constant mission to simply allow what was right in front of me, to stay in the moment. Any other strategy felt like it would kill me. To worry about how we were going to pay the bills when the savings ran out, to worry about what was next for me, or to worry about starting completely over when I was about to turn forty—none of this would my consciousness allow. I was in a forced state of benevolent numbness, that place of *peaceful whatever*, something Arya had taught me on the road.

Years ago, when a coworker had learned that I had never tried marijuana, he said to me, "You are a walking poster child for the need to legalize pot," because I was so strung out and stressed all the time, suffering from just about every anxiety disorder in the manual. What would he think of me now, I wondered? Stress was literally impossible for me in this soggy butterfly state; my only agenda was sitting on this flower, fanning, fanning my wings, not even thinking about where I would fly next, not even wondering if these new wings could carry my weight.

My OCD was quiet. I had no desire to clean the countertops

ninety times a day. My house was a little messy and I didn't care. My obsessive compulsion no longer had much to say. I seemed to have spontaneously healed from something that had plagued me my entire life. No more chronic croupy cough either, thanks to my encounter with Lozen. Had it been stress related all along? Or had her spirit literally cured me?

I did at this time feel more isolated than I ever thought possible. There was no context for what I had been through in the Western medical paradigm. I couldn't speak about much of this to anyone but a select few—a couple of best friends, my sister, and husband—and even those conversations I had to censor for fear of scaring them.

They didn't truly understand. Sharing what had happened to me elicited feelings of longing. As if getting access to this nonordinary reality was something everyone was desperate for. I wanted to shake them, to yell, "You have *no idea!*" It felt equal to somebody telling me they had their arm ripped off in a farming accident and me sighing, "Gee, I wish I could experience that," as I gazed wistfully into the distance, only half listening. I came to understand how desperate we are to connect with our own versions of the great mystery.

This isolation and confusion as to what the hell, on a scientific level, could possibly be the explanation for this, gave me a new full-time purpose: an intense desire to find answers. My voracious research uncovered the answers in the connections among indigenous cultures: Buddhism, Shamanism, and Christian mysticism; these were all doorways that led me to transpersonal psychology, which had actual terminology for what I had been through. Called the "spiritual emergency," or spiritual crisis—an awakening that blows up all at once, rather than gradually—mine (likely because of my history of chronic repression) took the form of a spontaneous shamanic initiation, an archetypal event that millions have experienced. I was finally given the gift of context.

One of the founders of the field of transpersonal psychology, psychiatrist Stanislav Grof, described the Shamanic Initiatory Crisis as being, "an altered state of consciousness that traditional Western psychiatry sees as a manifestation of serious mental disease. It includes visionary experiences of descent into the underworld, attacks from demons, and inhuman tortures and ordeals, followed by a sequence of dying and being reborn and subsequent ascent into celestial realms." He went on to say that if the crisis is successfully overcome and completed, it results in profound personal healing, superior social functioning, and the development of intuitive abilities. I was the Phoenix, rising from the blaze of my own smoking psyche, transcending that pile of smoldering ashes.

From that research, I made the commitment to get a master's degree in psychology—and devote my life to understanding transpersonal explanations of life experiences, to being a resource for others—that hand reaching into the darkness to offer light to another in need—all the while remembering the circumstances of my own dismemberment experience in Silver City. I had to always know my limits. I had to completely heal my own brokenness, which manifested as a savior complex with control issues, lest I risk being torn apart by life.

Were my experiences real?

I believe they were. I also believe I was only able to experience them because my mind temporarily broke, and that breaking permanently changed me on many levels.

But I wouldn't hold it against anyone who assigned an explanation of insanity to all of it, especially given my tragic beginnings. Believe me, as I navigated all of this, I myself wasn't sure.

Around this time I read a fable called *The Four Rabbinim* by Clarissa Pinkola Estés. In the story, there were four rabbis visited by an angel who awakened them and carried them to the Seventh Vault of the Seventh Heaven. It was here that they witnessed the fire of the glorious Wheel of Ezekiel. Minds blown, they were returned to Earth.

Having experienced such a phenomenon, the first rabbi completely lost his marbles and spent the rest of his life wandering, frothing and foaming at the mouth, the object of pity and scorn. The second rabbi became cynical, allowing his analytical brain to explain it all away as something he'd merely imagined. The third rabbi became full of ego, shouting from the mountaintops how he had been gifted with this visitation which made him the man to listen to, destroying and betraying his own faith in God. But the fourth rabbi—well, he disappeared into the beauty of the world, finding new words to describe the joy in his heart, his love for humanity, the power of compassion and the gifts of nature. He quietly wrote poetry.

This small fable profoundly affected me, because I felt that on some level, through this experience, depending upon the day, I had been all four *rabbinim*. I also knew which one I aspired to be. I wanted to simply write about what I had experienced without obsessing about it, or labeling myself this or that, becoming ego, or forcing understanding.

Meanwhile, things quieted, and I continued to recover. No more voices. No more astral traveling or the buzzing cicadas of channeled words. No more spirit sightings or trying to connect with the dead through sleep. I spent most of my time wandering my enchanted Minnesota forest, experiencing no further spectral visits, only the beauty of Mother Nature.

My phones, however, were still enchanted. I couldn't talk on either my landline or my cell phone without terrible crackling static occurring, especially if I got emotional in any way. Like a virus, this strange phone phenomenon spread to my friends' phones too. I felt bad for that. It got so severe with one friend that she had to call the phone company. He could find nothing wrong with her phones or her lines. "One of those unexplained phone mysteries," he said with an apologetic shake of the head. I told her it was a Fox spirit, Maggie Fox in fact, showing her presence for a little while longer.

My ghostly cell phone would also dial two of my best friends at random intervals. The phone wasn't ever on me, it would just be resting across the room, when I'd hear a muffled, "Hello? Kristy? Are you there?" Shari and Ann found humor in the strangeness and it all eventually stabilized as I further integrated the experience and grounded my energy. At one point, Aaron questioned me about an enormous cell phone bill with a 400-minute call, which we tracked down to that hellish night in Silver Springs. I wonder who I was trying to contact. I had no memory of a phone call that night, especially not a 6-hour one. It made me feel a little heartbroken, knowing what was happening that night, as if a part of my being was desperately reaching out. Was it Maggie trying to get help for me?

I began dreaming of light, oftentimes being gifted something of gold, once a gold necklace from an ancient Incan, and another time a painting my mother had done with an elaborate gilded frame. When I was shown the object in the dream it was always too bright to look upon. With these dreams I'd wake up with the physical memory of that eye strain but feel fulfilled and nourished.

Another recurring dream started around this time as well. I'd find a secret room filled with riches. There would be a small door that had always been in my house, but that I had somehow missed until one day, moving the piano to dust behind it, I would find this tiny doorway. Each time I entered I'd be stunned to see that although I lived in a small house, this secret room was the size of a football field, stacked floor to ceiling with glorious jewels and artifacts, pieces of my karmic history over hundreds of lifetimes. I was recovering pieces of my own inexhaustible, priceless soul, which had been available to me all along; I just wasn't aware I'd had access.

But it wasn't all peaceful. Occasionally I'd have dark visitations in the middle of the night and feel panicked that something was in the room, standing there, watching. I would be so terrified I couldn't move. I was usually too afraid to even think of calling for help. But this was when the Bobcat would step in, seemingly embodying Camille, one of my cats—or was it that my cat was embodying the Bobcat? I can't say. She'd never had much affection for me before, probably because of the stressed-out, maniacal freak of anxiety-related illness that I had been. She had avoided me and was much more affectionate with my husband. That all changed when I did. The night this fear first enveloped me, Camille showed up out of nowhere, the cavalry to the rescue, jumping onto my chest where I lay in the darkness. A tiny, gentle, black and white thing, she perched there, purring loudly. And the darkness evaporated in terror of her feline power. And to this day, years later, she sleeps by my side every single night, never having done so even one time prior in all her eight years with us. I recognized Camille to be somewhat of a shapeshifter. I'd see her in every room of the house simultaneously. If I was cleaning the house, she'd be downstairs lounging in the den, then in the kitchen on the top of the fridge, then jumping off the washing machine in the utility room, all the while sleeping on her kitty tree in the bedroom. It was something I easily accepted. I knew she hadn't changed. I had.

There was one thing I could not accept, even after so much phantasm and mystery, and that was the disappearance of the *cadejo* tile my friend Lisa had given me. Was that tile an admissions ticket, like the twenty bucks I had given to the disappearing man? Did they take it, the *cadejos*? I searched furiously for it, practically tearing the floor out of my car and ripping the dashboard off, trying to make sense of its disappearance. I still fantasize that it will somehow come back to me, but I know that can't be true. There were things lost to me on the New Mexico road that weren't meant to be returned.

Over the next six months I continued to recover. I continued to sleep almost constantly, and when I wasn't sleeping I kept reading and researching. My words became mine again, and I found my ability to write once more. I put myself back together, and from formless I became formed. When I struggled to make sense of what had transpired, I would remember the words of my beloved Mangas who had said, "You know nothing." I understood this to mean that there are things the human brain isn't engineered to understand. Maybe we will evolve to understand such things. Maybe quantum physics will finally give us the clues to make sense of some of this. Maybe in one hundred years this magic will be mundane, science catching up with all of it, if it hasn't already.

Blessed was I to have a friend who knew the Bible word for word, cover to cover. I never did, nor would I ever, have much interest in religious texts. But he sensed he knew what the message, "You carry the seed" was meant to convey. He read it to me and I cried, feeling the truth of it.

> "How will we liken the Kingdom of God? Or
> with what parable will we illustrate it? It's
> like a grain of mustard seed, which, when it
> is sown in the earth, though it is less than all
> the seeds that are on the earth, yet when it is
> sown, grows up, and becomes greater than all the
> herbs, and puts out great branches, so that the
> birds of the sky can lodge under its shadow."

> —Mark 4:30–32, World English Bible

I was growing my own version of Paradise inside of me. I was healing. I was creating circumstances for my life that would work for me. I was building a new world for myself. This human experience, it has no limits. The path out of hell is right there inside of us. All it takes is a little faith—in ourselves, in our capacity, and in the loving, benevolent universe. All we have to do is ask.

I remember the angel silently giving me the choice to live or die, to stay or go. I chose to live, because in all that I had witnessed, as terrifying as much of it was, I had faith in myself. I had faith that I could navigate through any terror, I could live through any threat. After what I had been through, so much of it a beautiful, celestial magic carpet ride, I couldn't bear to miss what might possibly come next, and it's true that plenty of adventures were awaiting me.

I had been dismantled and made complete again. It took

the hands of Heaven and Hell to sufficiently tear me apart so I could be put back together, reassembled and forged from truth, for the first time whole.

◎ ☉ ◉ ❋ ▣ ▦ ▢

*"Are you afraid?" she asked in turn. She put
her bowl aside and stared into my eyes.*

"No," I said.

"Why?"

"I don't know," I said.

*"I will tell you why," she smiled. "It is because
good is always stronger than evil. Always
remember that, Antonio. The smallest bit of
good can stand against all the powers of evil
in the world and it will emerge triumphant."*

~ Rudolfo Anaya, from Bless Me Ultima

Epilogue

Aaron had the day off, and we languished in bed, committed to a lazy day, with nothing on the agenda but enjoying each other. His phone rang.

"Don't answer it," I said.

"Uh, I think you'll want me to," he said, as he checked the screen to see who it was. He picked up the call and jumped out of bed, alert and pacing like a nervous lion.

I tried to listen in, to decipher who it was. Over the course of the past couple of months, Aaron had requested transfers to locations all over the southern edge of Colorado. He worked for the United States Postal Service, having pulled the same stunt I had years earlier and left his despised career in the field of physical therapy to follow his bliss. For him, that happened to be delivering mail. He socialized with an entire community of people who loved him, had nobody breathing down his neck, listened to books and podcasts all day, and remained super-fit walking ten miles daily. It was all he needed.

Because of everything that had happened to me in New Mexico, Aaron was reluctant to live there. But he knew I was infected with a primal longing to return, so he thought he could relocate right to the edge, close enough for me to dip my toe in the water but not drown.

New Mexico doesn't compromise. It's a jump-in-the-deep-end kind of place.

He applied to nearly twenty towns in Colorado, and one in New Mexico—Raton, right on the Colorado border, where

Mangas Coloradas had momentarily hijacked my reflection. Because I had such a strong intuitive hit that we were meant to live there, he played along, still not sure he wanted anything to do with the place.

I listened to Aaron laughing, charming someone with his kindness, confidence, and wit.

"Okay, well I really appreciate it, and very much look forward to meeting you. Thank you so much. It's been a pleasure."

He hung up the phone with a trickster's grin.

"Well?!" I said, unable to wait another second.

"We're moving to New Mexico," he said.

With Recognition and Gratitude

Years later, when I finished a master's degree in transpersonal psychology—having thoroughly studied the academic intricacies of the spiritual emergency—I understood how masterful my loved ones were in guiding me through my own. Supposedly this mastery was unintentional as none of the major players in my life had any cognitive idea what was happening with me, but I consider their place in my life to be nothing short of karmic. They felt the truth of this journey for me, even through the painful witnessing of what appeared to be my psychological demise. They never panicked, and they never lost faith in me.

To my husband, Aaron Tompkins, who listened tirelessly, who strained to stretch his mind to understand the new language I was speaking, you gave me the space and the strength to open my wings.

To Shari Vaccaro and Ann Campbell, you constructed an invisible net of support underneath me as I learned to fly, and I felt you always by my side. From the first moment I met you, I knew you were my sisters.

To Jill Lenzmeier, you were my love and daily nourishment. Listening generously, you evolved with me, remaining attentive yet silent through my sometimes seemingly never-ending manic discourses on the blossoming of the human spirit. You can't possibly have known how important that was, but you provided the healing space for me to put my mind back together. You never judged me. You simply held me with your open heart.

Of course to Arya, whom I credit for keeping me alive through those initial days in New Mexico. I have no words to describe what you will always mean to me. Your soul essence has eternally fused with mine, intertwined, like golden threads, my sacred cherished spirit companion.

And to all the spirits, the universal and divine beings who orchestrated and guided this journey, those cosmic and earthly...to you I devote my life, my work, my every breath. With my entire existence, I thank you with eternal devotion. You turned a monochrome life into an explosion of rainbow kaleidoscope color.

For everyone who is documented within the pages of *Stark Raving Zen*, named or unnamed, let this be a permanent love letter to you. Each and every person mentioned, even if I never knew their name, provided a critical hand hold which allowed me to crawl out of this experience alive. You are all living prayers to me. Particularly to Lisa and Harry, who fed me, rested me, guided me, and loved me.

And finally, for their deeply loving support, I would like to thank Nina Brown, Valentine McKay, Tracy Sweetland Phillips, and Amy Tompkins, as well as all of my beta readers who provided invaluable feedback in service to the impossibly difficult task of completing this profoundly personal memoir. To my editors, Ellen Kleiner and Joanne Sprott, there would be no book without your masterful guidance. To Nana Nishigaki who brilliantly and intuitively designed *Stark Raving Zen*, bringing to glorious sentience my life's soul journey. And to Shawn Richardson, my proofreader, who not only exquisitely polished this entire book, but did so with never-ending love, grace, and support.

To my readers, I hope you see a glimmer of your story in mine. And I hope you know how loved you are and how imperative your story is to others.

About the Author

Kristy Sweetland is a writer, teacher, and coach of transpersonal growth and transformation. She holds a master's degree in psychology and is professionally credentialed as a transformational life coach. Kristy writes exclusively on the subjects of freeing the human spirit, and healing and growth through creative expression. She considers Mother Nature to be one of her greatest teachers, and utilizes ecopsychology, animism, and feminine mythology in much of her work. Kristy has a private practice in northern New Mexico where she assists others through their own spiritual transformations. When not writing, teaching, or coaching, Ms. Sweetland can be found with her husband and cherished dogs, hiking the gorgeous canyons around her home, day-tripping to the glorious Sangre de Cristo mountain range, weekending to the Colorado Rockies, or scrambling around Ancestral Puebloan ruins in the Jemez Mountains. She also shares her life, if not her hiking adventures, with two magnificent indoor felines who appreciate being mentioned. Kristy Sweetland has previously co-authored a book with Nina Brown, called *The Fascinated Observer.*

CPSIA information can be obtained
at www.ICGtesting.com
Printed in the USA
LVHW050737070522
717695LV00002B/11